HUMANITY WITHOUT DIGNITY

HUMANITY *without* DIGNITY

MORAL EQUALITY, RESPECT, *and* HUMAN RIGHTS

ANDREA SANGIOVANNI

Harvard University Press

Cambridge, Massachusetts & London, England

2017

per i cicci

Copyright © 2017 by the President and Fellows of Harvard College
All rights reserved
Printed in the United States of America

First printing

Library of Congress Cataloging-in-Publication Data
Names: Sangiovanni, Andrea, author.
Title: Humanity without dignity : moral equality, respect, and human rights /
Andrea Sangiovanni.
Description: Cambridge, Massachusetts : Harvard University Press, 2017. |
Includes bibliographical references and index.
Identifiers: LCCN 2016046030 | ISBN 9780674049215 (alk. paper)
Subjects: LCSH: Equality—Philosophy. | Human rights—Philosophy. |
Dignity—Philosophy.
Classification: LCC HM821 .S17 2017 | DDC 305—dc23
LC record available at https://lccn.loc.gov/2016046030

CONTENTS

PART II. HUMAN RIGHTS

PREFACE

"Humanity" has two sets of meanings. The first refers to the human race, or to those attributes that make us, as human beings, distinctive. The second refers to a virtue—*acting with humanity*.[1] This book argues that to understand our commitment to moral equality, we must seek an account of humanity as a virtue rather than as a property. We treat each other as moral equals, I claim, when we treat each other with humanity. On this view, treating another as inferior is wrong when and because it is inhuman, a kind of cruelty, rather than because it overlooks a special worth, or dignity, that, like "a jewel . . . shines by itself."[2] We respect another's equal moral status not when we bow before their capacity to choose in accordance with reason, but when we recognize the vulnerability to which they are subject as beings who must, as Rousseau remarks, "live in the eyes of others."[3]

I have spent many years thinking through these issues. I am not sure I have gotten them right, but I have many people to thank for preventing me from going too far astray, and who have, along the way, given me not only invaluable advice and criticism but also encouragement and warmth. I would like to thank Chuck Beitz, Duncan Bell, Colin Bird, Jude Browne, Ian Carter, Emanuela Ceva, Rowan Cruft, Sylvie Delacroix, Tom Dougherty, Daniel Elstein, Sarah Fine, Miranda Fricker, Pablo Gilabert, Ulrike

Heuer, the late Istvan Hont, Arnon Keren, Matt Kramer, Gerald Lang, Kasper Lippert-Rasmussen, Tim Macklem, Matt Matravers, Christopher McCrudden, Eliot Michaelson, David Miller, Bence Nanay, Martin O'Neill, David Owens, George Pavlakos, Mark Philp, Tom Pink, Costanza Porro, Amit Pundik, Massimo Renzo, Arthur Ripstein, Martin Sandbu, Marco Sangiovanni, Jennifer Saul, Christian Schemmel, Tom Sinclair, Quentin Skinner, John Skorupski, Matthew Noah Smith, Bob Stern, Annie Stilz, Jesse Tomalty, Richard Tuck, Pekka Väyrynen, Daniel Viehoff, Leif Wenar, Jo Wolff, Lorenzo Zucca, and Federico Zuolo.

I would also like to thank my colleagues and friends in the Department of Philosophy at King's College London as well as Desiree Lim, who helped me put together the index and who offered many excellent comments along the way. I cannot think of a more supportive or collegial group of philosophers, and I am deeply in their debt. I am also deeply in debt to participants at a colloquium on the book manuscript organized by Rainer Forst at Goethe University, Frankfurt, in June 2015, and especially to Albena Azumova, Mahmoud Bassiouni, Allen Buchanan, Thomas Christiano, Dimitris Efthymiou, Dorothea Gädecke, Stefan Gosepath, Tamara Jugov, David Miller, Darrel Moellendorf, Peter Niesen, Miriam Ronzoni, Antoinette Scherz, John Tasioulas, and Laura Valentini. The comments and criticism I received at that colloquium (and beyond!) helped me to rethink and refine several key features of the arguments I present here. I am profoundly grateful to all of them, and especially to Rainer, for dedicating their time and intelligence to the manuscript. I would also like to thank Michael Aronson and Ian Malcolm at Harvard University Press for their faith, hard work, and, indeed, patience.

This book is dedicated to my children, Amalia and Luca, and to my wife, Mette.

HUMANITY WITHOUT DIGNITY

No animal could be as cruel as man, so artfully, so artistically cruel.

—IVAN TO ALYOSHA, from Fyodor Dostoevsky, *The Brothers Karamazov*

INTRODUCTION

LIBERALISM AND OUR modern allegiance to human rights rest on a foundational commitment—often voiced but little understood—to moral equality. Name any valued human trait—curiosity, intelligence, wit, charm, strength, inventiveness—and you will find an inexhaustible variety and complexity in their expression across individuals. These traits mark us out both in our own eyes and in those of others. They establish a powerful basis for differential concern and esteem in friendship, work, family, and society. And yet we insist that such diversity does not provide grounds for differential treatment *at the most basic level*. Whatever merit, blame, praise, love, hate, concern, or care we receive as beings with a particular past and a particular constitution, we are always and everywhere due the same respect merely as *persons*. Our humanity, it is often said, provides us with a status that demands recognition—a status that demands certain kinds of treatment from others, and perhaps more importantly, prohibits a range of things others may, with justification, do to us.

It is, however, mysterious what grounds this status. Indeed, it is mysterious what kinds of action and attitude this status demands of us, and who has the status. (I have spoken, thus far, of persons and human beings as if they were the same thing, but might some human beings lack this status, or other animals possess it?)[1] Gregory Vlastos powerfully expresses the predominant way of trying to resolve this mystery. He begins with a description of the commitment:

> To be sincere, reliable, fair, kind, tolerant, unintrusive, modest in my relations with my fellows is not due them because they have made brilliant or even passing moral grades, but simply because they happen to be fellow members of the moral community. It is not necessary to add "members in good standing." The moral community is not a club from which members may be dropped for delinquency. Our morality does not provide for moral outcasts or half-castes. It does provide for punishment. But this takes place within the moral community and under its rules. . . . Here, then, as in the single-status political community, we acknowledge personal rights which are not proportioned to merit and could not be justified by merit.

And he then claims that the *only justification* for such rights is the dignity of the human being:

> Their only justification could be the value which persons have simply because they are persons: their "intrinsic value as individual human beings," as Frankena calls it; the "infinite value" or the "sacredness" of their individuality, as others have called it. I shall speak of it as "individual human worth"; or "human worth," for short.[2]

The idea of human worth, or *dignity*, establishes the outer boundaries of what we may do to one another, applies to all and only human beings, is possessed to the same extent by every human being, and is grounded in our most distinctive human capacities. And, as Vlastos also mentions, it establishes the basis for a set of personal, individual rights—human rights—possessed by us in virtue of our humanity.

In this book, I challenge the predominant view. I will argue that the idea of dignity cannot sustain our commitment and its corresponding rights. But if not dignity, then what? Must we abandon our basic commitment, and claim that there is really no injustice in, say, racist views, or views that affirm a fundamental difference in status between women and men? Must we abandon, in turn, any reasoned defense of human rights? Or must we, alternatively, affirm our commitment and its correlative rights on the basis of nothing more than blind faith or political expediency, declaring, like Martin Luther, that here we stand, and can do no other? No. I will argue, however, that we need to take a different route to the conclusion that we are moral equals, and that, once we do, we will find ourselves rethinking, sometimes in fundamental ways, the content, grounds, and scope of both the commitment itself and the human rights that are said to go along with it.

The first step is to abandon the search for some set of natural psychological capacities in virtue of which we all have an infinite, absolute, and incommensurable *worth*. We ought to abandon, that is, the attempt to explain why, and in virtue of what, we have a special and privileged place in the order of nature. Instead the key to moral equality, I will claim, lies in seeking a more direct, less transcendent explanation of when and why it is wrong *to treat another as an inferior*.[3] On the view I will defend, our commitment to moral equality is therefore explained in terms of a rejection of inequality rather than the other way around. This is important: I do not mean merely that our commitment is more easily understood via an understanding of what's wrong with inequality; an interpretation of the phenomenon *treating as inferior* is not merely a heuristic device. Rather, I mean that the wrongness of treating another as inferior is *prior* to an affirmation of the idea of treating another as an equal. Our commitment, I will argue, is both *defined in terms of* and *grounded in* a rejection of inequality.[4]

This way of proceeding creates a puzzle. Consider that hierarchies in power, esteem, and status are an essential part of all human societies.[5] Relations between superiors and inferiors within any formal hierarchy will therefore always be marked by an asymmetry. Military officers, for example, have powers and privileges of control and office that privates do not. The same is also true of more informal and temporary hierarchies in power, esteem, or status. A kidnapper, for example, exerts power over the kidnapped (even if they do not possess greater esteem or status). In most social situations, a person that holds a high political office commands superior esteem, status, and power when compared with a member of the public. Thus, there will always be, in any human society, some who treat others as inferior. This will be the case any time the officer gives a command, or the kidnapper brings the captive something to eat, or the official addresses a member of the public. But, crucially, not all such forms of treating others as inferior are wrong. And not all wrongful treatment as an inferior will be, more narrowly, a violation of our status as moral equals. Our question then becomes: When and why is treating as an inferior a violation of our status as moral equals, and wrongful for that reason?

The answer to this question, I will suggest, has two parts. First, we need to examine paradigmatic instances of treating another as an inferior in a way that violates equal moral status, or treating another as an inferior, as I will sometimes say, *in the relevant sense.*[6] This part is primarily interpretive and descriptive. We aim to characterize the phenomenon we are interested in through a rich description of the practices in which it figures. Such practices, I will contend, include torture; slavery; rape; segregation and apartheid; caste societies; persecution and invidious forms of discrimination; demeaning forms of paternalism; concentration and death camps; genocide; cruel, inhuman, and degrading treatment. I will argue that each of these paradigmatic cases is characterized by institutions and relations that either enable, express, or instantiate one or more of the following inferiorizing modes of treatment: *stigmatization, dehumanization, infantilization, instrumentalization,* or *objectification.*

The second part is to explain when and why these inferiorizing forms of treatment are wrong. Is there a feature that is shared by all of them, and that can be used to illuminate the grounds, content, and scope of our basic commitment? To illustrate: Torture is wrong in part because of the pain, but the mere fact of causing pain is insufficient to explain its equal-moral-status-violating wrongfulness. To capture the wrongfulness of torture, we must explain the sense in which the infliction of pain is used *in the service of* dehumanizing, instrumentalizing, and objectifying another. Similarly, genocide is wrong in part because it is an instance of mass murder, but that does not explain its equal-moral-status-violating character. Otherwise, how could it be in a class with invidious racial discrimination, which doesn't necessarily involve mass murder, and yet still seems wrongful *qua* violation of equal moral status? I will argue that essential to any adequate explanation of the wrongness of genocide—and also essential to any adequate explanation of the wrongness of invidious racial discrimination—is the way that mass murder in one case and comparative disadvantage in the other are used to stigmatize and dehumanize.

But what contribution do dehumanization, instrumentalization, stigmatization, infantilization, and objectification make to the wrongfulness of these acts? I will claim that what best explains when and why each of these inferiorizing modes of treatment is wrong is their embodiment of a particular kind of *cruelty*. Delineating what this kind of cruelty is, and why it, in turn, is wrong, holds the key to resolving our initial puzzlement.

I do not travel this road alone. Judith Shklar once proposed that liberalism is ultimately grounded in a rejection of cruelty.[7] Citing Montaigne, she argued that cruelty "is the worst of all vices."[8] It disfigures and destroys the humanity of both the perpetrator and the victim, and flourishes with astonishing regularity and vigor in political life. I think Shklar was right, and this book can be read in many ways as an exploration of that insight, though not so much for liberalism broadly as for our conception of moral equality and its connection to human rights.

We can anticipate the conclusions I will draw by turning briefly to the Stoics, to whom we largely owe our contemporary conception of the "unity of mankind," the idea that all human beings share a fundamental status that binds us together as a species. Most who turn to the Stoics turn to the Stoic conception of the *cosmopolites,* or citizen of the world.[9] The Stoics believed that human beings have a special place in the universal order in virtue of our rationality, which allowed us to participate in a world mind. The world mind is like a world republic: as participants in it, we acquire a special status and a special value, a dignity that raises us above the rest of nature.[10] But there is another, often overlooked, aspect of Stoic thought that I think is more revealing, namely the Stoic theory of man's *sociability*.[11] Human beings naturally seek out other human beings for companionship and communication, and this fellowship is at the root of all morality.[12] But our search for others can also become destructive, especially when in the grip of false opinions about what is really essential to a flourishing life and what we need to realize it. What makes us uniquely human can also make us inhuman. It is no surprise, therefore, that the Stoics were the first to write against cruelty. Seneca, like Cicero, comments on the nature of cruelty in his essays *On Mercy* and *On Anger*, both dedicated to Nero. "Cruelty," Seneca writes, "is the least human sort of evil and unworthy of the gentle mind of man; it's a bestial sort of madness . . . to cast[] off one's humanity and assume the character of some woodland creature."[13] The opposite of cruelty is not mere "kindness" or "generosity" but *humanity* understood as a virtue rather than as a property.[14] As we will see, we act with humanity when we see things from another's point of view, and seek an "accord and symphony,"[15] a reconciliation, with the other's perspective. Humanity is therefore also the virtue that we display when we act against cruelty, when we respond to others' suffering by seeking to understand and then to alleviate it rather than to reinforce or remain indifferent to it. It is Montaigne's allegiance to this aspect of Stoicism that reflects his own rejection of cruelty, and in turn Shklar's. Traveling a similar road, I will conclude that our commitment to moral equality, and hence our commitment to fundamental human rights, is not ultimately grounded in our *rationality* but in our *sociability*.

GUIDE FOR THE READER

The book has two main parts. Part I, "Foundations," argues against dignity and in favor of my own conception of moral equality, which I call the Negative Conception. Chapter 1 sets out the three main traditions of thinking on dignity, namely the Aristocratic, Christian, and Kantian. I argue that all three fail. I spend the most time on the Kantian version, since that is the one that has, I believe, the most going for it—although arguably it is the Christian view that has been the most influential. Chapter 2 provides a defense of the Negative Conception. Chapter 3 turns to a case study, namely discrimination, in an effort to show how the conception can be used both to illuminate a particular area in which moral equality is important and to expand and broaden our analysis of the five forms of inferiorization already mentioned. This chapter can also be read as an independent contribution to debates on the moral wrongfulness of discrimination.

No account of moral equality would, however, be complete without a consideration of its role in our understanding of human rights. As the quote from Vlastos already suggests, the idea that we are of infinite worth is intimately tied to our understanding of human rights. Part II, "Human Rights," offers the Negative Conception as a lens through which to reinterpret human rights without the idea of dignity, and therefore addresses what are sometimes referred to as the "deep foundations" of human rights, rather than their history or significance in contemporary politics.

Chapter 4 is on the concept of human rights. In this chapter, I try to move beyond the current impasse between so-called Political and Orthodox accounts. Chapter 5 begins by arguing that one of the central functions of the international legal human rights system is to protect our status as moral equals. Drawing on Part I, I then argue that the central place of equal moral status in the system is well-deserved: states and citizens have duties to protect both their own citizens and residents and those in other states from public, systematic, and pervasive forms of cruelty typical of life in a state system. Chapter 6 concludes the book by reflecting on how the moral rights constitutive of our status as moral equals delimit a subset of *fundamental* human rights, or rather a subset of fundamental human rights *violations*. In Chapter 6, we therefore broach a topic—hierarchy among human rights norms—that has been little discussed by philosophers of human rights.

A NOTE ON METHODOLOGY

The argument presented in this book is an inference to the best explanation.[16] To illustrate: my wallet is gone. It could either be that someone has broken into my house and stolen it, or that my children have hidden it, or that I have misplaced it. Upon further reflection, I conclude that it must be that I have misplaced it (my children are too young, there is no evidence of a break-in, and I am often absent-minded). In inferences like this, the phenomenon to be explained counts as one of the argument's premises, and the explaining theory is taken as the conclusion. Inference to the best explanation is pervasive in moral and political philosophy. We often take some considered conviction or judgment as (provisionally) given, and then seek the combination of values or theories or principles that best explains, from a normative point of view, why we might think so-and-so.[17] For example, we think slavery is wrong, or that we have a human right to bodily integrity, or that no one should die of starvation in a modern constitutional democracy, and we seek the principles or values that best explain such judgments given everything else we believe. In the same way, I begin with a rich description of our commitment to moral equality by examining our rejection of inferiorizing treatment, and then ask: What, if anything, might best explain that commitment?

The answer I provide has constantly in view the dominant alternative, namely an analysis of moral equality and inequality in terms of dignity. Throughout, and in different ways, I aim to show that my account supplies a better explanation because it avoids common objections to dignitarian views, illuminates our social practices and their limits in ways that dignitarian views cannot, and has independently appealing, and perhaps unexpected, implications for a range of further commitments, including for our understanding of discrimination and human rights.

The argument, therefore, is not deductive. I do not begin from widely held premises and derive moral equality as a conclusion. Beginning in this way might give rise to a worry: Don't I simply beg the question? Shouldn't I argue *to* moral equality rather than *from* it? After all, the definition of a circular argument is that the conclusion is found among the premises, and I have granted outright that our commitment to moral equality is, indeed, a premise of the argument. This objection rests on a mistake about the scope and aim of the arguments I present in this book. I agree with John Rawls that "justification is argument addressed to those who disagree with us, or to ourselves when we are of two minds. It presumes a clash of views between persons, or within one person, and seeks to convince others, or ourselves, of the reasonableness of the principles upon which our claims and judgments are founded."[18] So who are those with whom I disagree? The arguments I present are not addressed to those who are enemies of moral equality (such as, say, Nietzsche, or those who have argued for the subordination of women or the enslavement of entire races). My arguments are addressed to those, like us, who already affirm a commitment to moral equality, but are unsure regarding its foundations. This explains why I offer my theory throughout as an alternative to dignitarian views of various kinds, and why I spend little time discussing philosophical and political views that reject moral equality.

However, if my arguments are sound and illuminating (even if, at points, radical and unsettling), and if they are coherent and consistent with the rest of what we believe, then this should strengthen our commitment in moral equality itself.[19] This is because our commitment to moral equality would no longer look like an isolated, poorly supported, or inert node within the scheme of values and principles with which we guide our lives. Rather, it would begin to look like a commitment that both flows from and actively contributes to that scheme. If the account is successful, then enemies of moral equality would have to attack not just the commitment, but the entire network of further beliefs and commitments upon which it, in turn, rests.

PART I

FOUNDATIONS

1

AGAINST DIGNITY

"Dignity" was included almost by accident in the original UN Charter and the Universal Declaration of Human Rights (UDHR). Penned by Jan Smuts, the South African prime minister at the time, the original preamble to the Charter listed a series of objectives that the UN was to pursue. The UN was "to re-establish faith in fundamental human rights, in the sanctity and ultimate value of human personality, in the equal rights of men and women and of nations large and small."[1] Virginia Gildersleeve, part of the US delegation and dean of Barnard College, proposed a revision, which was accepted (without comment) by the drafting committee. The final and definitive version reads: "to reaffirm faith in fundamental human rights, in the dignity and worth of the human person, in the equal rights of men and women and of nations large and small." In Gildersleeve's version, "dignity" took the place of "sanctity"; the rest stayed mostly the same. The rapporteur mentioned, as a motivation for the revision, the need to "awaken the imagination of the common man," but the revision did not trigger any further discussion at the time.

Yet today the idea of dignity is widely invoked as the animating foundation of human rights—the value through which our commitment to such rights can be ultimately explained and justified. Since the adoption of the UDHR, the concept of dignity is used regularly across domestic, regional, and international jurisdictions. Courts around the world routinely refer to the protection of human dignity in important cases involving the beginning and end of life, prostitution, free speech, disability, forced labor, war crimes, genocide, adverse possession, and many others.[2] And dignity appears as a central value in numerous international legal instruments, including the two major human rights covenants, the Geneva Conventions, the Helsinki Accords, the American Convention on Human Rights, the African (Banjul) Charter of Human and Peoples' Rights, and the European Union's Charter of Fundamental Rights.

But can the concept of dignity bear so much normative weight? In this chapter, I will argue that it cannot. This may seem like a setback for a theory of human rights. In the rest of the book, I will contend that, when appropriately understood, it need not be.

DESIDERATA

Most skepticism about dignity has been motivated by the shapelessness of the term, or, similarly, by the fact that there is such a variety of (correct) uses of the term that it can seemingly be deployed to defend almost any conclusion.[3] This is not the charge that I will bring. All evocative and powerful values have a variety of meanings and uses to which they can be put. Think, for example, of liberty, equality, or autonomy. This is not surprising: concepts like these have formed not one but many battlefields on which myriad political, social, and cultural struggles have unfolded. Philosophically articulated conceptions, therefore, must reflect that history and must be understood as particular positions within that history (whether consciously or not). So the fact that dignity is such a historically contested term, and that it therefore carries many latent, incompatible, and open-ended possibilities within it, is no objection at all. It is an invitation to further reflection and an invitation to see in what guise it can best do battle.

My argument will therefore be another one. I will claim that the major traditions in which the value has played a central role cannot meet two desiderata.

1. The account must explain the sense in which we are *equal* in dignity. *(Equality)*
2. The account must explain *why* and *in virtue of what* we have dignity. *(Rationale)*

Let us explore each one in more detail. As I will elaborate in greater depth later on, human rights are egalitarian in an important and often overlooked sense.[4] They are not egalitarian merely in the sense that all human beings have the *same* rights. For example, all human beings might have the same right to enslave prisoners of war, yet no one would say that such a right was compatible with the commitment to moral equality at the heart of human rights. The egalitarianism of human rights is a *substantive* rather than merely *formal* constraint. This is why the most prominent theories of dignity might seem to offer a promising foundation for the moral egalitarianism of human rights. Kantian theories of dignity, for example, assert that we are moral equals in virtue of being equal in *worth*. This worth is of a type that calls for, indeed commands, a certain kind of respect from all rational beings. From this point of view, enslaving prisoners of war is wrong because and insofar as it is a fundamental violation of the respect owed to a person's humanity—the dignity *qua* worth of their capacity for rational choice.

Rationale is also important. Any plausible theory of dignity should be able to explain why some psychological capacity or set of capacities gives beings that bear it an absolute and unconditional worth that is not only higher but also incommensurable with the value of all other things in the world. Or, as we will see in particular with certain types of contemporary Kantianism, the theory should be able to ground our obligation to treat others with dignity (or, equivalently, in accordance with their dignity) as a necessary presupposition of an activity—such as mutual address or mutual justification—that we cannot but engage in.[5] If the theory cannot provide this basis, then it cannot provide a rationale for which human rights we ought to respect and why.

In this chapter, I discuss three different traditions of thinking about dignity: Aristocratic, Kantian, and Christian. These are traditions in the broadest sense of the term: structured patterns of argument, each with a particular history, organized around a central theme and displaying many internal variations. My aim is to identify the central theme that animates each one and to demonstrate that none of them can meet both desiderata. I have chosen these three traditions because of their importance in our contemporary understanding of dignity. They are not meant to be logically exhaustive. But if I am right that none of them can meet our desiderata, then it might be worthwhile to look elsewhere for a theory of moral equality that can undergird human rights, if such a theory exists.

THE ARISTOCRATIC TRADITION

In the Aristocratic tradition, dignity is used to refer to three aspects of an elevated role or position. First, dignity can refer to the *elevation* of the role in question. A role that has *dignity*, or someone who is a *dignitary*, has a high rank, and deserves respect in virtue of that rank. Today, for example, we might speak of the dignity of a judge. In the Renaissance, we might speak of the dignity of a prince or courtier. Second, dignity can refer to the duties, attitudes, virtues, and bearing that ought to characterize those who occupy the higher-ranking role. According to this usage, the dignity of a prince, for example, will include the duties, attitudes, bearing, and virtues that flow from his higher position and are definitive of it. So a prince can act below his dignity, or "outside" or "against" his dignity. This would imply that he has violated a role obligation or duty, or acted without virtue in some domain connected to his role, or failed to act in a way that is appropriate to his rank. Third, dignity can refer to the *higher value* or *worth* of the office itself or of the actions performed in accordance with it. This is closely connected with ideas of rank and desert.[6] The rank is higher not only because it involves, let us say, authority over others, but also because the role requires actions and virtues that both are more demanding than other, lower-ranking roles and serve greater or more worthy ends. So when someone acts with dignity in this sense, one acts in accordance with the demands of a higher rank or position. One then deserves esteem as a result of one's virtue or action in accordance with the role, which is seen as especially valuable because of its demandingness, difficulty, worthiness, or rarity.

The language of Aristocratic dignity was born in the crucible of late classical antiquity, especially via Cicero, and formed and shaped into our contemporary usage by the Renaissance and its courtly life. In this tradition, it was Aristotle, and in particular Aristotle's discussion of the "great-souled man," or *megalopsychos,* that set the terms for the discussion. The great-souled man[7] is the man "who thinks himself worthy of great things—and is indeed worthy of them." The most important among those great things, Aristotle claims, will be public honors worthy of his greatness, the "prize for the noblest achievements." He will always aim for those honors that are truly worthy, and that are therefore sought by the most worthy, and never because they are merely popular. He will aim to set himself apart and therefore show disdain for things that only people less worthy desire or can attain. He will show resolve and courage in the face of great dangers and never face a trivial danger if he can avoid it. He helps others readily but rarely asks for anything. Frank and open, he shows great self-command and is never servile or dependent on others, quickly forgetting harm that has been done to him but never overlooking the good. Even though he pursues honors as the crown for his virtue, he will take bad and good fortune in his stride and have a measured attitude toward wealth, power, or influence. He will therefore seek honor—which depends not only on his own worth but also on external circumstance—without either grasping for it or relying on it. Those who exhibit greatness of soul will, in turn, invariably be those who are well-bred, since being well-bred instills in one the desire for superiority and equips one with the external goods required for it. The great-souled man, in other words, is a man of dignity, the *kalos kagathos,* or gentleman. It is no surprise then, that in the most widely read medieval Latin translation of Aristotle's *Nicomachean Ethics,* Robert Grosseteste translates one who "deems himself worthy of great things" (or *megalon auton axioun*) as *qui magnis se ipsum dignificat.*[8]

But no book had greater influence on the ethics of the gentleman (and indeed ethics generally), and hence on our modern conception of dignity, than Cicero's *De Officiis,* in which classic themes regarding greatness of soul, the relation between the honorable and the beneficial, justice, and so on, are treated within a mainly Stoic frame. *De Officiis,* dedicated to his young son Marcus (see also I.78), was in many ways a book for educating the Roman gentleman into the civic and political duties that his social standing (his *dignitatis*[9]—or dignity in the first sense) required of him. The parts that are most relevant to our theme are the ones on greatness of soul and on *decorum*, or "seemliness." The chapters on greatness of spirit share much with Aristotle, though with a typically Stoic emphasis on the disdain for externals, such as money, influence, and power. The great-souled man seeks only what is honorable and does "not yield to [any] man, not to agitation of spirit, nor to fortune." Though he seeks glory, his desire for it does not overrun his imperturbability and restraint. What most distinguishes Cicero's treatment, however, is his concern with the greatness of soul required of those who seek and maintain public office. And here Cicero is anxious to identify the dangers of public rule, and what it takes to be worthy, or *dignus,* of that elevated office. He asks, for example, whether the "great-spirited and courageous" statesman should be angry with his opponents and responds that "nothing is more to be praised, nothing more worthy of a great and splendid man [*nihil magno et praeclaro viro dignius*] than to be easily appeased and forgetting" (I.88). What we have here, once again, is an identification of the duties, attitudes, and bearing (dignity in the second sense) required of the man who is worthy (dignity in the third sense) to play an elevated public role (dignity in the first sense). The same usage is prevalent throughout his discussion of *decorum*, which lays out the demands of "seemliness."[10] Here Cicero discusses, among other things, the kind of house appropriate to a man of standing, maintenance of one's external appearance, and the art of civilized conversation—all standards of conduct and appearance for the gentleman.

In both the Latin Aristotle and Cicero, therefore, the idea of dignity was closely associated with the virtues, attitudes, actions, and bearing of those who have an elevated *social* standing. But there is one (very Stoic) passage in particular that might suggest a more universalist reading—a reading that might seem to bring Cicero closer to the understanding of dignity implicit in our modern conception of human rights.

> It is a part of every enquiry about duty always to keep in view how greatly the nature of a man surpasses domestic animals and other

beasts. They perceive nothing except pleasure, and their every in-
stinct carries them to it. A man's mind, however, is nourished by
learning and reasoning; he is always enquiring or acting, he is led
by a delight in seeing and hearing. And furthermore, even if anyone
is a little too susceptible to pleasure (provided that he is not actually one of the beasts, for some are men not in fact, but in name
only), but if he is a little more upright than that although capti-
vated by pleasure he will deceitfully conceal his impulse for it
because of a sense of shame. From this we understand that bodily
pleasure is not sufficiently worthy [*dignius*] of the superiority [*pra-
estantia*] of man and that it should be scorned and rejected.[11]

In this passage, Cicero argues that our capacity to reason, to wonder and
inquire, and to act in accordance with a conception of what is good gives
us a special, and more elevated, position in the universe, and in particular with respect to other animals.[12] But this notion of our superiority
does not give rise, in Cicero, to any rights that we possess merely in virtue
of our humanity. And nor does it give rise to the idea that *all* human beings *actually* have more worth than animals (hence his joke about some
human beings being human "in name only"). All it says is that our nature as rational and intelligent generates a duty to act in accordance with
the order we perceive in the natural world—a duty, in short, to act in accordance with nature (and hence our own nature). This is a classic piece
of Stoicism and is well reflected in Cicero's earlier discussion of the origin of the four categories of duty, all of which emerge out of our natural
sociability and capacity to reflect on our place in the universal order.[13]
There is no suggestion that everyone can realize the virtues that he
will go on to expound (many of which, as we have seen, require one to be
eligible for public office or of otherwise high social standing),[14] and no
sense that we ought to esteem, let alone respect, any individual who fails
to realize the virtues. I return to this below.

The Aristotelian and Ciceronian models of *decorum* and greatness of
spirit, as I have said, cast a long shadow over etiquette books in the Renaissance, where our own understanding of dignity was refined. There is
no better place to look for these developments than Castiglione's *Book of
the Courtier* (1528), which was read for centuries as setting forth the

exemplar of the courtly gentleman and lady.[15] It is also useful for our purposes because it demonstrates how the three uses are not distinct and only contingently connected—as is often implied by recent historical treatments of dignity[16]—but are unified by their essential reference to the qualities inherent in the elevation of a role or position. There are many places in which Castiglione, via his courtly interlocutors, is concerned to identify how the Courtier may preserve his *dignità* (understood in the third sense as his worth, public standing, and reputation) when engaged on public occasions, and hence mingling with inferiors, as well as when he is dealing with his prince, and hence his superiors. In each of these occasions, the Courtier must be careful to act in accordance with his rank (dignity in the first sense), and the self-command, restraint, beauty, and nonchalance [*sprezzatura*] that is essential to it (dignity in the second sense). For example, Federico discusses what kinds of activities a Courtier may pursue alongside peasants at public festivals, which allow a "charming liberality" in one's bearing. He agrees that it is appropriate for the Courtier to "run, jump, and wrestle" with peasants, but, at least in wrestling, "he must be well-sure of winning, else he ought not to enter in, because it is too unseemly [*troppo male*] and too ugly a thing, and quite without dignity [*fuor della dignità*], to see a gentleman defeated by a peasant."[17] Here we have a standard for dignity in the second sense, and hence dignity as a set of criteria of virtue, bearing, and action for those of elevated rank, blending into dignity in the third sense, or dignity as value or worth. So we can construe Federico's claim in this way: should a gentleman lose in a wrestling match with a peasant, he would be failing to live up to standards of bearing, reputation, and virtue intrinsic to his elevated role, and hence would not merit the esteem or worth that meeting such standards would otherwise earn him.[18]

But these distinctions and their relations are also clear in Books 2 and 3 of the *Courtier*, in which the disputants take up the classic *querelle des femmes*.[19] The question the Duchess sets them to argue is whether women are, as Ottaviano declares, "very imperfect creatures, and of little or no worth [*poca o niuna dignità*] compared with men, . . . of themselves . . . not able to do any worthy thing [*atto alcun virtuoso*]." Ottaviano argues that they are of lesser dignity, and Giuliano defends them. But how does the defense unfold? Giuliano clarifies that the dignity of women (in the third sense) must be established relative to standards that are appropriate to their role or station (in the second sense) as not only women but also "Donne di Palazzo," just as the bearing, attitudes, actions, and virtue of men were established in relation to their role as Courtiers. Whether women deserve esteem and respect, in other words, is determined by whether they are up to the task of acting and bearing themselves in accordance with the aims and goods definitive of the Court Lady. "But if things were to be made equal," Giuliano declares, we must "imagine a Court Lady with all the perfections proper to a woman, just as they have imagined the Courtier with all the perfections proper to a man."[20] Ottaviano argues (in classic Aristotelian fashion) that women's deliberative capacity is imperfect, which diminishes their ability to act virtuously. Giuliano powerfully denies this, and goes on to paint a portrait of the ideal Court Lady to match that of the ideal Courtier. For our purposes, the important point is that the dignity *qua* worth (and hence dignity in the third sense) of women is determined by inquiring whether they are able to act according to the dignity of their role as Court Ladies (and hence dignity in the second sense). Again, the three uses of dignity form three aspects of the very same thing, namely (in this case) the elevated rank of Court Lady (hence a role that has dignity in the first sense).

Finally, it is worth noting the metaphorical uses to which the language of dignity was put in the Renaissance, especially in discussions of the *paragoni,* or comparisons, which reinforces the interpretation I am pursuing. The *paragone* was a central trope of Renaissance discourse, in which two (usually) esthetic genres were compared to determine which was of greater "dignity." A good example is the *paragone* between painting and sculpture.[21] Leonardo treats this classic *paragone* in his *Trattato della Pittura* (which he wrote as notes at around the same time as Castiglione began to put together the *Book of the Courtier,* namely 1508).[22] He writes:

> The sculptor claims that his art has more dignity [*essere più degna*] than painting because sculpture is more lasting and suffers less from humidity, fire, and hot and cold. To him we respond that this does not attest to the dignity of the sculptor [*non fa più dignità nello scultore*], because such permanence is a result of the material

and not a result of his own making; indeed, such dignity [*la qual dignità*] can also be attained by the painter by painting on metal or terra cotta with colors made from glass . . . as one sees these days in . . . Florence, especially in the excellent workshops of the Della Robbia family.[23]

Here the purported dignity of the sculptor is associated with his ability to make things that are imperturbable, permanent, and incorruptible, just as the dignified gentleman is meant to be. But even more revealing is Leonardo's depiction of the sculptor and the painter in their studio. To prove the greater dignity of the painter, Leonardo pokes fun at the physical strain and disheveled appearance of the sculptor:

> In producing his works of art, the sculptor must exert himself to a much greater extent physically than mentally; for the painter, it is exactly the reverse. This is easily seen by the fact that the sculptor must use the strength of his arms and hammer through layers of marble, or other stone, to liberate the figure enclosed within. This is an extremely mechanical activity, most often accompanied by heavy sweating—a sweating so heavy that it transforms what was mere dust on his face into a layer of plaster. With his face thus floured and battered, he takes on the appearance of a baker, and with his body all covered in marble chips, he looks as if he has been caught in a flurry of snow. And this is not to mention his house, which is a mess, submerged as it is by stone chips and dust. The situation of the painter couldn't be more different (and here, I remind the reader, I am only speaking of the best painters and sculptors). The painter, well-dressed, sits calmly before his easel and moves his brush with light, airy movements, using the most delicate colors; he dresses and adorns himself how he pleases. His house is clean, full of charming paintings, and his own work is usually accompanied by music or by readings of the most varied kind. He takes delight in all of these activities, which are heard without the din of hammers or other noises.[24]

In this passage, Leonardo uses the "mechanical" and physical aspects of sculpture to lampoon the bearing of the sculptor, who is, we are led to believe, but a kind of skilled, but still manual, laborer. The painter, on the other hand, is graceful and aristocratic, dignified in bearing and station. The association of dignity with elevated status and the worth that comes from this status are here used to prove the higher value or esteem in which we should hold painting.

So far we have seen how the Aristocratic conception of dignity centers on the bearing, conduct, virtues, and attitudes required of the gentleman (and lady) of social standing. And we have seen how the idea of dignity as a kind of worth is closely connected to the esteem that the man or woman of social standing merits when he or she acts in accordance with his or her role. We have also noted the extension of this basic concept in the Stoic idea of the human being and his elevated place in the order of the universe, and in more metaphorical uses applied to genres such as painting. This history sets the background against which contemporary discussions of dignity must distinguish themselves. And so now we are in a position to return to our concern with dignity as a foundation for human rights and ask: What, if anything, does Aristocratic dignity have to do with the human dignity invoked in the modern practice of human rights?

In an article elucidating our contemporary understanding of dignity, Aurel Kolnai memorably begins by outlining the qualities of the dignified person, which include

> composure, calmness, restraint, reserve, and emotions or passions subdued and securely controlled without being negated or dissolved . . . distinctness, delimitation, and distance. . . . Dignity also tends to connote the features of self-contained serenity, of a certain inward and toned-down but yet translucent and perceptible power of self-assertion: the dignified type of character is chary of emphatic activity rather than sullenly passive, perhaps impassive rather than impassible, patient rather than anxiously defensive, and devoid but not incapable of aggressiveness.[25]

These are precisely the characteristics of the gentleman that emerge from the long Aristocratic tradition tracing back to Aristotle that we have just outlined. The only difference is that the association with elevated social standing has been removed. Everyone can be dignified in this way. Kolnai thus resolves—in a universalist direction—the long-standing ambiguity in the Aristocratic tradition regarding whether *anyone* can aspire to the virtues of greatness of soul and self-possession (as, for example, the Stoics believed) or whether only those of a certain sex or social background can (as Cicero, and perhaps Aristotle, implies).[26] Kolnai then goes on to wonder about the relationship between dignity as a "quality" and the idea of "human dignity." One might initially think that there is no connection, that the idea of "human dignity" and "dignity as a quality" are entirely separate usages, but I believe that Kolnai is right to assert that there is a connection (at least on one understanding of "human dignity"; we turn to another in the next two sections). He notes that human dignity is not something earned or merited in the way the esteem or respect shown to the man of dignity is earned. It is rather a quality that is "ascribed" to every human being merely in virtue of being human. But it is, *like* dignity as a quality, something that can be lost or impaired or destroyed. Kolnai gives the examples of torture and slave camps. I think the best way to make sense of Kolnai in these passages (which are elusive and elliptical) is this: torture and slave camps undermine the human dignity of victims by stripping them of the *very ability* to act in a dignified way; they strip them of the ability to "stand tall," to maintain composure, distance, delimitation, and so on. In torture, one is invariably reduced to a whimpering, broken shell; one might beg to be released; one might soil oneself. One is reduced to one's merely animal condition. And so it is with slave camps. "Deficient, alas, in heroic virtue and not of the stuff martyrs are made of, I would most likely ingloriously collapse under torture and fail to stand up to pain, fright and benumbing poisons: I would then be ready to behave, perhaps without even feeling that it matters much, in a fashion incompatible with 'Human Dignity.' "[27] By implication, we can entertain the possibility of a man or woman so strong that they can maintain their composure even in the face of torture and slavery. This man or woman, according to Kolnai, would therefore succeed in *maintaining* their human dignity despite the great adversity they face. So, it seems, for Kolnai, "human dignity" refers to one's *capacity* to carry oneself in a dignified way—which everyone, including the undignified, is supposed to have, at least in normal circumstances (hence the appropriateness of ascribing human dignity to everyone)—and the dignified behavior itself (what Kolnai calls "dignity as a quality").

The concern for one's human dignity (in this sense) also makes an appearance in reflection on human rights. Often one reads—in human rights reports, for example—of the *squalor* of conditions in, say, a refugee camp. Or, similarly, one often reads that one of the fundamental aims of human rights is to provide people with the conditions for living a minimally decent life, where standards of decency are defined relative to societal conventions.[28] Martha Nussbaum, in turn, defends a set of human rights—in Nussbaum's case, rights grounded in capabilities—as rights that are necessary for people to live lives "worthy of dignity."[29] In these and other cases, it is clear that something like the image of a dignified man or woman, and the related idea of a capacity to live such a dignified life, plays a role. The person who lives in squalor lives a life "beneath the dignity" of a human being; such squalor makes him or her incapable of acting in a dignified or "decent" way; people in such conditions are not living lives that are "worthy of dignity"—worthy, that is, of their higher place in the order of nature.

If I am right about the connection between the Aristocratic notion of dignity and views of this sort regarding human rights, then they strike me as implausible. First, assuming that "human dignity" in the sense articulated can be something that can be lost, it is not clear how we gained it in the first place. Did we gain it by acting with some modicum of dignity in the full sense? Or is it something we suppose that all human beings simply have when they are not living in situations of great adversity? Let us assume it is the latter. The view therefore urges us to look at the ways in which others can destroy our capacity to act in this (minimally) dignified way. By forcing people to live in squalor, or by throwing people into slave camps, or by torturing them, we make it impossible for them to retain their dignified bearing, to "stand tall" among others.

There are three problems with this view. First, the view seems to place the wrong involved in slave camps, torture, and so on, in the wrong place. Is the wrongness of torture or slave camps really contained in the fact that it makes it hard for us to maintain a dignified bearing? That seems hard to believe. It is the suffering, the humiliation, and (as we will see in Chapter 2) the cruelty involved in cases like these that matters, *not* our dignified bearing. Second, the view has the odd implication that someone who is very poor (or living in "squalid" conditions), and who as a result does not "stand tall," *lacks* dignity or, in Nussbaum's phrase, is "unworthy" of dignity, or, alternatively, must be living an "indecent" life. To illustrate: If one says that "having at least this much is required for a life that is worthy of dignity," then it follows that *not* having this much entails that one's life must be *un*worthy of dignity, or otherwise *in*decent. Otherwise, where does the demand come from? But does the view in question really want to be committed to this conclusion? And it also has the odd implication that someone who is strong enough to *withstand* an assault on his or her dignity doesn't have a claim against his or her oppressor, since, if the claim is based on the worth of living with "human dignity," then his or her human dignity has not been set back at all. (Indeed, we may think it has been *heightened* by their fortitude [which is, incidentally, exactly what the Stoics believed].[30]) For these two reasons, the account therefore fails the Rationale Desideratum: it cannot explain how the importance of having a dignified bearing grounds our commitment to moral equality.

Third, the account fails to meet the Equality Desideratum. To see this point, return to the question: In virtue of what is it wrong to attack someone's "human dignity"? The account answers in a Ciceronian vein: "It is wrong because it is an attack on our capacity to live dignified lives, which is of value in itself (as the realization of what makes us distinctively human)." The problem here is that the value, or dignity in the third sense, seems to reside in the *realization* of the capacity rather than in the mere possession of the capacity itself. So, if that is true, then why does everyone have an *equal* claim, or *right*, to have their "human dignity" respected? Why shouldn't those who have realized their human dignity to a greater extent have more of a claim than others? Even if, somehow, the account were to emphasize the value of the capacity rather than its realization, we may still wonder: "Yes, but don't individual capacities to live in accordance with 'human dignity' vary? And, if that is true, shouldn't their claims vary too?" Recall that Cicero was no rights theorist and certainly no egalitarian.

In this section, I have reconstructed the origins of what I have called the Aristocratic tradition of thought on dignity. Dignity, in this tradition, always refers to one of three aspects of an elevated role or position, namely either the elevation itself, or the bearing, virtues, and conduct appropriate to those who occupy it, or the value or worth of those who occupy it *well*. This is important not only because it forms the background to our own contemporary usage but also because it plays a perhaps unexpected role in some current conceptions of "human dignity," namely those which treat human dignity as something that every person has a right to but that can be lost in conditions of severe adversity. In the next two sections, we turn to the most popular contemporary accounts of dignity, namely the Christian and the Kantian ones. In both of these traditions, dignity is treated as a kind of inner transcendental kernel that can be violated but, in contrast to the Aristocratic conception, never lost.

THE CHRISTIAN TRADITION

The dignity of the human person is a central value among contemporary Christians, especially within the Catholic tradition. According to the Vatican II document *Gaudem et Spes* (1965), which typifies the contemporary Catholic approach to the connection between human dignity and human rights: "there is a growing awareness of the exalted dignity proper to the human person, since he or she stands above all things, and his or her rights and duties are universal and inviolable." The basis for this exaltation is, as the papal encyclical *Evangelium Vitae* (1995) puts it, the "life which God gives man," which

> is quite different from the life of all other living creatures, in as much as man, although formed from the dust of the earth (cf. Gen 2:7, 3:19; Job 34:15; Ps 103:14; 104:29), is a manifestation of God in the world, a sign of his presence, a trace of his glory (cf. Gen 1:26–27; Ps 8:6). This is what Saint Irenaeus of Lyons wanted to emphasize in his celebrated definition; "Man, living man, is the glory of God." Man has been given a sublime dignity, based on the intimate bond which unites him to his Creator: in man there shines forth a reflection of God himself.

In short, the church's reverence for human dignity—and hence for human life, community, and faith (and, more recently, for those human rights that protect each of these)—is grounded in the fact, if it is a fact, that man's rational and volitional capacities are manifestations of the special bond that connects him to God, with whom he shares an image and likeness shared by no other creature.

I have stressed the *contemporary* Catholic celebration of human dignity and human rights. I did so because the central place accorded to the dignity and inviolability of the individual human person (as opposed to the dignity of the *species*)[31] in Catholic doctrine, and even more so the adherence to human rights, is of more recent vintage.* We can see some of the first modern Catholic uses of human dignity in Pope Leo XIII's important encyclical *Rerum Novarum* (1891), which is one of the founding documents of modern social Catholicism. Discussing the relations between capital and labor, the owner and the worker, Leo argues against the injustice of long working hours under severe conditions and in favor of a day of rest:

---

* This is not to overlook the theory of natural rights as it was developed by the School of Salamanca, and in particular Vitoria and Suarez. For Vitoria, as he made clear in *De Indis* (lectures delivered in 1532, published in 1557), the possession of natural rights depended on the capacity to exercise dominion, and hence on the possession of those rational faculties necessary to exercise a power to do or to refrain from doing in accordance with reason. His argument was then (roughly) that the Amerindians did not lack this power (e.g., he pointed to the cities and communities the Amerindians had built), and so their rights must be respected. In an interesting passage, he also discusses whether children who cannot yet exercise reason can have dominion, and therefore rights. And here he answers affirmatively, first on the basis of the law of inheritance and the legal relation between a guardian and ward, but then, more significantly for our purposes, he claims that children "can suffer wrong; therefore they have rights over things," and then goes on, "the basis of dominion is in the possession of the image of God, and children already possess that image" and therefore, unlike an "irrational creature," a "boy does not exist for the sake of another, as does a brute, but for his own sake" (*De Indis*, §21). (It is an interesting further question, not addressed by Vitoria, *on what basis* the child bears the image of God, since, in many cases, they won't have any rational capacities to use yet. More on this below.) In any case, this tradition of natural rights was not deployed to any polemical use by the nineteenth-century church, in which the language of natural rights was associated with the modern natural rights tradition encompassing thinkers such as Hobbes, Pufendorf, Grotius, Locke, and Rousseau, and influential in the American and French revolutions. It is also worth remarking that nowhere did the School of Salamanca refer to

The working man, too, has interests in which he should be protected by the State; and first of all, there are the interests of his soul. . . . It is the soul which is made after the image and likeness of God; it is in the soul that the sovereignty resides in virtue whereof man is commanded to rule the creatures below him and to use all the earth and the ocean for his profit and advantage. . . . In this respect all men are equal; there is here no difference between rich and poor, master and servant, ruler and ruled, "for the same is Lord over all." No man may with impunity outrage that human dignity which God Himself treats with great reverence, nor stand in the way of that higher life which is the preparation of the eternal life of heaven. Nay, more; no man has in this matter power over himself. To consent to any treatment which is calculated to defeat the end and purpose of his being is beyond his right; he cannot give up his soul to servitude, for it is not man's own rights which are here in question, but the rights of God, the most sacred and inviolable of rights.

It is noteworthy here that Leo clarifies that these rights to a day of rest are not in the first instance rights belonging to workers but rights belonging to God in his creation.[32] This is not by chance.[33] The church in the nineteenth century was hardly a friend to either socialism or liberalism, often inveighing against the selfishness and individualism of the rights of man proclaimed in the French Declaration and in the revolutions of 1848.[34] The nineteenth-century church, furthermore, had at most an ambivalent relationship with democracy (e.g., the widening of the franchise), religious freedom (e.g., the separation of church and state),

---

these natural rights as grounded in the "dignity of the human person." The association of dignity with the inviolability of the individual human person is, as I have suggested, of much more recent vintage. As far as I am able to discern, the closest the Spanish Thomists come to the modern Catholic usage is in passages like the following, from Bartolomé de las Casas (1992, p. 39): "Even though these peoples may be completely barbaric, they are nevertheless created in God's image. They are not so forsaken by divine providence that they are incapable of attaining Christ's kingdom. . . . Consequently, to these men who are wild and ignorant in their barbarism we owe the right which is theirs, that is, brotherly kindness and Christian love."

and the natural liberal rights that had come to the fore in the wake of the American and French revolutions.[35] By emphasizing the rights of God in his creation, Leo reminds his flock that all genuine rights ultimately rest on a foundation in Christ and the church rather than in the individual *as such*.[36]

Even Jacques Maritain, who was to become such an influential figure in the drafting of the UDHR, was, in 1925, a somewhat reluctant advocate of modern natural rights. In *The Three Reformers,* he wrote:

> In the social order, the modern city sacrifices the person to the individual; it gives universal suffrage, equal rights, liberty of opinion, to the individual, and delivers the person, isolated, naked, with no social framework to support and protect it, to all the devouring powers which threaten the soul's life, to the pitiless actions and reactions of conflicting interests and appetites, to the infinite demands of matter to manufacture and use.[37]

As Samuel Moyn convincingly argues, it was only later in the 1930s that both Maritain and the church began more firmly to tie together the dignity of the human *person* (as opposed to the human *individual* championed by the liberal) to modern natural rights.[38] As the situation of Catholics in Germany worsened after Hitler breached the *Reichskonkordat* of 1933, the language of modern natural rights came to be seen by the church as a bulwark against both totalitarianism (in both fascist and communist forms) and liberalism. They could be mobilized to protect the inviolability of the human person—but the human person conceived of as embedded in ties to community, society, and church rather than as isolated and alone in a sea of unbounded possibility. As Eugenio Pacelli, who was soon to become Pope Pius XII (and who was instrumental in the drafting of the anti-Nazi encyclical *Mit Brennender Sorge* [1937]), warned in 1937,

> A vast conspiracy . . . threatens the inviolability of the human person that, in his sovereign wisdom and dignity, the Creator has honored with an incomparable dignity. . . . [I]f a society believed it could diminish the dignity of the human person in refusing all

or some of the rights that come to it from God, it would miss its goal.[39]

Then, in a radio message on June 1, 1941, for the fiftieth anniversary of *Rerum Novarum*, Pacelli, now as Pope Pius XII, declared: "To protect the inviolable field of the rights of the human person and facilitate the fulfilment of his duties, should be the essential task of every public authority." Natural rights had become *human* rights grounded in the inviolable dignity of the person as created in the image and likeness of God. From then onward, and especially after Vatican II (in which, *inter alia,* the church's ambiguity with respect to religious freedom was resolved in a liberal direction), the alliance between dignity, human life, and human rights became in many ways the lodestar of modern Catholic ethics.

But what of its philosophical basis? Can the Catholic argument in favor of human dignity be used to explain our commitment to moral equality, and then, separately, to human rights? And, for our purposes, can it do so without appeal to revelation or a God-creator? For the church's underlying philosophical theology, we must look to neo-Thomist theorists of natural law.[40] And, indeed, many contemporary neo-Thomists have claimed that moral equality can be grounded in a robust notion of human dignity that is neither Kantian nor sectarian. Here I will focus on two such recent accounts of human dignity in the Thomist tradition, namely Patrick Lee and Robert George's "The Nature and Basis of Human Dignity"[41] and various articles on euthanasia by John Finnis.[42] These arguments are particularly interesting for our purposes because they attempt to ground human dignity in an account of the worth of human potentials (or, as Finnis puts it, "radical capacities") to act freely and to reason. In this section, I make two counterarguments. First, I argue that their accounts depend on a metaphysical view about the relation between the soul and the body called "hylomorphism" (from *hylē,* body, and *morphē,* or form). I will then claim that, for their argument to work, the soul must be an organizing principle that guides our biological development and that is metaphysically prior to whatever accidental form we happen to have as a result of our genetic makeup. The argument puts them on the horns of a dilemma. Either they maintain the soul-based hylomorphism, but at the cost of a contentious view about the soul, or they abandon the soul-based hylomorphism but then cannot explain how all human beings, whatever their natural capacities, have equal dignity. Second, I then argue that without appeal to the idea that our soul is created in the image and likeness of God, they cannot explain why we have noninstrumental, unconditional, and absolute value (let alone equal value), i.e., a dignity.

Lee and George's argument can be summed up in the following way:

1. Rationality leads us to seek things that are not just good because we desire them or because they are instrumental to attaining what we desire, but that are good in themselves.
2. The realization of the goodness of such activities requires that we choose and pursue them for the right reasons.
3. Therefore, we must value our own capacity to rationally participate in them, since such participation enables us to participate in something intrinsically good (and good for us).
4. Therefore, we must value the capacity of others who rationally participate in them, since such participation enables something intrinsically good (and good for them).
5. All and only human beings have a capacity to participate in such activities, and all human beings possess that capacity to the same extent.
6. Therefore, every human being must be valued and respected as a being who has the potential to participate in things good in themselves, and therefore as having an equal dignity.

Let us first challenge the conclusion at (6) by challenging premise (5). In what sense of capacity do *all* human beings have the capacity to participate in the rational activities of the kind identified (what about, for example, the severely disabled)? And don't people who are not disabled vary in their capacity to engage in such activities? Lee and George write:

> It might be objected against this argument, that the basic natural capacity for rationality also comes in degrees, and so this position (that full moral worth is based on the possession of the basic

natural capacity for rationality), if correct, would also lead to the denial of fundamental personal equality. However, the criterion for full moral worth is having a nature that entails the capacity (whether existing in root form or developed to the point at which it is immediately exercisable) for conceptual thought and free choice—not the development of that basic natural capacity to some degree or other. The criterion for full moral worth and possession of basic rights is not the possession of a capacity for conscious thought and choice considered as an accidental attribute that inheres in an entity, but being a certain kind of thing, that is, having a specific type of substantial nature. Thus, possession of full moral worth follows upon being a certain type of entity or substance, namely, a substance with a rational nature, despite the fact that some persons (substances with a rational nature) have a greater intelligence, or are morally superior (exercise their power for free choice in an ethically more excellent way) than others. Since basic rights are grounded in being a certain type of substance, it follows that having such a substantial nature qualifies one as having full moral worth, basic rights, and equal personal dignity.[43]

This is Thomism through and through, and depends on a hylomorphic view of the soul as a spiritual substance. The key is when they deny that the capacity for conscious thought and choice is an "accidental attribute" (i.e., something that derives from, say, one's particular genetic makeup); that capacity derives, they claim, from our having a "substantial nature"—the fact that our nature as human beings is necessarily directed toward the development of those capacities. But in what sense of "substantial nature" are we so directed? The essential Thomist idea on which they are drawing is this: All human beings have a soul, which is the substantial form of their body.[44] A substantial form configures prime matter into a functional arrangement, composed of parts organized to achieve some purpose. More specifically, a substantial form makes a material composite a member of the species to which it belongs. Rationality is the differentia that marks out the species "human being" (genus = animal); therefore, the soul, *qua* substantial form, organizes the parts of a human being into a rational whole. The way the soul does this is by conferring *potentialities* on the matter it structures, even defective matter (though less than perfectly). An ill-built house, for example, is still a house in virtue of its having a functional arrangement of parts whose purpose is to function as a well-built house. Similarly, all human beings, even embryos and severely cognitively disabled infants, are functionally organized to become fully rational beings; we might say that their parts are so organized as to be internally directed toward the development of rationality, even if they never develop it. This is what makes them, in the proper sense, *human beings*. Notice that the argument relies on the thought that we have a soul (*qua* substantial form) independent of our genetic makeup that guides and structures—even in defective cases—the development of our biological existence. This soul is the seat of dignity. Because every human being has a soul, and therefore a rational form, and because such a form confers the same potentialities, every human being therefore has the same dignity.

The problem with the view is that, if the soul is merely the form of an organism that explains how its parts are connected to perform some function, then it is not clear how *all* human organisms have the *same* underlying form. A fetus that lacks a genetic basis for higher brain growth, for example, does not and will never have the potential to acquire a biological organization that will make it capable of rational thought and reflection. The only way to sustain the thought that such a fetus does in fact have a potential to develop rationality is to say that, despite lacking a genetic basis for consciousness or rationality, it possesses a soul *qua* "organizing principle" that is *independent* of its actual material constitution. But this would be to invoke the soul as *more* than merely the form of some matter and so to adopt a highly sectarian conception of the soul as an immaterial substance.

John Finnis, in responding to an argument by John Harris, makes much the same argument as Lee and George:

> Like Harris, the tradition considers that self-consciousness and intelligence are "criteria for personhood" in one sense of that very elusive phrase. To be a person is to belong to a kind of being which is characterised by rational (self-conscious, intelligent) nature. To have a particular nature is to be so constituted, dynamically inte-

grated, as to have certain capacities (e.g. for self-awareness and reasoning). But if being a person ("personhood") were not as radical and fundamental to one's dynamic constitution as being a human being is, but were rather an acquired trait—something as extrinsic and therefore potentially transient as, say, the magnetism of a piece of iron—then one's being a person would not have the significant depth, the dignity, which even Harris acknowledges. . . . Harris fails to understand organic identity, and the substantial change of organic identity. . . . He misconceives the relevant point as a claim that "since the fertilised egg is potentially a human being we must invest it with all the same rights and protections that are possessed by actual human beings." The argument instead claims that the embryo is actually a human being because it already possesses, albeit in undeveloped or immature form, all the capacities or potential that any other human being has. . . . [Harris] fails to grasp the difference between an active capacity and a vulnerability or susceptibility. An organic capacity for developing eyesight is not "the bare fact that something will become" sighted; it is an existing reality, a thoroughly unitary ensemble of dynamically inter-related primordia of, bases and structures for, development.[45]

Since the last sentence (which obscurely invokes a "thoroughly unitary ensemble of dynamically inter-related primordia") cannot refer to genetic makeup (which is as "accidental" as the "magnetism of a piece of iron") it must refer to the rational soul as a substantial form; otherwise the argument is unintelligible. The Finnis argument is, in other words, exactly the same as Lee and George's. The argument, I conclude, either must also depend on a sectarian conception of the soul or cannot explain why dignity doesn't vary along with variation in rational capacity (and hence would fail the Equality Desideratum).

The second point I want to make with reference to the neo-Thomist argument is that it cannot explain why our rational nature (granting for the sake of argument that it is possessed in equal measure by all and only human beings) has a distinct kind of absolute, unconditional, and incommensurable value, or dignity. The argument as I reconstructed it above at most establishes that rational nature is instrumentally or perhaps constitutively good (as part of activities that are intrinsically good). What it doesn't establish is how this evaluative fact explains the kind of respect that is owed to a being possessing it. Why, for example, is rational nature itself valuable in a different way than, say, the reading of a good book (an activity which has, according to the Thomist argument, intrinsic, noninstrumental value)? Why, in other words, does the *capacity* to engage in an activity have a different and higher kind of value than its *realization* in the activity itself? I do not see how this further bridge in the argument can be crossed by the secularizing neo-Thomist.[46] Official Catholic doctrine, on the other hand, does have such an argument: rational nature has a different kind of value than anything else in the world because it bears the image and likeness of God, whose own rational nature is the source of all value in the world.

In the next section, we turn to the Kantian position, which, on one reading, has a structural similarity to the Catholic view, with an important difference. Where the Catholic claims that our rational nature has absolute, unconditional, and incommensurable value as a result of bearing the image and likeness of God, whose own rational nature is the source of all value in the world, the Kantian argues that our rational nature has absolute, unconditional, and incommensurable value because *we* are the source of all value in the world.

THE KANTIAN TRADITION

In this section, I assess two readings of the Kantian Tradition: the Regress reading and the Address reading. The Regress reading holds that rational beings are essentially evaluative beings, and our capacity for valuing things necessarily presupposes that we, *qua* valuers, must possess a different kind of value from everything else in the world, which Kant called *Würde* or dignity. The Address reading, on the other hand, eschews the appeal to a special kind of value presupposed by our rational choice. Instead, it holds that our valuing, justifying, moralizing activity necessarily presupposes the equal and reciprocal *authority* of those whom we address through that activity. Dignity is then understood as the name given to that equal and reciprocal authority. I will argue that neither reading can meet the Rationale and Equality Desiderata. I do not hope to trace every possible variant of the Kantian position. The positions addressed are the ones that I believe have the most promise.

The Regress Reading

The Formula of Humanity requires us to treat our own and others' humanity always as an end, and never merely as a means. The Formula permits me to treat you in all sort of ways based on your particular interests, merits, character, goals, and so on. I can select you for a prize because of your searching novels, or elect you to a post that you are best placed to fill, or find special ways to make you happy. Indeed, for Kant, I may even treat you as a means—rather than *mere* means. I might peer over to look at your watch for the time, or hire you because you will make my business grow. In each of these cases, I treat you on the basis of some particular property that singles you out among persons: *your-wearing-a-watch-that-I-can-see* or *your-ability-to-program-computers* or *your-prize-worthiness.* But I can only do so if, at the same time, I treat your humanity, understood as your rational nature, as an end. I may not, for example, threaten to break your legs unless you work for me or steal your watch. In acting toward you on the basis of such particular properties, I must always also respect your humanity; I must, that is, treat you in ways compatible with your universal status as a rational chooser, and hence as the only one who has the authority over your own life.

We will return to the idea of treating as mere means in Chapter 3. What I want to focus on in this section is Kant's proposed basis for the conclusion that we must always treat humanity as an end-in-itself. Humanity, for Kant, is our capacity to freely choose ends on the basis of reasons.[47] It is this capacity—rather than, say, our capacity to suffer—that demands universal respect, and demands it equally. Why? On one popular reading, Kant's claim is that our humanity alone has absolute, unconditional, and incommensurable value. Its value is absolute because it cannot be overriden; its value is unconditional because it does not depend on the value of any other thing; and its value is incommensurable because it cannot be graded on a single scale of value with anything else. Things of only conditional value have therefore what Kant calls a "price": they can be treated as mere means, traded, abandoned, compared. Our humanity alone has what Kant calls "dignity." Things that have dignity cannot be traded, exchanged, or abandoned without violating their higher status *qua* incommensurably, absolutely, and unconditionally good. And things that have dignity, like a higher position or rank, demand respect from ourselves and from others.[48] Hence Kant's injunction always to treat the humanity in others and ourselves as an end—i.e., as having a dignity—and never as mere means—i.e., as having a price.

But what is the argument for the claim that our humanity has dignity? A powerful reading of this argument, due to Christine Korsgaard, has the following form.[49]

1. Every time we commit ourselves to some particular activity, plan, or action, we must presuppose—*qua* rational, reflective, and hence evaluative beings—that the end is worthy of our pursuit.

2. It is incoherent, however, to claim that a thing's goodness is among its intrinsic, nonrelational properties; a value untethered from the particular perspective of a *valuer* is unintelligible as a value.[50]

3. Therefore, what we value must be worthy of pursuit, ultimately, because *we* value it.

4. If (3) is true, then we must presuppose that the exercise of our rational, evaluative, reflective capacity itself—the same rational capacity that makes valuation possible in the first place—ultimately bestows value on all our chosen ends. Put contrapositively: if we proceeded on the basis that our capacity for rational choice wasn't itself a source of value, then (given [2] and [3]) we couldn't coherently suppose that our choice to pursue any particular end had value, and so we couldn't be committed to the end (in the way that our choice itself demands).

5. We must therefore presuppose that our capacity for rational choice has *unconditional* value since its value is the condition for the value of everything else. As Korsgaard writes, "you must value your own humanity if you are to value anything at all."[51]

6. As an unconditional value, it must also have a value that is *incommensurable* with all conditional values, which merely derive their value from it.

7. As an unconditioned and incommensurable *source* of all value, we must presuppose that our humanity *qua* capacity for rational choice must, therefore, have a value that is of a higher and different order than anything else in the world. It must have, that is, a *dignity,* like the God in the Christian version of the argument.[52]

To bridge the ravine that takes us to equality, we can add the following argument:[53]

8. When we choose in accordance with reasons, we must presuppose that our choice is uncaused by anything other than our will, and hence free (we must act "under the idea of freedom").
9. Therefore, we cannot coherently suppose that any one valuer is more free than any other, and so we cannot coherently suppose that any one valuer has a greater rational capacity to make rational choices than any other.
10. All valuers must, therefore, possess equal dignity.

I will make two counterarguments. The first questions (5), and claims that, without it, the argument fails the Rationale Desideratum. The second questions (8), and concludes that the argument fails the Equality Desideratum. Developing these counterarguments will also allow us to present some of the assumptions about value that will become important again in Chapter 2.

Let us grant that, when we pursue something as choice-worthy, we must presuppose that we have good reason to do so. (Of a bona fide choice, we can always ask—Why did you do that?—and expect an answer that makes sense of the action as choice-worthy under some description.) Let us further grant that the idea of a value untethered from the existence of a valuer is unintelligible. The point is not (or not only) that a valuer is necessary for any given value to be recognized. That much seems analytically true. The point is rather that there is *no such thing* as value without valuers. Values only come into the world when valuers do. This entails that a thing's goodness cannot be among its intrinsic, nonrelational properties. We can also concede the further thought that, because goodness is not a nonrelational, intrinsic property of things, then moral properties must be, as Korsgaard writes, "projections of human dispositions."[54] There are no intrinsically normative entities in the world to be discovered by an exercise of theoretical reason; it is false to affirm that "we have normative concepts because we've spotted some normative entities, as it were wafting by."[55] Normative concepts are practical concepts, which only exist because "we are normative animals who can question our experience."[56] The statements in which such concepts figure therefore express practical states of mind rather than assert beliefs about the normative properties of things in the world.[57]

Korsgaard goes on to claim that if we grant these premises, then we must also grant (3), namely that things—such as projects and plans—must ultimately possess value because *we* value them—because, that is, we reflectively endorse them: "Kant saw that we take things to be important because they are important to us—and he concluded that we must therefore take ourselves to be important."[58] The reason seems obvious: if a thing's value is not a nonrelational, intrinsic property of it, and if all valuing expresses an attitude of reflective endorsement from a particular perspective, then a thing's value must be a *product* of our reflective endorsement. But the argument only appears to succeed because the assertion that "things have value because we reflectively endorse them" is equivocal.[59] It is one thing to say:

3a. Valuing consists in the expression of an attitude of reflective endorsement rather than the assertion of a belief about a nonrelational, intrinsic normative property.

And another to say:

3b. I take this project, plan, or thing to be valuable because I reflectively endorse it.

The first is a statement about what valuing in general consists in. It is a *metaethical* statement regarding the meaning or metaphysics or ontological commitments of value judgments. The second is a *first-order ethical* statement about what makes something good. But one doesn't follow from the other. To illustrate: When I yell, "You should have picked up the children!" I express anger as well as my reflective endorsement of a set of parental norms, but I do not claim (or presuppose) that either my anger or my reflective endorsement *makes it the case* that you ought to pick up the children.[60] If this is right, then Korsgaard's rejection of the claim that goodness is not a nonrelational, instrinsic property at most allows her to move from (3) to (3a) rather than to (3b).

But then what of (4), which claims that our capacity for rational choice—which enables us to commit to things like parental care—must therefore be a *source* of value? Step (4) inherits the ambiguity of (3): where (3) says that things have value because we value (i.e., rationally choose) them, (4) says that we, *qua* rational choosers, must therefore be the source of their value. But if (3) is a statement about what valuing consists in, rather than a statement about what makes things valuable, then (4) must also be. So (4) at most establishes that valuing *consists in* rational choice (i.e., rationally governed reflective endorsement). What it doesn't establish is that we must take rational choice to *make* any particular end good. And, if that is true, then (5)—and so the rest of the argument—looks to be in trouble. We might grant that if we believe something makes something else good, then we must take the former to be good also; it would be incoherent *(ex hypothesi)* to say that the goodness of something derives solely from the *badness* of something else. So, if (4) was a statement about what makes things good, then the argument would go through. But (4) only establishes what valuing consists in. It doesn't establish, as I have argued, what makes things valuable. Therefore, (5), which is a first-order statement about what we must take to have value (namely our capacity for rational choice), doesn't follow. In a nutshell: From "valuing consists in an expression of reflective endorsement," we cannot get: "therefore, we must presuppose that reflective endorsement (let alone the capacity for such reflective endorsement) is valuable."

To make this more concrete, let us work through our example regarding parental duty. Suppose some third party to our familial dispute asks me why I think that we, as parents, ought to have picked up the kids in the first place. I say, "Because we are their parents!" The person then wants to know the grounds for my adherence to such parental norms, and hence the grounds for my identifying with my role as a father. I explain my grounds in terms of importance of love and the reasons that loving someone gives. The person then asks about what makes love good. Suppose that, at this point, I answer with a buck-stopper, such as: "love is one of the most important goods in a human life—a good, in turn, whose value does not derive from, or depend on, its contribution to the good of anything else."

Does this commit us to the view that love's objective goodness is among its nonrelational, intrinsic properties, and that we are warranted in our assertion because we have reliable intuitive access to this property? In short, no. The problem with the argument is, as before, that the rejection of the claim that goodness is a nonrelational, intrinsic property does not tell us anything about what has value or what makes things valuable. So there is no contradiction in saying that love is both nonderivatively and noninstrumentally valuable and saying that love's goodness is not among its nonrelational, intrinsic properties (either because there is no such property[61] or because the property is neither natural nor nonrelational[62]). When I say that "love is one of the most important goods in a human life—a good, in turn, whose value does not derive from, or depend on, its contribution to the good of anything else," I am saying something about the role that love ought to play in a human life, and what love's relationship to other goods is, in an attempt to show you that you, too, have reasons to endorse my claim. I am not saying that love would be good even in a world with no valuers, or saying anything about what goodness as a property consists in. It is thus consistent to say that love is nonderivatively and noninstrumentally good, while also holding that love couldn't be good at all unless we were around to value it.[63] When the Regress argument affirms that if love is good then it must be good ultimately because of some necessary feature of how we value it, we can agree, but clarify that the "because" does not refer to our reasons for affirming that love is good, but to what valuing, as an activity, consists in. If this is right, then the Regress reading collapses: the conclusion that, in valuing anything at all, we must presuppose the dignity of humanity does not follow. The Regress reading fails Rationale.

There is a much more straightforward reading of the argument that might seem appealing, and that does not go via a rejection of the claim that goodness is not a nonrelational, intrinsic property. The argument has this form:

> I value X;
> X (practically, conceptually, or logically) requires (or presupposes) Y;
> Therefore, I must value Y as well.

The argument, at first glance, seems invalid. I value mercy; mercy practically, logically, and conceptually requires (or presupposes) wrongdoing, so I must value wrongdoing. There is a quick fix: "valuing mercy," we might say, practically, logically, or conceptually requires (or presupposes) that I value wrongdoing *only insofar* as mercy requires (or presupposes) it. This gives me no reason to value wrongdoing *as such*. Similarly: Playing football (conceptually or practically) requires the use of a football. I must therefore value the football that enables me to play football but *only insofar* as it enables me to play football. The additional clause beginning "insofar as . . ." (just as in the mercy case) is required because I might have other, independent, reasons for valuing (or not valuing) footballs *as such*. The argument only establishes, therefore, that I must value footballs only when and insofar as they enable me to play football.

In the same way: I value love, or football, or anything at all. My valuing conceptually (or, perhaps better, practically)[64] requires that I have the capacity for rational choice. I must therefore value my capacity for rational choice (insofar as it enables me to love, etc.). I think this version of the argument is valid. But what does it really show? It only establishes that the capacity for rational choice must be valued *only insofar* as it is an enabling requirement for the realization of loving relationships, football, etc. What it doesn't show is *either* that the capacity for rational choice is a source of all value, *or* that it has value as such and hence in its own right, *or* that it has a value that is higher and of a different order than the value of anything else, *or* that its value is unconditional. It doesn't show, that is, that our capacity for rational choice, and hence our humanity, has *dignity*. To check this, take a staple of Kantian ethics: suicide. Suicide is a paradigmatic case of a person violating the

dignity of their own humanity. Using the argument we have just canvassed, however, would only give us the conclusion that the person must
value their capacity for rational choice *insofar as it enables them to end
their life*. There is thus no rational contradiction involved in their
choosing to die. There is only such a contradiction if we suppose that
their humanity, *qua* capacity for rational choice, has a value that is both
incommensurable and of a higher order than the value of anything else
(including their mere desire to kill themselves). But this conclusion is
not delivered by the simple argument just canvassed.

There is another, more subtle variant of the simple reading—due to
David Velleman—that deserves discussion.[65] The argument goes like this.

1. We believe that either our own or another person's good matters,
   and hence stakes a claim on others for attention and concern.
2. A person's good matters only if and because the person whose
   good it is matters.
3. Therefore: "Value *for* a person stands to value *in* the person roughly
   as the value of means stands to that of the end: in each case, the
   former merits concern only on the basis of concern for the latter.
   And conditional values cannot be weighed against the unconditional values on which they depend. The value of means to an end
   cannot overshadow or be overshadowed by the value of the end,
   because it already is only a shadow of that value, in the sense of
   being dependent upon it. Similarly, the value of what's good for a
   person is only a shadow of the value inhering in the person, and
   cannot overshadow or be overshadowed by it."[66]
4. Therefore, (a) the persons themselves must have value independently of whatever is good for them (and hence independently of
   their interests), (b) the person's value must be incommensurable
   with the value of what is good for them (and hence their interests),
   and (c) the person's value must be of higher value than what is
   good for them (and hence whatever is in their interest).

Velleman concludes that our value as persons, and hence our dignity,
makes it impermissible for us, for example, to take our own life simply
because we believe that doing so will make us better off. That would

place the value of our flourishing (which is interest-relative and conditional) above the value of our person (which is both interest-independent and unconditional), and that, the argument asserts, is to contradict what valuing our own and others' good must commit us to.

The argument only succeeds by *assuming* that there must be a bearer of value—a person, understood as a being with a rational nature—separate from the particular cares and concerns that make up a human life and for the sake of which we act. But nothing in the argument requires us to accept this assumption. Indeed, if we don't assume that our rational nature as such can be a bearer of value apart from our flourishing, then a similar argument goes through, but with a very different conclusion. Compare:

1. We believe that either our own or another person's good matters, and hence stakes a claim on others for attention and concern.
2. Our individual interests matter only if and because our flourishing matters.
3. Our individual interests—including our interests in love, friendship, pleasure, knowledge, rational capacity, and so on—are constitutive elements of our flourishing rather than means to its realization.
4. Therefore, our capacity for rational choice matters because it is a constitutive part of our flourishing.

This argument, of course, does not establish that our or others' flourishing matters (but neither does Velleman's).[67] What it does establish is that, *if* and *when* we believe our interests matter, we are not *required* to assume that our capacity for rational choice has a value that is independent of, of higher value than, or incommensurable with our interests (which are constitutive of our flourishing). Indeed, this argument establishes that personhood—understood as rational agency—matters insofar as and because the agent's flourishing matters *rather than the other way around* (below, in discussing the grounds of basic moral status, I argue that we have good, independent reasons to accept this conclusion). To be sure, the idea that something is good *for* a person presupposes a *point of view*—in the case of a rational agent, a self and sense of self in the terms I will present in Chapter 2—from which we can make sense of the goods in question *as* goods and therefore as contributing to a flourishing life.[68] But, given the alternative argument I have just canvassed, I don't see why we *must* then conclude that this point of view *as such* has some kind of interest-independent, incommensurable, or unconditional value that commands reverence.* If this is right, then there is no contradiction in suicide. We might be gravely wrong about whether killing ourselves will make us better off, but we do not somehow wrong ourselves as rational choosers if we go ahead and do it. Suicides are, in most cases, horribly tragic, but nothing in Velleman's argument forces us to concede that they are morally blameworthy attacks on the dignity of our rational nature.

I now turn to the second counterargument against Regress arguments. As I anticipated in the Introduction, the capacity to make rational choices varies among human beings. Some of us are better at making rational choices, others worse. Our capacities for rational choice will vary along with, as Bernard Williams puts it, "intelligence, a capacity for sympathetic understanding, and a measure of resoluteness."[69] But if we have value in virtue of our capacity for rational choice, then it must also be true that variations in our capacities will produce variations in our value. It would seem that those with greater rational capacity ought therefore to be treated as having greater intrinsic value, and hence dignity, than those with lesser.

---

* Cf. Scanlon 1998, p. 104: "Appreciating the value of human life is primarily a matter of seeing human lives as something to be respected, where this involves seeing reasons not to destroy them, reasons to protect them, and reasons to want them to go well. Many of the most powerful of these reasons, however, are matters of respect and concern for the person whose life it is rather than of respect for human life, or for this instance of life, in a more abstract sense." What Scanlon says here strikes me as exactly right. Contrast the Kantian view, as adumbrated by Velleman 1999a, p. 365: "But when the object of our love is a person, and when we love him as a person—rather than as a work of nature, say, or an aesthetic object—then indeed, I want to say, we are responding to the value that he possesses by virtue of being a person or, as Kant would say, an instance of rational nature." And, finally, consider, on this point, Michael Rosen's reading of Kant, which is insightful: "What has intrinsic, absolute value, for Kant, is not our *lives* but our personhood— 'humanity in our persons'—and . . . our personhood and our lives [for Kant] are not the same thing" (M. Rosen 2012, p. 152).

To avoid this unwelcome conclusion, Regress Kantians have one of two routes available. First, they can argue that, although there is natural variation in rational capacities, above a certain threshold that variation ceases to matter. Or, second, they can argue that our capacities for rational choice are in fact *equal*. John Rawls's brief discussion in *A Theory of Justice* offers an example of the first path.[70] Rawls's argument, and the many who have followed him, makes use of the idea of a "range property." I will adapt an example from Jeremy Waldron to unpack this idea.[71] From a legal point of view, we are equally on English territory when we are in Newcastle (toward the border) as when we are in Birmingham (in the middle). "Being on English territory" is therefore a range property: it holds of all geographical points within the English border—the "range"—even though it supervenes on a set of scalar coordinates, namely geographical position. According to Rawls, "moral personhood" is a range property in the same way as "being on English territory" is: being a person with a minimal ability to understand and assess reasons supervenes on a scalar, namely degree of rational (and emotional) capacity, but it does not vary with respect to one's distance from the threshold dividing those who are and those who aren't moral persons. Above the threshold, those with great rational and emotional capacities are just as much moral persons—who can understand and evaluate the moral character of their own choices and those of others—as those with capacities much closer to the threshold. The idea, then, is that dignity is a function of the range property, which doesn't vary above the threshold, rather than a function of the subvening psychological capacities, which do.

The view has been much criticized already, so I won't spend much time discussing it.[72] The most important problem is the following. Why, if worth depends on possession of some (minimal) degree of rational capacity, does variation above the threshold suddenly cease to matter? In response, one needs to explain why the range property, but not the scalar variable on which it supervenes, is dignity-bestowing. But why focus our attention on someone's possession of moral personhood but *not* on their degree of rational and emotional capacity? An advocate might respond that we ought to focus on moral personhood because its appearance in the world strikes us with awe. And, as something awesome, it commands our reverence and respect. "Before a humble common man," Kant writes, "in whom I perceive uprightness of character in a higher degree than I am aware of in myself *my spirit bows,* whether I want it to or whether I do not."[73] Or think of our impression of the awesome expanse and sublimity of the aurora borealis. Kant writes: "Two things fill the mind with ever new and increasing admiration and awe . . . : *the starry heavens above and the moral law within me.*"[74] We *might* agree. But this provides no reason to focus on the range property—namely the bare fact of moral personhood, the minimal ability to make and respond to moral judgments—rather than the expression of those rational and emotional capacities on which it supervenes. Indeed, by Kant's own admission we ought to bow before the common man's uprightness of character to a *much greater extent* than we ought to bow before Kant's. Why shouldn't, therefore, the common man deserve greater respect or reverence than Kant? And, even if we were to focus on moral personhood, why shouldn't a *greater* ability to make and respond to moral judgments affect the dignity we command? Fixing our gaze on moral personhood as a range property rather than as a scalar also seems *ad hoc.*

The second path open to the Regress Kantian is, I believe, the more interesting one, though less often discussed. For Kant, our capacity for rational choice is a transcendental aspect of the will. We have our rational capacities, on this response, in virtue of our transcendental freedom. Transcendental freedom is our capacity to make our will an uncaused cause of our actions. Though we cannot definitively *know* that we are free in this sense, there is no inconsistency in acting *as if* we were.[75] And because we cannot, for practical purposes, act *without* assuming that we actually do have this freedom, then we cannot act without assuming that all persons must also have the *same* freedom.[76] We might then reason that our capacity to make specifically *rational,* and hence moral, choices must therefore be as unconstrained as our transcendental freedom.[77] But all unconstrained, unhindered, uncaused freedom must—precisely because it is unconstrained, unhindered, and uncaused—be *equally* free. And so, the argument concludes, our capacities for rational choice must also be equal.

But then how do we explain the evident fact that our (empirical) capacities to make rational choices vary? The Regress Kantian might here say that our unconstrained, transcendental capacity for rational choice (*qua* member of the intelligible realm) is *masked* by our empirical capacities (*qua* members of the sensible realm).[78] Characteristics—such as, for example, a lack of resoluteness—might dispose us to act in more (and less) rational ways, but do not undermine our transcendental freedom. On this picture, our empirical selves are like fetters worn by our noumenal selves.

One problem is that the argument ties the defense of moral equality to the existence of transcendental freedom. Yet we seem to have reason to be committed to moral equality whether or not we turn out to have such freedom. It is not as if it would become permissible to torture or otherwise degrade human beings were we to find out that transcendental freedom is an illusion. Another problem is that it commits those who make it to the existence of noumenal selves that stand over and apart from our phenomenal selves. But if such selves exist, where do we locate them? Naturalists balk.[79] These are commonly recognized problems with this version of Regress Kantianism (the latter which, I believe, could be resisted using the idea of a masked ability in the way mentioned above). But these are not the problems I want to focus on. Rather, I want to focus on a distinct problem that is, unlike these two, internal to the Regress Kantian apparatus.

The problem emerges for the Regress Kantian because of the way value is supposed to follow from capacity. The argument is supposed to demonstrate that all of our relative ends (happiness, virtue, pursuits, activities) have value only when they are chosen in accordance with the laws of rational agency. This entails, the Regress Kantian argues, that rational agency itself must therefore have *unconditional* value (as the condition for the value of every other end). As Kant writes in the *Groundwork,* "Now, morality is the condition under which alone a rational being can be an end in itself, since only through this is it possible to be a lawgiving member in the kingdom of ends. Hence morality, and humanity *insofar as it is capable of morality,* is that which alone has dignity" (emphasis added).[80] But if our value is supposed to follow from our capacity to be moral, then why should we focus on the capacity as it would be *unmasked,* rather than *masked?* Why focus on the capacity that we would be able to exercise in the absence of the phenomenal self—or at least unhindered by the phenomenal self—rather than the capacity we actually do exercise in the here and now? Suppose I try out as a goalkeeper for Arsenal (I am not a very good goalkeeper). And suppose that I don't do very well. I claim: "I didn't do very well, but this is only because my real ability is masked. I always practice—in fact, because of the way I am, I can't but practice—as if I were a premier league footballer, which, if I wasn't hindered by my lack of skills, I would be." Arsenal wouldn't be very impressed: I have value to them only insofar as I am actually capable of keeping balls out of the net; it is *that* ability—rather than my counterfactual ability—that confers value on me as a player. Why should anyone put any value on the fact—assuming it is a fact—that I could play like a premier leaguer if I had been unhindered by my lack of skills? Or that, in one (modal) sense of "capacity," I do have a capacity to keep goals out of the net since nothing in the laws of nature or logic prevents me from doing so? For Kant, humanity has value *only insofar as it is capable of morality*. This follows from the fact that chosen ends have value only if they are willed in accordance with the moral law. But if that is true, then it must also be true, for the same reasons, that it is my *actual* rather than *counterfactual* capacity to act rationally and hence morally that bestows value, and hence dignity, on me. Absent some other way of demonstrating that our transcendental freedom gives us dignity, the Regress Kantian strategy for satisfying the Equality Desideratum must therefore fail.

The Address Reading

The Address reading abstains from any appeal to the *value* of our capacity for rational choice. Rather, it points to our equal and reciprocal *authority* to make claims on others instead. Because this reading grounds our moral equality not in a value we are meant to possess equally but in the capacity to address and respond to others' claims, it is more promising. But I will argue that it, too, fails the Equality and Rationale Desiderata, though in a more interesting and ultimately more productive way than the Regress reading. Our discussion of the Address reading will then open up a new way of conceiving of basic and equal moral status, which I will go on to elaborate in Chapter 2.

Rainer Forst and Stephen Darwall's versions of the Address reading are paradigmatic of this approach. Darwall's presuppositional analysis is best summarized via one of his preferred examples, namely a sergeant addressing a private by commanding him. Imagine you are the sergeant and I am the private. You to me: You issue a demand (e.g., "do ten pushups"). Darwall argues that you must presuppose

a. ... that you have the authority to make this demand;
b. ... therefore, that you are giving me a second-personal reason to comply with the demand;
c. ... therefore, that I have the capacity to acknowledge the force of the demand as grounded in your authority and to comply with it for this reason (rather than, say, out of fear);
d. ... therefore, that I am accountable for failing to comply (both to myself and to you)—you can thus blame me for not complying (and I can blame myself);
e. ... therefore, that you and I share a (role-independent) normative point of view from which we can both see that I have a reason to do what you demand, and
f. ... that you have a reason not to overstep your authority (for example, by coercing me without justification);
g. ... therefore, that I have an equal authority to make demands on you, as you have on me.

The idea is that when you address a claim or make a demand on someone, you commit yourself to a series of "normative felicity conditions" that must be met for the claim to create a genuine (second-personal*) reason

---

* A second-personal reason is a reason that takes the form of an address to a specific person, and that presupposes that the force of the reason derives directly from the (practical) authority of the addressor to issue the demand. The contrast with epistemic authority is useful: if an expert tells you not to take a certain pill, you now have a reason, in virtue of that very demand, not to take the pill. Though the address and demand are second-personal, the basis for the authority of the expert is *third*-personal: her authority, that is, rests on her relation to the facts and evidence on the matter, rather than on her specific relation to you. Second-personal authority, on the other hand, is second-personal,

for the person addressed to do as you say. The normative felicity conditions are listed in (c)–(g). You must presuppose that the person addressed has *competence* to take your demand as a reason, that both you and the person addressed are *accountable* for failing to live up to the demand or failing to have the requisite authority to make the demand in the first place, that you and the person addressed share a *normative point of view* from which to assess whether the demand is legitimate, and that you and the person addressed are both *equal* authorities in making this assessment. If we understand dignity as a kind of moral standing, and we understand the idea of moral standing in terms of the authority to make moral demands on others, then, if the argument goes through, we must therefore all be (as [g] concludes) equal in dignity; as Darwall often puts it, following Kant, we then share in the legislation of a "kingdom of ends" in which we are equally and mutually accountable.

For Rainer Forst, the recognition of the reciprocal, general, and equal authority of others is a constitutive standard of justification. Forst writes,

> My own proposal starts from the assumption that the analysis of the moral point of view should begin with a pragmatic reconstruction of moral validity claims and, proceeding recursively, inquire into the conditions of justification of such claims and of the construction of norms. . . . If, starting from [the moral] validity claim, we inquire recursively into the conditions under which it can be redeemed, then the validity criteria of reciprocity and generality take on the role of criteria for discursive justification. It follows that, in justifying or problematizing a moral norm (or mode of action), one cannot raise any specific claims while rejecting like claims of others (reciprocity of contents), and one cannot simply assume that others share one's perspective, evaluations, convictions, interests, or needs (reciprocity of reasons), so that, for ex-

---

as Darwall often says, "all the way down." All purely second-personal authority (of which moral standing is one type) ultimately depends, for Darwall, on the specific normative relations between the individuals involved rather than on their relation to an independent order of facts. See, e.g., Darwall 2006, p. 12.

ample, one claims to speak in the "true" interests of others or in the name of an absolute, unquestionable truth beyond justification. Finally, the objections of any person who is affected, whoever he or she may be, cannot be disregarded, and the reasons adduced in support of the legitimacy of a norm must be capable of being shared by all persons (generality).[81]

The idea, I take it, is this. We find ourselves necessarily implicated as human beings in practices of discursive justification, some of which require one to justify one's actions in specifically moral terms. Put another way: If someone asks us—"With what right do you act in such and such a way?"—we must answer. And, once we do, we become enmeshed in practices of moral justification. Moral discourses of justification, in turn, have a certain normative structure, which can be reconstructed by considering what is (necessarily) presupposed in "redeeming" a claim to rightness. This is what makes them practices of *justification* rather than, say, forms of command, advice, warning, exhortation, or questioning. If we do not respect the standards internal to justification as a practice, we must therefore fail in justifying ourselves to others, and hence fail in something we must do. As Forst writes in the first passages from *The Right to Justification:* "Human beings" are "justificatory beings. . . . If we want to understand human practices, we *must* conceive of them as practices bound up with justifications; *no matter what we think or do,* we place upon ourselves (and others) the demand for reasons, whether they are made explicit or remain implicit."[82] As in the passage quoted above, Forst then claims that such practices, given their structure, necessarily presuppose that the reasons we offer others must meet criteria of generality and reciprocity, and hence equality. In recognizing others' right to justification, we must thereby recognize them as moral equals, and hence as bearing a dignity that demands respect.[83] Like Darwall, Forst thus proposes an argument that goes from a form of moral address—or justification—to a claim about the moral equality of all persons.

Let us take Darwall first. If Darwall's argument is to work, he must be able to show the practical incoherence of any relation of second-personal authority that is not, ultimately, compatible with the equal moral standing of its participants. To see the difficulties, let us work through two examples, both considered by Darwall: the first regarding God, and the second regarding slavery. One possible relation of second-personal authority is between a party who claims unlimited and eternal authority over another, much as the Christian God does over his subjects. Must God's second-personal claims on his subjects necessarily presuppose their equal authority to make reciprocal claims on him? Must God's commands to his subjects presuppose, that is, their equal moral standing? This is not a theological question but a question about the normative structure of moral address and mutual accountability. And it is a question that Darwall's own account invites. In chapter 5, Darwall argues that theological voluntarism is put under "heavy pressure" once it is forced to explain the sense in which God's authority over us is grounded in his normative power to bind our will rather than in his sheer causal power to coerce us. To explain such normative power, the voluntarist must grant (as [c]–[e] express) that God's commands bind only if we, as his subjects, have a second-personal competence to hold ourselves and each other accountable, and hence only if we are able to share, as it were, God's normative point of view, from which we can see the justification of his authority as unlimited and eternal. In this way, we "enter into moral community with God."[84]

Let us grant that (c)–(e) are true. How do we then make the jump to (f) and (g)? Take, for example, (f). In the theological context, (f) implies that, in virtue of his recognition of our second-personal competence to take his commands as reasons to do what he says, God must also accept (*qua* "normative felicity condition") that he has reasons to recognize the limits of his own authority, and that, therefore, as (g) holds, that we have authority to call God to account for respecting those limits as equals in the domain of reasons. But how do these further claims follow? By hypothesis, God's authority is unlimited and eternal. While we can recognize, as (e) affirms, that we share a normative point of view with God, such that we can see that he has unlimited and eternal authority over us, this does not entail that he must also *therefore* recognize that he is (in fact) limited in his powers, or that he must be accountable to us for what he does, or be obligated to work only within the bounds of his authority (given that there are no such bounds). And, *ipso facto*, he is also therefore not obligated to see himself as our equal in moral standing.

Why is this important? It is important because the conceptual and practical possibility of God's unlimited and eternal authority demonstrates that there is nothing in the logic or practical structure of second-personal address that *necessarily presupposes* equal accountability, equal authority, or equal dignity. Even more strongly, there is nothing in the structure of second-personal address that necessarily presupposes that the commander is accountable—in any egalitarian *or* nonegalitarian sense—to the commanded. All the argument shows is that God must presuppose that we can understand his commands as obligatory, that such commands are grounded in his eternal and unlimited authority, and that we can hence blame ourselves for not complying with them.

This has significant consequences for our second example, which allows us to bring the discussion back to earth: the master and slave. If Darwall's account is to meet the weakest possible interpretation of equal dignity (and hence the Equality Desideratum), it must be able to rule out slavery. But can it? Suppose the slaveowner claims to have unlimited authority over the slave *just as God is traditionally conceived to have unlimited authority over his subjects.* He issues second-personal commands to his slave, expects him to comply, believes the slave is obligated to submit, and so on. What mistake has he made? Why, according to Darwall's argument, must he—when and because he issues second-personal commands—presuppose that the slave is a moral equal? To be sure, I have granted that the slaveowner must presuppose that he and the slave can share a normative point of view from which they can both assess the practice (claim [e] above). But this claim is not sufficient to demonstrate that the authority of the slaveowner is limited in any particular way (claim [f]). And it is also not sufficient to show that the slave has a standing to hold the slaveowner accountable for violations (i.e., that he can be wronged by the slaveowner) let alone that he and the slave are equal in their authority to make claims on one another (claim [g]). Put another way: Something more is needed to show that, when taking up a shared normative perspective, the slaveowner's reasons for wielding unlimited authority over the slave (say, because the slaveowner won the war) are not *good* reasons for the slave to submit.[85]

Darwall is alive to this worry. He writes:

> It is . . . no objection to the argument of this chapter that the argument would entail that practices like slavery are impossible, necessarily conceptually confused, or pragmatically self-contradictory. The argument does not have these consequences or presuppositions. In fact, I am not even here claiming that slavery is immoral. Although I certainly endorse that substantive normative thesis, my argument in this chapter does not depend on it. My claim, again, is only that any address of a second-personal reason, including any from a master to a slave, is committed to the presupposition that addresser and addressee share an equal normative standing as free and rational persons.[86]

This is a puzzling concession. If an account of the ground and nature of equal dignity—which I have been assuming Darwall is offering—cannot explain the sense in which slavery is wrong, then I submit that it is not, in fact, an account of moral equality or equal dignity at all. So what is the most charitable reading of this passage?

To see how difficult it is to provide such a reading, note that, to make the account intelligible, we must construe the terms "free," "rational," and "equal"—and the concepts thereby invoked in the quoted passage—in such a way that they are *compatible* with the most extreme forms of slavery. Here is my suggested reading: Darwall has not shown that we are moral equals, or equal in dignity, or that we have equal moral status. Rather, he has shown that, when we address others second-personally, we must presuppose that they have *a* moral standing, a standing to demand *some* justification that is intelligible and consistent. When we address others second-personally, we must presuppose, that is, that they can understand what we have said and comply with it on the basis of our purported authority, and that we can share a normative point of view to assess this claim (claims [c]–[e]). The most perspicuous way of making this point would be to drop claims (f) and (g), which might otherwise lead one to believe (falsely) that Darwall has provided something more than he has in fact provided. The account therefore fails the Equality Desideratum.

But note how limited even this conclusion in fact is. Notice, in particular, that it is conditionally stated: *if* we address others second-personally, then we must presuppose (c)–(e). What it does not tell us is that we must address others second-personally in the first place.[87] For example, if the slaveowner never addresses any commands at all to his slave—if he simply keeps him, say, locked in a cell—then Darwall has no basis for claiming that the slaveowner has violated the moral standing of the slave *even in the limited sense we have just outlined.* Of course, I have no doubt that Darwall would object to the treatment; my claim is that he cannot do so by using the concepts of "freedom," "equality," "dignity," or "rationality" deployed in the book. Once again, Darwall strikingly concedes the point:

> The slaveholder's approach to the slave may not even purport to be second-personal address in our sense. He may simply be attempting to force the slave's submission or compliance in one way or another that doesn't even purport to address a second-personal reason. To be sure, the most interesting and disturbing cases of domination include second-personal traces or simulacra, such as a humiliating mutual acknowledgment of the slaveholder's power to subjugate the slave. But even here, if there is nothing that purports to be authentic second-personal address of the kind we have been concerned with, *the argument simply does not apply.*[88]

So Darwall has only offered an argument showing that the slaveowner owes a justification to his slave, and hence that his slave has basic moral standing, only if he addresses him. But the argument doesn't show that he does any wrong in *not* addressing him. The argument therefore also fails the Rationale Desideratum.

Does Forst's view offer a better account of the Address reading? I will argue that it does, but only by relying on a set of very un-Kantian premises. Recall that Forst claims that the very structure of our practices of justification—our practices of giving and offering reasons—necessarily commits us to criteria of generality and reciprocity, and hence equality. These criteria then recursively apply to the very reasons exchanged as standards: if the reasons offered do not meet the standards, then they are not genuine reasons; they carry, that is, no normative force over those to whom they are addressed. "Morality," Forst writes, "is merely the form of this 'justifying' existence in a particular practical context."[89]

Here's the problem. Are the higher-level, formal criteria of generality and reciprocity presupposed by the giving and taking of reasons enough to ground a substantive commitment to moral equality, such that it could rule out slavery? In much the same way as we pressed Darwall, we can press Forst. We might grant that the slaveowner owes a justification to the slave for his ownership, and we might also grant that the justification must be shareable by both the slave and the slaveowner from a general and external point of view. But why can *only* reasons that respect the slave as an equal in our more substantive sense be admissible from this general and external point of view? The slaveowner, after all, can give a *general* justification of his right to enslave: for example, he could argue, as ancient slaveowners often did, that one has a right to enslave any population that has been overcome in a war. This justification makes no use of proper names, is consistent, and is no less general than its opposite, namely that "victors do not have a right to enslave those conquered." And it is *reciprocal* because the slaveowner recognizes that, had *he* lost the war, then he could have rightly been enslaved. There is, in other words, no special pleading involved.* There is therefore nothing in the practice of ancient slavery that seems to contradict any logical or formal feature of reason-giving or justification.

Forst will want to respond by saying that the reasons given by the victors for the enslavement of the vanquished cannot be shared *in the*

---

* The enslavement, furthermore, is not based on any culpable ignorance or insincere beliefs about the inherent racial inferiority of those enslaved. I have focused on ancient slavery precisely because it does not (in every case) depend on false beliefs about the attributes of the enslaved (i.e., many who defended such slavery did not do so on the basis that some were born natural slaves, as in Aristotle's account, but that they were conquered in war). See, e.g., Garnsey 1996. But even if we were to focus on later forms of chattel slavery in Africa and the Americas, which often were based on such false beliefs, the wrongness of those practices does not rest, as we will see in Chapter 3, primarily on the fact that slaveowners had a bad or culpable epistemic position with respect to slaves. Even if the groups in question did have the qualities attributed to them, it would still not justify enslaving them.

appropriate sense by the latter. But why not? The answer, I am suggesting, must point to some substantive wrong-making feature of the relation between the slave and the slaveowner that cannot be derived directly from the purely formal characteristics of reason-giving and justification. Slavery is wrong, we might say, because of the kind of domination, coercion, violence, and vulnerability to which the slave is subject. But, as we have just seen, there is nothing in the mere idea of *giving a reason* or *providing a justification* that implies that—or more importantly *when*—domination, vulnerability, violence, or coercion are objectionable from a moral point of view.

One might think that practices involving coercion, violence, vulnerability, and domination (including slavery) are *ipso facto* incompatible with practices of reason-giving and justification. For example, if you are coercing someone (or dominating them, using violence against them, or exploiting their vulnerability), then you are, *by that very fact,* failing to offer reasons or justifications for your actions. But the Kantian must be careful. If coercion, violence, vulnerability, and domination are *necessarily* incompatible with reason-giving and justification, and hence wrong for that reason, then *any* coercion, violence, vulnerability, or domination must be wrong. But surely there are *legitimate* exercises of coercion, just as there is legitimate violence, vulnerability, and domination (at least if we take some degree of coercion, violence, vulnerability, and domination to be a necessary feature of many legitimate hierarchies of power, such as those between, say, a state and its citizens). To allow for cases like these, the Kantian must say that coercion, violence, vulnerability, and domination can be legitimate if adequate reasons, and hence adequate justification, can be given for them. But this concession would only serve to bring into further relief the point I am pursuing: the mere idea of reason-giving, and hence justification, can do little normative work on its own. We need something else to explain not only *why* but also *when* violence, domination, vulnerability, and coercion are wrong, and, *a fortiori,* something else to explain in what sense we are moral equals.

As with Darwall, I think Forst's Address reading thus far establishes, at most, that practices of reason-giving and justification presuppose that the person addressed has a competence to understand the reasons offered and respond accordingly. The reason-giver must presuppose that the person to whom reasons have been given must therefore have *a* moral standing—a standing, that is, from which they are expected to understand the reasons as moral reasons, and rationally guide their responses accordingly from a shared normative point of view.[90] When given a command, the other can therefore ask why, and expect an answer that provides a standard that they should both accept for the authority of the reason-giver. But, once again, the mere idea of a shared normative point of view does not exclude even the most extreme forms of slavery, and so does little to establish on what basis we are moral equals in the substantive sense that we are searching for.

At this point, however, we run into the same difficulty that Darwall's account faced. So far, Forst's argument is entirely conditional: *if* we provide reasons or justifications to others, then we must presuppose that they have a moral standing in the sense outlined. But why *must* we provide reasons or justifications in the first place? Recall the imprisoned slave, who was offered no reasons, no commands, and hence no justifications. Notice further that the Kantian cannot respond to this critique by saying that, by imprisoning the slave in a cell, the slaveowner thereby *implicitly* provides a reason or a justification for doing so. The reason is this. Imagine that someone imprisons, for example, a toy robot that he or she can't figure out how to shut off. If shutting the slave in a cell implicitly communicates a reason, then so would imprisoning the robot. The argument only works because it already assumes that the slave is not a robot and deserves to be treated with respect and concern as a moral equal. What it doesn't do is to show that, by imprisoning the slave, we thereby express reasons and therefore justifications, and must *for this reason* presuppose that the slave is our moral equal.[91] The argument therefore also fails to satisfy Rationale.

The Distinction between Basic Moral Status and Equal Moral Status

With this critique of the Address reading at our shoulders, we are now in a position to draw a fundamental distinction between what I will call *basic* moral status and *equal* moral status. Basic moral status refers to a being's moral standing to be treated only in ways that we could justify from a common perspective. Equal moral status refers to a being's moral claim to be treated as an equal. As we have seen in our discussion of Darwall and Forst, the Address reading establishes at most that, if a person is addressed second-personally, or is offered a justification, then the addressor must presuppose that those addressed have a basic moral status. However, the argument cannot establish, I argued, that persons are moral equals in the substantive sense required, for example, to rule out slavery. We then went further. Address readings only establish the truth of a conditional: *if* one offers second-personal commands, reasons, or justifications, then one must presuppose that those one addresses have a basic moral status. But they could not explain why anyone has a reason to offer commands, justifications, and reasons *in the first place*. What moral mistake does the master who locks the slave in a cell make? The Address reading, I argued, must remain silent in response to this pressing question. I now want to offer an explanation of our commitment to basic moral status that does, I believe, better than the Address view, and that will open a new avenue for addressing moral equality, to which we will then turn in Chapter 2.

Above I mentioned that Forst's view had the resources to point us toward a solution, but that the solution relied on a set of very un-Kantian premises. I now want to make good on that claim. At a critical point in *The Right to Justification,* Forst explicitly recognizes a series of difficulties facing alternative Kantian views. Referring to purely "transcendental-pragmatic" justification of morality (including Apel's discourse ethics and Korsgaard's Regress reading), he argues that they make failures to take the moral point of view into failures of "rational self-relation." For discourse ethicists like Karl-Otto Apel, Forst worries that violations of moral duty cannot be explained merely by a kind of pragmatic or rational incoherence.[92] I read Forst's rejection of Apel in the following way: that an act is morally wrong gives us a reason not to do it—but that reason cannot simply be: "don't do it because otherwise you will find yourself contradicting what is pragmatically presupposed by your own speech acts." The failure to "see another as a human being" (as Forst often writes), as one does in violating the most important moral obligations, is a wrong that cannot be reduced to a form of communicative incoherence, as if our reasons for not doing what is morally wrong were of the same character as our general practical reasons for ensuring that we are understood by others. Similarly, against Korsgaard, Forst contends that important violations of the moral law cannot be explained solely as failures to see that our valuations and commitments necessarily presuppose that *we* are of value (and only by extension, and hence derivatively, that other people possess the same value). What is missing from both accounts is an explanation of how the *other* enters into moral reflection as more than merely a refraction of a relation we have fundamentally to *ourselves* (let alone a relation we have to our speech acts).

Forst's alternative is complex and nuanced, but I believe it not only points him well beyond his own Kantian starting point but also risks making that starting point otiose. It is worth quoting him in full:

> This reflection on the capacity for being a "rational animal" is bound up with the reflection on being a "social" and also a "natural" animal: not only a justifying being but also a being who *needs* reasons. . . . For one owes other humans reciprocal and general reasons not only as autonomous beings but also as finite beings with whom one shares contexts of action in which conflicts are unavoidable.
>
> [The insight into finitude] is an insight into the various risks of human vulnerability and human suffering, bodily and psychological. Without the consciousness of this vulnerability and the corresponding sensibility . . . , moral insight that is an insight into human responsibility remains blind. A morality of justification also rests therefore on the insight that human beings as vulnerable and finite beings require moral respect and thus justifying reasons; and in this sense this is not a morality for mere "rational beings" but for those who have a sense of the evils that follow from denying someone's right to justification and not being respected as an author and addressee of validity claims.[93]

The way I read this passage is that others' moral standing is presupposed by any recognition of that other as a vulnerable, suffering, finite being. On this view, when you fail to take that standing into account, you fail to recognize the (vulnerable, finite, suffering) humanity of another person *directly* (rather than merely failing to recognize your own capacity to set and pursue ends, and the other only derivatively).

But why, we might wonder, is the other's moral standing always already included in any such recognition? Here Forst makes, I believe, a false move. He writes, referring to Levinas: "It is the 'face' of the other that makes clear to me where the ground of being moral lies, namely, in a certain fundamental understanding of what 'being human' means. It makes sense to describe this phenomenon as one of both cognition and recognition. For morality is concerned with the cognition of a human being *qua* human being."[94] What force does "being human" have? Forst here seems to be appealing to something like the concept of "being human," as if reflection on what we mean when we refer to human beings as human beings requires us to recognize them as finite, suffering, and vulnerable. This is certainly true, but how does that recognition require us to treat them a certain way? And why *only* human beings? Sometimes Forst refers to Wittgenstein and the idea that when we recognize another as a person, we must recognize that the other is not merely an "automaton" but a being with a "soul."[95] Yes, but the idea of possessing a "soul" seems merely metaphorical in this context: What is intended by use of the term "soul," exactly, if not something like what Christians believe animates our body (and survives the body after its death)?

To resolve this puzzle, let us return to the master who shuts the slave in a cell without offering justifications, reasons, or commands. He sees the slave as no more than an automaton. What moral mistake has he made? What has he failed to see in the slave? Why is he wrong to believe that the slave lacks a moral standing to demand a justification and expect a response from a perspective that they both can share? We have seen that merely appealing to what he must presuppose in justifying himself, or in addressing the slave, cannot work. He does neither. And appealing to the idea that the slave is created in the image and likeness of God cannot work either, given its sectarian character.

As Forst intimates in the passages quoted above, the best response, I now want to argue, is that the slaveowner fails to see that the slave's finitude, vulnerability, and suffering *itself* calls for a response. More specifically, the argument will come to the conclusion that the slaveowner, in recognizing the slave's evaluatively laden perspective on the world, must also recognize that the slave has a basic moral status, in its own right and for its own sake, to be treated only in ways that we could justify to him from a shared perspective. This will not yet be a demand to be treated as a moral equal, but it will at least be enough to close the gap left open by Darwall's and Forst's Address readings.

Above I followed Forst in emphasizing finitude, vulnerability, and suffering. But why these three? Plants, for example, are both vulnerable and mortal. Suffering seems to make up the relevant difference. But why does the capacity for suffering make a difference between a being that matters morally in its own right and one that doesn't? One response that has seemed attractive, especially among some utilitarians, is to argue that only conscious mental states that involve pleasure and pain (and hence suffering) can have morally relevant value or disvalue in their own right. The reason is that such mental states together constitute a point of view from which a being sees the world and through which the world begins to matter *to* the being. I will argue that such utilitarians are right to emphasize the idea of an *evaluative point of view* but wrong that only mental states can be bearers of moral value.

To see the extent to which utilitarians are right, consider that a being capable of some kind of mental representation is not enough. It is not enough for a being to be in states that have semantic content (that can refer, have truth-conditions, be accurate, and so on). Even robots can represent the world in this sense. The being must also be (phenomenally) conscious of those representations. But even such consciousness is not enough. We might imagine conscious creatures that could perceive the world through their senses, but for whom all such perceptions were entirely evaluatively neutral. For such a being, nothing would appear *as* good or bad, to-be-sought-after or to-be-avoided. While it would have a (phenomenal) perspective onto the world, it would not have any reaction to aspects of that world as being hospitable or inhospitable to it.[96] Such a being does not matter morally in its own right because, while it does have a point of view, its point of view is entirely passive and inert from an evaluative perspective. For this reason, it is no more morally significant than a robot. It is only when the creature's conscious life gives rise to an *evaluative* stance on the world that it begins to matter morally in its own right; it is only when a being reacts to the world with, for example, fear, desire, repulsion, disgust, joy, or attraction that it should register noninstrumentally in our reflections on what to do morally with respect to it. A being matters in its own right only when things matter *to* it.[97] We can then say that the being matters not only *in its own right* (i.e., not merely instrumentally) but also *for its own sake* (i.e., from its own point of view). On this view, suffering then appears, in fact, as only *one* of the many different ways a being might respond evaluatively to the world through their experience of that world.

So where is the hedonist utilitarian's mistake (at least with respect to basic moral status)?[98] The mistake is to argue that a being's conscious, evaluatively laden mental states must be the only bearers of moral value. The hedonist utilitarian arrives to this conclusion by reasoning that, since such mental states are constitutive of a being's point of view, and hence of its mattering morally, then our moral relations to beings of this sort must ultimately be solely a function of the quality, quantity, and duration of those mental states. But we can grant that the character of a being's conscious mental life is constitutive of its having a point of view, and hence of its mattering morally, but resist the conclusion that *therefore* our moral relations to it must be a function solely of its relevant mental states. We can do this, first, by emphasizing that what makes a being morally matter in its own right and for its own sake is a being's point of view, but that it is a mistake to argue that the (morally relevant) good for a being of this kind must be confined to whatever it is that constitutes the point of view in the first place. An analogy: It is one thing to argue that the game of chess is constituted by its basic rules, and quite another that the good of chess as a game can only be a function of the rules themselves. In determining the good of chess, it also matters what those rules enable one to do, and the kinds of social and cultural practices that grow up in virtue of chess as it is actually played over time and with others. To be sure, none of these further goods would be possible without the constitutive rules that make chess what it is, but these further goods are not properties of the rules themselves, but of the activities made possible by the rules. The same thing is true of conscious, evaluatively laden mental states. While those conscious mental states constitute an evaluative point of view on the world, their particular properties do not exhaust what is good for a being *from* that point of view. What matters morally with respect to beings with conscious, evaluatively laden mental lives will therefore depend on what it is like to live the life of a being of that kind, including the goods made possible by the kind of conscious mental life it is.* Any plausible morality will therefore be a function of (among other things) the full range of goods available to beings from their particular point of view, rather than merely a function of the quality, quantity, or intensity of the pain and pleasure of the mental states experienced by them.†

---

* I leave open here how an account of the "goods available to individuals from a particular point of view"—an account, that is, of its flourishing as a conscious, evaluatively sensitive being—might include the goods that it cannot now, but will in normal circumstances later enjoy (as with healthy infants). And, even more radically, I leave open how the kinds of goods it *could have* enjoyed in an identity-preserving way (even if it cannot ever enjoy them in the future) might also play a role in moral justification. The idea of what kinds of goods a being could have enjoyed is particularly interesting when we consider the claims that severely cognitively disabled human beings have on us. For an account of such "modal personism," see Kagan 2016; for criticism, see McMahan 2016. It is noteworthy that on my account (unlike Kagan's) we do not say that conscious, evaluatively sensitive nonpersons that could have been persons (e.g., severely cognitively disabled human beings) have a *higher status* than conscious, evaluatively sensitive nonpersons that couldn't have been persons (e.g., dogs). Rather, we say that a justification of what we can (and cannot) do to them should take into consideration goods that they cannot now or ever enjoy, but could have enjoyed in normal circumstances. We might say, for example, that severely cognitively disabled human beings are relevantly *worse off* than normal dogs, all else equal, simply as a result of missing out on what they could have been, and that this makes a moral difference to what we must, and may permissibly, do with respect to them.

† This account therefore extends to nonhuman animals that respond to the world in the evaluative sense we have identified, which is coextensive with the class of sentient beings. With respect to those beings, I say that we must have reasons for what we do that take into account their basic moral status; we must act, that is, toward them in ways that we could justify from a perspective that takes into account their good. If the beings in question are persons, and hence can understand reasons and justification, then we also say

So far, I have argued that the reason we have to treat an individual as a being that matters in its own right and for its own sake—and hence as a being with a basic moral status—is that it has an evaluatively laden, conscious point of view on the world. At this point, one might wonder what further considerations one might adduce in favor of this reason. Is it, for example, itself grounded in further reasons? In short, no. The reason is basic and nonderivative. It neither follows from acceptance of any higher-level practical principle nor can it be explained in terms of any further reasons one might have (for example, to do what one desires or would desire on reflection). But this is not the end of the story. Just because the reason is not itself grounded in any further considerations doesn't mean that we can't try to justify our commitment to it by considering the role it plays within a broader scheme of values. We must not, that is, confuse the *evidential support* for a claim about the reasons we have and an account of a reason's *grounds*.[99]

What might such a further argument look like? Many who have balked at the existence of basic, nonderivative reasons have worried that a proponent cannot explain the "grip" that such reasons could possibly have on the agents they are meant to guide.[100] But the idea of "grip" is ambiguous. Is an account of the reason's "grip" meant to provide an account of the reason's normative authority over us? Or is it meant to demand an account of how we could be motivated by it?[101] If the former, then we might reasonably wonder what it would mean to provide an account of a reason's normative authority, if not to point to the still further reasons on which it, in turn, rests (but then what of *those* further reasons?). To stop the regress, the Kantian wants to claim that there are practical reasons whose force we *cannot deny* on pain of rational or practical contradiction. I have, however, doubted whether they can

---

that we owe them a justification from a perspective that can be shared with them. This difference between "owing them a justification from a shared perspective" and "acting in ways that we could justify from a perspective that takes into account their good," I believe, does not mark any difference in status, only in how we express that status in our actions. It is a further question, to be answered in Chapter 2, what kinds of beings we ought to treat as moral equals, and in what sense. Here we offer only a criterion for *basic* moral status.

make good on this claim. I have suggested, instead, that the regress can simply stop at a reason we find compelling and basic enough to provide an ultimate ground; as I have already mentioned and as we will see in a moment, however, this does not imply that we cannot say anything else to support our belief that the reason is genuine. We can profitably seek such a supporting account, I now want to argue, by answering the *latter*, motivational question.

At first glance, the motivational question might seem too psychological, asking for merely contingent facts about how different people might be led to affirm practical reasons rather than why they have some further normative reason to affirm them. I believe there is much more to be said for the normative rather than the merely psychological relevance of the motivational question. But it must be understood in a different way. Providing an account of how one could be motivated by a reason or a set of reasons can serve an *evidential* rather than a *grounding* role. We do not, that is, point to facts about motivation to explain in virtue of what further considerations the reason has normative authority over us. Rather, we assume the reason's moral authority and ask instead whether its acceptance is part of our good. What is the shape of a life in which such a reason figures? And what of a life in which the reason does not? We then wonder what *independent* practical reasons we might have—independent, that is, of the reason's own autonomous claim on us—to endorse a life with that shape, or to reject a life without it. If we do have such independent practical reasons, then we have provided further support for the reason—further evidence, we might say—that the reason is genuine and that its role in our scheme of commitments is deserved.[102]

This is what I want to do with respect to our reason to treat another as bearing a basic moral status. Let us return to the slaveowner and ask: What rational pressure—independently of simply pointing to the fact that the slave has a conscious, evaluatively laden perspective on the world—can we create on the slaveowner to see the slave as a being with a perspective on the world that matters in its own right and for its own sake? It is important here that we are not asking or searching for considerations that even the amoralist must accept. If the amoralist has a tin ear for morality in general, then we will need to adduce some further *nonmoral* considerations to take the slave into account. But we may reasonably doubt that there are any such nonmoral considerations. We may think that there is no vindication of morality from outside of morality.[103] We are also not seeking to show that the egoist—the person who is committed to doing what is best for himself, narrowly understood— should take others' good into account because it will make his life better. Rather, we try to show that accepting the reason to take another's good into account on the basis that the other has a point of view on the world is *itself* a constituent part of his good.[104] We assume, that is, that the slaveowner has a normal range of moral sentiments and reactive attitudes that allow him to engage as a participant in social and moral relations with others, and see where we can go from there.

Once we have put things in this way, we proceed by pointing to the rest of the slaveowner's life, and to what gives it integrity and meaning. From this point of view, we characterize the slaveowner's failure as a failure of *humanity*, where we understand humanity as a moral virtue rather than an attribute possessed by all and only human beings. Humanity is the disposition to projectively imagine the world from another's point of view, and then to seek an "accord and symphony"[105] of your and the other's perspective on the world, a reconciliation that seeks a harmony of perspectives rather than division. The person who acts with great humanity is the person who is able to leap into and embrace others' point of view, and, in the case of rational beings, to seek ways of reconciling multiple and conflicting perspectives into a single one that can be shared by all. Humanity is, in this sense, the disposition displayed by the person who recognizes another's evaluatively laden perspective on the world as a reason to treat it only in ways that one could justify to it as a being that matters in its own right and for its own sake. Humanity is a natural consequence of accepting our basic reason as a ground for reflecting on what to do and what we owe to others.

At the center of humanity, understood as a disposition, is therefore empathy. Notice, furthermore, that it is this disposition that explains our capacity, as human beings, for friendship, love, conviviality, and, indeed, morality.[106] And it is empathy that explains why we normally have such a strong desire to be, as Mill writes, at "unity with our fellow creatures."[107] Like Adam Smith and Hume, I believe that this desire is explained by our capacity to enter projectively into others' point of view, and, in turn, to imagine what we must seem like from that perspective.[108] We seek an accord and symphony with others' perspectives because we must inevitably see ourselves as we appear in their eyes. The thought of how we must appear to others brings with it not only the possibility of love and conviviality, but also shame and the pain of disapproval.[109] Without empathy, and without the mutual reconciliation that it naturally seeks, we would therefore be incapable of engaging reciprocally in any of the practices that makes a human life good. Insofar as[110] it is part of the essential and sustaining infrastructure of many of the most important goods in a human life, empathy is itself good, and the disposition to project ourselves into others' situations and seek a reconciliation with them from that perspective therefore a virtue.

So the slaveowner's failure, on this view, is not only a failure to respond to a self-standing reason to treat another as bearing a basic moral status; it is also, more broadly, a failing that implicates the ethical integrity and moral tenor of the rest of his life. To the slaveowner, we say, "Your inability to 'see' your slave as a being with a rational, evaluatively laden point of view, and hence as a being that deserves reasons and justification, is a failure of humanity understood as a virtue. Don't you see that you are failing to use your capacity to projectively identify with others' perspectives, which underlies all the most important relationships in which you stand to others? Don't you realize that the slave also has a point of view on the world just as the most important people in your own life do?" This isn't, of course, yet a reason to, say, free the slave, or, therefore, a reason for affirming moral equality. Similarly, this isn't a reason that is somehow *inescapable:* there is no logical or practical contradiction if the slaveowner doesn't recognize it. I have argued that the search for such inescapability is chimeric, and even if it weren't chimeric, it would offer the wrong kind of reason. But the further reason offered is, I believe, none the less powerful for that. By questioning how he can live with himself, given the place of empathy in the rest of his life, given the way that empathy promotes his good and given that all of his most important commitments and cares must rely on it, we put pressure on his own sense of humanity. We urge him to see that his humanity, so evident in the rest of his life, compels him to seek a reconciliation with the slave through a justification that can be shared with him.

This way of proceeding allows us to respond to what might seem like an objection, but upon further reflection is not. In a recent discussion of moral equality, Thomas Christiano writes:

> It is hard to see why having seen things from the other's point of view by itself implies that I should then be concerned to advance the concerns that manifest themselves from that point of view. . . . [T]he mere fact of being able to identify with someone else's point of view does not give us reason to value what is valued from that point of view.[111]

One might think of this as an objection to the argument I just canvassed. After all, I have said that our capacity for empathy, and our recognition of that capacity's role in any flourishing life, gives us independent reason to see that beings with a conscious, evaluatively laden perspective on the world deserve justification for what we do to them that takes into account their interests as mattering in their own right and for their own sake. But does it imply that we therefore should be "concerned to advance the concerns that manifest themselves from that point of view," including "giving us reason to value what is valued from that point of view"? *No.* I agree with Christiano that it is a mistake to draw an inference from the former to the latter. But that is precisely the point: an account of basic moral status, in my terms, tells us that we must act only in ways that we could justify from a perspective that takes into account the other's good as mattering in its own right and for its own sake (and so mattering in ways that a robot or a rock does not), but it doesn't yet tell us much about the content of the justification that is due to it; it doesn't tell us what reasons we have (or lack) to act on their behalf, or to value what they value, just as it doesn't tell us that, for example, enslaving them is morally wrong; and neither does it tell us, more generally, which kinds of instrumental treatment violate its basic moral status and which ones don't.[112] For that, we need a further stretch of moral argument, to which I turn in Chapter 2. That is why I have emphasized that an argument for *basic* moral status doesn't imply or presuppose a commitment to *equal* moral status. So Christiano is right.[113]

2

MORAL EQUALITY, RESPECT, AND CRUELTY

THERE IS NOW almost universal commitment to the idea that we are moral equals. Human beings, it is said, have an equal and inviolable dignity or worth that limits what any agent may do to them. Most of us take these ideas so for granted that we have stopped asking three basic questions, namely: In virtue of what do human beings have this worth? Do all and only human beings possess it? And what kinds of attitudes and actions does an appropriate regard for this worth require of us? These are three of the most difficult and perplexing questions in moral and political philosophy.

As we have seen in Chapter 1, philosophers who have answered these questions—the most influential have been either Kantians or Christians—have searched for some morally significant, value-bestowing natural property shared in equal measure by all and only human beings. They have argued that our commitment is grounded, for example, in the interest-independent, incommensurable, and intrinsic value of our capacity to make choices for reasons, or in our more general capacity to think, reflect, or love. It is these capacities, such philosophers argue, that give us dignity—a fundamental worth or value, in turn, which not only commands everyone's respect but also commands it equally. Both

Kantians and Christians thus defend *dignity-first* accounts; they explain the grounds of human dignity first, from which an attitude of respect is said to follow.

In this chapter, I set off on a different track. I abandon the search for a natural property or set of such properties that might explain why and how persons have dignity. Instead, I will argue that our commitment to moral equality is best explained and justified by careful consideration of our practices of treating each other as moral equals, and, more specifically, by examining the normative role that reactive attitudes such as respect play within those practices.[1] I will also argue that the most fruitful way to develop such a conception is to explore what is at the heart of *denials* of moral equality—to explore, that is, what it is to treat someone as a moral *un*equal, and hence as an *inferior,* and why such treatment is wrong.

The strategy pursued here is similar to the one adopted by P. F. Strawson regarding the problem of moral responsibility.[2] If you want to understand the grounds of moral responsibility, Strawson argued, don't begin with puzzles about free will and determinism, but begin instead with the reactive attitudes that constitute our practices of assigning responsibility. In a similar spirit, I propose that we avoid intractable puzzles regarding what we must presuppose about our own and others' value when we exercise our capacity to choose freely, or metaphysical puzzles regarding God's love for humanity. Rather, when seeking to understand the grounds of moral equality, we should aim to provide an account of the roles played by the reactive attitudes governing our practices of treating each other as equals. According to this hypothesis, the justifiability of those attitudes does not turn on whether they respond adequately to facts about our dignity or about the character of God's love. Their justifiability turns on whether and how they structure relations of mutual concern that are valuable in their own right.

TREATING AS INFERIOR

What is it to treat someone as a moral *un*equal, as inferior in that sense, and why is it wrong? It is not always wrong to treat someone as an inferior. Every instance of hierarchy, whether it is hierarchy within a company, hospital, university, military, sporting ground, state, and so on, involves both exercises of power of some over others and differences of esteem and rank. Yet not all hierarchies of power, esteem, and rank are illegitimate. So what makes the wrong involved in treating someone as a moral unequal, as an inferior *in that specific sense,* distinctive? Why and when is it wrong?

There are at least five paradigmatic and interrelated types of action that are instances of treating others as inferior in the relevant sense (from now on, I will simply say, "treating as inferior" to refer to this kind). First, we can treat others as inferiors by treating them *like animals* in need of the restraint and control of a superior, and hence as if they lacked typically human characteristics of self-control and self-consciousness. Such treatment, we say, *dehumanizes.* Second, we can treat others as inferiors by treating them *like children,* in need of the help or supervision of someone who knows better. Such treatment *infantilizes.* Third, we can treat others as inferior by treating them like *objects,* as lacking in subjectivity or interiority, or, fourth, as *instruments,* as we would a tool. And fifth, we can treat others as inferior by treating them as *polluted,* as bearers of what Erving Goffman called a "spoiled identity," marked out for special types of exclusion, disdain, or contempt on account of properties of their physical aspect, character, or background.[3] Such treatment, we say, *stigmatizes.* Consider also a nonexhaustive list of paradigmatic instances of treating others as moral unequals, all of which involve one or more of these types of action: torture; slavery; rape; segregation and apartheid; caste societies; persecution and invidious forms of discrimination; demeaning forms of paternalism; concentration and death camps; genocide; cruel, inhuman, and degrading treatment.

Any successful account of moral equality should be able to identify a unified set of wrong-making properties that explains why and when each of these paradigmatic types of action (and their corresponding practices) is wrong *qua* violation of equal moral status. Merely pointing to the idea of dehumanization, for example, is not enough. A police officer, for example, might herd people out of a stadium without the slightest regard for their self-consciousness or self-control. Yet, we wouldn't normally call such action wrong, let alone a violation of equal moral status. Similarly, it is not always wrong to use someone as an object or as an instrument. Think, for example, of peeking over to check the time on someone else's watch. In this case, we use them like a clock. When is treating as an object, or as a tool, wrong in the special sense we have identified, and why is it wrong? Similar things can be said both with respect to infantilization (think of a child) and stigmatization (think of a murderer).

As we have seen, dignity-first accounts, such as Kant's, will say that each of these types of action is wrong when and because it overlooks a transcendental fact about the power of rational choice: in acting and choosing, we must necessarily presuppose that our power of rational choice, and hence our humanity (in the Kantian sense), has an unconditional, interest-independent, and incommensurable value.[4] Christian accounts, similarly, will say that each of these actions is wrong when and because it fails to treat persons in accordance with the dignity inherent in their rationality, or capacity for free choice, both of which mark us out as beings created in the image and likeness of God.[5]

As I said, this is not the approach I will take. Rather, I ask: How do these types of action and the practices exemplifying them change the nature of the social relations in which people stand to one another? It strikes me that the most salient feature shared by all instances of treating as an inferior in the relevant sense is their *cruelty*. I will suggest that understanding what kind of cruelty is involved in such cases, why it is wrong, and what means we have of protecting ourselves against it, is the key to understanding our commitment.

CRUELTY

At the most abstract level, cruelty always involves the unauthorized and wrongful use of another's vulnerability to cause severe harm or suffering.[6] There are, however, many different conceptions of cruelty, each one of which illuminates a different aspect of cruelty or a different way of being cruel. Most traditional accounts of cruelty, for example, focus on cruelty in which the type of severe suffering or harm inflicted is not as important as the mental states or dispositions of the perpetrator. Such accounts emphasize, for example, the pleasure the perpetrator takes in inflicting suffering or pain, or his or her indifference.[7] But there is another conception of cruelty that, while still being sensitive to the quality of the perpetrator's will, focuses more prominently on what the perpetrator can reasonably be taken to be doing *in* causing severe harm, and hence on what we might call the objective social meaning of the action.[8] Cruelty of the kind I have in mind, which I will refer to as social cruelty, involves the *unauthorized, harmful, and wrongful* use of another's vulnerability to attack[†] or obliterate their capacity to develop and maintain an integral sense of self.* It is a rejection of this type of cruelty, I will argue, that stands at the center of our rejection of treating as inferior in the relevant sense. This is perhaps most evident with torture, whose purpose is not simply to inflict severe pain or suffering but to narrow the social, physical, and interpersonal world of the victim to such an extent that their own body becomes an enemy and their mind a surrogate of the torturer's.[9] But it is also evident at Winterbourne, where eleven care workers were filmed slapping vulnerable residents, soaking them in water, trapping them under chairs, taunting and swearing at them, and pulling their hair.[10] In cases like this, the care workers' actions strike us as cruel whether or not the care workers derived pleasure from their actions, and whether or not they lacked remorse or empathy for their victims. What matters is that they were

---

* By "wrongful," I mean that social cruelty is *(pro tanto)* wrong *because* it is a harmful attack on or obliteration of another's capacity to develop and maintain an integral sense of self rather than a harmful attack or obliteration that is wrong in virtue of some other feature of the action. An action's being a harmful and unauthorized attack or obliteration is what makes it wrong. Social cruelty, however, is a thick concept, so the precise extension of the terms "use of another's vulnerability," "attack," and "obliteration" as they are used in the formulation cannot be determined without doing some evaluation. This way of framing the issue can be accepted by both (sophisticated) reductionists and nonreductionists. See, e.g., Elstein and Hurka 2009; Roberts 2011.

† This formulation does not require that the attack be *successful*. It is enough if the attack on another's capacity to develop and maintain an integral sense of self is harmful *qua* attack. I turn to this below, in discussing Janie Crawford. By harm here, I mean a setback to interests. I discuss in more detail below which interests of ours are set back by attacks on our capacity to develop and maintain an integral sense of self, even in particular cases where our capacity to develop and maintain an integral sense of self survives the attack.

using the residents' vulnerable social position—their institutionally exposed weakness, age, and incomprehension—to destroy their capacity to develop and maintain an integral sense of self, their sense of being in control of their environment and their bodies in a way that preserved their ability to express a self-conception without fear of retribution. And it is also true of genocide, though this may be harder to see at first glance. The wrongness of genocide does not simply lie in its being an instance of mass murder. Genocide's distinctive wrongness is explained by the reasons for mass murder, which are grounded in an ideology that singles out a group of people as deserving extermination in virtue of who they are.[11] In every act of genocide, there are preceding events that aim to mark out a group within a community as subhuman, thus identifying those characteristics as marks of shame. Those affected can no longer appear in public without fear or maintain a social self that is (partially) defined or controlled by them. The only identity that matters in the community of which they were previously part is the one that marks them out for murder, exclusion, and revulsion. An essential aspect of genocide's cruelty (and the persecution that always accompanies it) is its use of a group's societal vulnerability to fracture and then obliterate the capacity to develop and maintain an integral sense of self.[12] It is no coincidence that victims of genocide are often portrayed as animals: they are animals because they have lost the right to define or express themselves as individuals and to claim recognition by the wider society on the basis of that self-definition. This aspect of genocide is also relevant to the social cruelty of slavery. Whatever else slavery is, it is a system maintained through deep and pervasive incursions on the slave's capacity to develop and maintain an integral sense of self, sustained by attacking one's sense of oneself as a participant in a wider society or community.[13]

Consider what is perhaps the paradigmatic instance of the kind of cruelty I am seeking to elucidate, namely the concentration camp. Of the "Musulmänner,"[14] what Levi calls "*i sommersi,*" the drowned, he writes that "one hesitates to call them living," but one also "hesitates to call their death death, in face of which they have no fear, as they are too tired to understand." They have been emptied of their sense of self, like "Zero Eighteen" who, Levi writes, was "nothing more than an involucre."

But this fracturing or obliteration of the self is not just suffered by the drowned, those who have given up. It is also experienced, though in a different way, by the saved. In one of the most powerful and ambivalent passages of *Se questo e' un uomo,* Levi writes of Henri, a "sane and civilized man," one of the "saved." He writes of speaking with him, feeling him warm and near, such that even

> affection is possible. One seems to glimpse, behind his uncommon personality, a human soul, sorrowful and aware of itself. But the next moment his sad smile freezes into a cold grimace which seems studied at the mirror Henri politely excuses himself *(". . . j'ai quelque chose à faire," . . . "j'ai qualqu'un à voire")* and here he is again, intent on his hunt and his struggle; hard and distant, enclosed in armour, the enemy of all, inhumanly cunning and incomprehensible like the Serpent in Genesis.
>
> From all my talks with Henri, even the most cordial, I have always left with a slight taste of defeat; of also having been, somehow inadvertently, not a man to him, but an instrument in his hands.
>
> I know that Henri is living today. I would give much to know his life as a free man, but I do not want to see him again.[15]

Along with Null Achtzehn, Levi expresses an ambivalent disgust toward Henri's inhumanity. But there is still the thought, which traverses the book, that though Levi was not Henri or Null Achtzehn, there was a part of himself that was, or that could have been. Henri's inhumanity, just like Null Achtzehn's lack of humanity, infects Levi's recollections and reminds him of the fragments of the self he has left behind. Philip Roth is right to call attention to the precision of Levi as chemist and observer, and to his "quantitative concern for the ways in which a man can be transformed and broken down and, like a substance decomposing in a chemical reaction, lose its characteristic properties."[16]

So far I have left the canonical formulation of social cruelty unpacked and merely alluded to the ways in which it can explain the cruelty in the class of paradigmatic cases mentioned above. I now want to give a more precise characterization of the most important elements of the formulation, starting with the idea of a "sense of self," which might otherwise seem obscure.

By "self," I do not mean one's personal or metaphysical identity, that which makes one numerically identical to one's past and future selves and nonidentical to another self. By self I mean what is sometimes called one's self-conception, one's conception of the values, commitments, and concerns that are central to one's life, the relationships and roles that make one the "kind of person" one is, including the qualities and defects of one's personality and character.[17]

But if that's the self, what does it mean to have a "sense" of self? Having a sense of self requires two aspects or points of view. There is the point of view of oneself as a creator and enactor and the point of view of oneself as what has been created and enacted. There is the self—or rather aspect of the self—that we might describe to another, that we might aspire to, or regret, and then there is the aspect of the self that does the describing, aspiring, and regretting. The two aspects—one active, one passive—are perhaps better described as two functional roles that we can assume. Our conscious life is a constant movement between one and the other. By acting, deciding, pursuing, we shape the kinds of people we are and can become, and by reflecting on who we are and can become, we give rise to our actions, decisions, and pursuits.[18]

Our *sense* of self, I want to claim, is an emergent property of this complex and variegated interplay. We develop a sense of self—a higher-level awareness of ourselves *as* selves—as we move into and out of the active and passive modes in the ways I have just described; it is in this way that our life becomes intelligible as forming *a* life rather than a disconnected series of life-fragments. When our sense of self maintains some minimum degree of reflective stability, consistency, internal coherence, and continuity across time and circumstance, we say that it has integrity. Rupture the process of (passive) reflection and (active) creation, and the integrity of our sense of self will suffer. It will be difficult to say, in general terms, how much reflective stability, internal coherence, continuity, and consistency is required. It will vary by person, according to our ability to integrate dissonant experiences, circumstances, and internal and external upheavals. Consider how our sense of self can be broken by internal and external events. Our sense of self can be broken, for example, by depression, which is often associated with a sense that one has lost oneself, a sense that one no longer knows oneself or knows how to continue given who one was. Great tragedies, such as the death of a loved one, can also break the integrity of one's sense of self, causing significant disorientation, including the feeling that one has lost one's identity.[19] A loss of social standing or recognition, triggered by unemployment or sudden poverty, can disrupt the integrity of our sense of self, as can grave physical or mental illness. Similarly, and as we will see in more detail below, oppressive socialization that undermines our capacity to reflect critically on our values, commitments, and concerns, or that leaves us with deep inner conflicts that defeat our attempts to make sense of our lives, can also fragment our sense of self. In all these cases, we are challenged to integrate those experiences, events, and circumstances as part of ourselves. Sometimes we can rise to the challenge and make them *ours;* at other times we will struggle to make sense of our situation and will feel nothing but loss or disorientation. Having an integral sense of self gives rise to a concomitant sense of ourselves as autonomous, or self-governing: our choices, actions, values, commitments, and concerns are our *own.* Losing the integrity of our sense of self gives rise, in turn, to the sense that we are not in control, that we are being determined by events or by others, that we are not ourselves; in laboring with a broken sense of self, the world becomes undone. In one mode, we create and are created and can therefore see ourselves reflected in our decisions, values, and commitments; in the other, we are only ever worked upon, and feel as if we are merely playing a part in a play that we don't understand.

It is important to emphasize that an integral sense of self, in my terms, does not require that we live our lives as the protagonists of a grand, historically unified narrative, or that we wholeheartedly embrace every aspect of ourselves or our lives, or that we seek to weed out all ambivalence.[20] The notion is much more modest and human.[21] All it requires is that our ambivalences, regrets, dependencies, and upheavals be integrated into our evolving self-conception—but there is no embargo on their being integrated *as* ambivalences, regrets, dependencies, and upheavals. A good example is provided by Maria Lugones's writings on the difficulties of affirming an identity as *both* Latina and lesbian. From the perspective of *Nuevomejicana* culture, lesbianism is considered shameful, an "abomination." From within the lesbian community, the *Nuevomejicano* way of life is alien, foreign, and dominating. Lugones cannot give up, she says, either side of her life without betraying the other. "I do not know," she writes, "whether the two possibilities can ever be integrated so that I can become, at least in these respects, a unitary being. I don't even know whether that would be desirable. But it seems clear to me that each possibility need not exclude the other so long as I am not a unitary but a multiplicitous being."[22] Insofar as Lugones sees her "multiplicity" as giving her life meaning and direction—indeed in part *because of,* rather than *despite,* the conflicts it creates—she acts from an integrated, rather than a fractured, sense of self.

A similar point can be made with respect to another class of cases, in which individuals find themselves divided between what they most care about and what they judge to be best, all things considered. Both the mother who cannot bring herself to give up her daughter for adoption, but who still believes that she has conclusive reasons to do so, and Huck Finn, who treats Jim with humanity even though he judges that he really ought to turn him in, provide examples.[23] In cases like these, we find that some of our deepest projects, values, and commitments lead us onto paths that we believe to be rationally objectionable, and yet we still identify with them—whether implicitly (like Huck) or explicitly (like the mother)—as expressions of what we most care about and hence what gives our life meaning. When we do so, we act out of an integral sense of self. Our sense of self fractures only when such inner struggles, conflicts, dissonant events, and circumstances cease to make sense to us—when, for example, we are paralyzed by them, or we cannot find ourselves in them, or we have become merely passive or rudderless with respect to them.

This brings us to a difficult question that is crucial to the account: What is the value of an integral sense of self? Think of the most important goods in a human life, those things we have most reason to value, such as knowledge, love, friendship, pleasure, the appreciation of beauty, the raising of children, accomplishment and skill. What contribution does an integral sense of self make to the good of each of these things for us? It might seem that the contribution is solely instrumental: an integral sense of self makes it causally more likely that we will be able to enjoy each of those things. But, on reflection, I think the connection is deeper: an integral sense of self is also a *constituent* of the good of each of those things. To see this, consider that we do not only want the *benefits* that knowledge, friendship, the raising of children, solitude, pleasure, skill, beauty, and so on, can bring. Their value for us is not merely in the *having* of them. Their value for us is fully realized only when we engage and pursue them through our own endeavor, choice, and commitment. To have value for us, to be meaningful to us, they must reflect who we are; we must be able to see ourselves *in* the pursuit and enjoyment of these goods. Knowledge, for example, is of course instrumentally useful (and also, I believe, good in itself), but knowledge that is acquired through our own pursuit and passion and engagement acquires a different and deeper value for us.[24] The same reasoning applies *a fortiori* to love, skill and accomplishment, and so on. Similarly, the good of many of these things for us can only be realized when they make sense in terms of other ends and the place they hold in our lives; the good of solitude, for example, can only be realized against the background of deep and layered relations to friends, lovers, and family, just as the good of such relations can only be realized when we also have solitude.[25] An integral sense of self is, therefore, a constituent ingredient and structural element of a flourishing life; while its value is *extrinsic,* it nonetheless plays an essential role in our enjoyment of the most important goods.[26] In laboring with a fractured sense of self, we lose the capacity to see ourselves in our pursuits, concerns, and cares and so we cannot participate in the most important goods that those pursuits, concerns, and cares make possible.

What, barring exceptional circumstances, are (empirically) necessary conditions for the emergence and maintenance of an integral sense of self understood in this way? I will not provide an exhaustive list. Instead, I will focus on three that, for our purposes, stand out. All three of them reflect our social and sociable nature and are expressly targeted by social cruelty. They are different components of our nature as *self-presenting* beings.[27]

The (dual) process I described above depends on and generates a self-conception. But, given our nature as sociable beings, such a self-conception must find some echo in the world of others. A gap between the way we see ourselves and the way the world sees us (as we perceive it) will cause dissonance and lead us to adjust or adapt.[28] Our capacity to develop and maintain an integral sense of self cannot long survive a widening gap between the two. This need for recognition is borne of our nature as self-presenting beings: we do not simply participate in the (dual) process of reflection and creation as Robinson Crusoes. We define and redefine our self-conception—which includes, recall, our place in a network of roles and relationships—in communication and interaction with others similarly engaged.[29] We are constantly involved in the presentation of a self to a world of other selves.

But which self? As everyone knows, one does not come unadorned or unmasked into society. There is the self that we present and the self that we conceal. One is no more "true" than the other; there is no dishonesty in presenting a self or self-conception that is not an image of the raw currents of our inner mental and emotional lives.[30] Indeed, the division between inner and outer, the shown and the concealed, is necessary for any kind of social interaction.[31] Our self, then, is doubly divided: once between the self-conception that we present to society and the one we hold to ourselves, and then again between its active and passive roles, which straddle the divide between inner and outer.

And so we come to the first condition for maintaining and developing an integral sense of self over all these divides. The first condition is that we can (partially)[32] control what is inner and what is outer, what is presented and what is hidden and, in turn, that we can (partially)[33] control the terms in which we are to be recognized by others. We not only want to be recognized as *this* or *that,* but we want to be recognized *as* self-presenting beings—as beings who have a say in how we are to be seen by others. It is no surprise, then, that the most systematic forms of social cruelty aim at breaking our sense of ourselves as self-presenting. Torture is perhaps the most obvious. In torture, our body is, as I have said, turned against us; our inward fears are exposed, and in exposing them we are turned, as it were, inside out; torture works by entirely dissolving our sense that we can control the border between what is inner and what is outer.[34] We might also consider the life within "total institutions," characterized as institutions in which groups need to be managed collectively over all aspects of their life—such as mental hospitals, slave plantations, care homes, prisons, concentration camps, convents, military camps, and so on. Erving Goffman notes that the most dysfunctional "disrupt or defile precisely those actions that in civil society have the role of attesting to the actor and those in his presence that he has some command over his world";[35] he considers the "various forms of disfigurement and defilement through which the symbolic meaning of events in the inmate's immediate presence dramatically fails to corroborate his prior conception of self."[36] In all total institutions, inmates are stripped of those aspects of their previous social roles and relations that made them who they were, and, most of all, stripped of those symbolic and material elements that are used to make up their self-presentations. They are, Goffman writes, "defaced." Inmates lose their names, civil standing, position, clothes, and personal property. And once in, they are no longer free to form intimate relationships beyond the gaze of staff, to develop or pursue independent activities without permission, or to care for their bodies without monitoring. The sense of a boundary between inner and outer slowly dissolves.

The second, closely related, condition is the presence of a sustaining social environment in which one is recognized as a member and participant. "Part of our existence," Levi writes, "lies in the feelings of those near to us."[37] We have already seen how both genocide and slavery aim to destroy the integrity of our sense of self by obliterating any connection the individual holds to the cultural life and sustaining social environment through and in light of which the individual forms a self-conception. And we have just seen how Goffman's total institutions often succeed in regulating "inmates" by doing the same thing. Torture works in the same way. Torture counts as treating as inferior in the relevant sense not because it is an infliction of pain *simpliciter,* but because of the way it destroys the social and physical world in which the victim usually acts. The point of the violence is to narrow the victim's sense of social space—the space of reciprocal self-presentation—until there is nothing left in that space except the torturer himself. Torture makes it the case that the torturer can say to the victim, "You are nothing; I am everything." As I will discuss in much more detail in Chapter 3, our central interest in a sustaining social environment can also be thwarted by the bearing of a stigma (something that marks one out as socially or ritually "polluted," such as a physical deformity, or membership of an "undesirable" race or class):

> The central feature of the stigmatized individual's situation in life
> can now be stated. It is a question of what is often, if vaguely, called

"acceptance." Those who have dealings with him fail to accord him the respect and regard which the uncontaminated aspects of his social identity have led them to anticipate extending, and have led him to anticipate receiving; he echoes this denial by finding that some of his own attributes warrant it.[38]

Societies that reproduce social stigma thwart our central interest in seeing our concerns and cares echoed by the communities on which we rely for the development and maintenance of an integral sense of self.[39]

Finally, another way we present our selves to others is via our body. Given the importance of this form of self-presentation, the third condition is that we retain (partial) control over how our self-conception is presented through our body. Once again, torture is paradigmatic. But so is rape. Rape is not only an incursion on one's bodily integrity, like breaking someone's arm. It is, more importantly, an incursion on one's capacity to develop and maintain an integral sense of self. It is in part through our sexual choices—through the way we express and embody our love and passion and desire—that we allow others to see us as we are and we are allowed to see them as they are. Rape dehumanizes by attacking one of the most intimate aspects of our self-expression.[40] The presentation of our body to others also critically matters to us as we approach death. The thought that we have no (partial) control over how we may die (as we are dying), or over how our bodies will be treated after death, can also threaten the integrity of our sense of self (or, if not ours, then those who are forced to witness the way bodies of those like us are treated after we are dead). Think, for example, of the mass grave.[41]

So far I have defended a novel conception of cruelty, explored the idea of an integral sense of self at the heart of that conception—including three social conditions (empirically) necessary for its emergence and development—and suggested why sustaining an integral sense of self is valuable. Notice that at no point have I invoked the idea of dignity. We have an understanding of social cruelty, I have suggested, that is *prior* to our understanding of dignity. It is prior in the sense that we can know what social cruelty is, and how it is wrong, without needing to explain in what sense we have dignity. It is enough that we see how social cruelty is an attack on one's capacity to develop and maintain an integral sense of self, and that such attacks threaten to destroy something of great value to us, namely our ability to enjoy and participate in those things we have most reason to value.

In the next section, I will draw together the strands left hanging by this account to show how they bear on our understanding of respect, and then from there to our commitment to moral equality. But before turning to that, I want to mention another part of the formulation adumbrated above, namely the idea that the attack on or obliteration of the self must be *unauthorized*. One might wonder what to say, for example, about institutions like monasteries, convents, and militaries, all of which involve what Goffman calls "mortifications" of the self. Must all such mortifications be socially cruel? No. As long as the attempted mortifications of the self are the result of genuine and ongoing* consent, then we have made them ours in the relevant sense. They therefore cease to be socially cruel. I return to this point below.

RESPECT

There are many different forms of respect. We respect, for example, the speed limit by observing it, or the rules of football by complying with them. Or we respect the storm by remaining moored in a sheltered bay. This is not the kind of respect we are interested in explaining. Here we are focused on the grounds for respecting *persons* rather than rules or forces of nature. But even here there is variety. For example, we might respect someone's estimable qualities. We respect them, in this sense, insofar as we hold their achievements or character in high regard, or

---

* It is important to emphasize the importance of *ongoing* consent in situations where the integrity of our sense of self is (voluntarily) threatened. Because of the effect of such mortifications, there is always a risk that consent will cease to be genuine. Hence the importance of giving those involved a chance of exit. (By "genuine," I mean that consent generates permissions, granted to those to whom consent has been given, to do what would otherwise be impermissible. So, if an act of consent fails to be genuine, then the actor who acts on that consent is a wrongdoer. Note that, depending on the context, the wrongdoer may be blameless.) I cannot here discuss what might make an act of consent invalid, since that would take us too far afield, though see the discussion of consent and its role in a theory of moral equality, both later on in this chapter and in Chapter 3.

treat them in accordance with the dignity of their office or position. The kind of respect for persons we are interested in is, however, owed to others simply as persons, and hence is not conditional on merit, position, or social status. It is a form of respect that Darwall calls "recognition respect."[42]

The key questions are: What *kinds* of claims must we respect in others for us to respect them in the appropriate way, that is, in a way that reflects our commitment to moral equality? And: What is the basis for this respect? As we have seen, most answers to this question have gone by way of the idea that persons have dignity. We proceed, instead, by pointing to the role that respect plays in securing the conditions for the development and maintenance of an integral sense of self. The rest of the chapter is dedicated to elaborating this idea.

Notice that respect is deeply imbricated with the functions that social roles play. Whenever there is a social role, there is a set of norms governing the modes of respect appropriate to it. Think, for example, of medical allocation decisions. There is only one organ to transplant. You are a doctor. Whom do you save? Do you make your decision on the basis of particular facts about how well people's lives are going, rewarding the happy and leaving the unhappy to the side? Do you take into account people's moral virtue, their intelligence, or their accomplishments? Do you take into account how many children they have, or by whom they are loved? Or do you make the decision solely on the basis of their prognosis, and on the basis of *general* facts about people's quality of life in different life stages? It seems that we do best by doing the latter. Why? We might say that information about how well people's lives are going, or how many people love them, or their moral virtue, is difficult to ascertain. But would it really make a difference if such information were readily at hand? Here's another explanation: We think of such private information as irrelevant to the decision because it reflects intimate features of people's lives that are central to their sense of self. Exposing people's inner lives to public gaze and evaluation, especially in decisions over their life and death, threatens at least two if not all three of the essential social conditions for developing and maintaining an integral sense of self. Such information ought, we might say, to remain opaque to the medical bureaucracy that allocates organs.

This kind of opacity is pervasive and central to the normativity of social roles. When we are students, we expect to be respected by our professors *as students,* and when we are professors, we expect to be respected by our students *as professors.* Our standing *as students,* we say, gives others reasons to treat us in ways that are appropriate to that standing. Acting in accordance with those reasons is acting with respect. But what is the specific form this respect takes? What are the reasons our standing or role as students, as professors, gives? Any information about our person that is not relevant to the fulfillment of our role gives others reasons not to treat such information as definitive of the relation unless they are authorized otherwise. But the same thing is true when we consider the attitudes that govern how we ought to treat persons *independently* of their particular interests, worth, character, and accomplishments as well as their roles. When you respect someone *as a person,* you do not treat who they are, what they have done, or where they come from as relevant to your interaction with them. To respect in this way just is, therefore, to treat the contingent aspects of their life and situation as opaque (unless we have been authorized to do otherwise), just as we did in the medical allocation case. It is worth reflecting on why this kind of respect, or *opacity respect* as I will call it, is so central.[43]

Notice that when we respect someone in this way, we do not engage their full personality. We maintain a reserve or distance and, above all, we sustain a kind of *restraint.* But why the distance and restraint? What purpose does it serve?[44] Of course, part of its purpose within social roles is just to allow people to get on with their jobs, to fulfill their roles given the special nature of the social practices in which the roles figure. Opacity respect, more generally, can also protect people against everyday forms of rudeness or discomfort.[45] These functions form, however, only a part of the explanation. At its most fundamental level, opacity respect, I want to suggest, also serves to protect us against social cruelty. This protective function, in turn, is an essential part of its justification.

This is easiest to see by considering not minor violations of opacity respect—those violations that only skirt the surface of our practices of respect—but deeper and more pervasive violations. Consider first a world without the restraint characteristic of opacity respect. In *The*

Scarlet Letter, Hawthorne describes Hester Prynne on the scaffold. Publicly marked by her crime and forced to carry her illegitimate son with her onto the raised wooden frame, she stood "fully revealed" with "the heavy weight of a thousand unrelenting eyes, all fastened upon her." Hawthorne writes: "There can be no outrage . . . against our common nature—whatever be the delinquencies of the individual—no outrage more flagrant than to forbid the culprit to hide his face for shame." As an object of contempt and public dishonor, Hester Prynne no longer merits the restraint implicit in opacity respect; she becomes, as a result, liable to the inferiorizing social cruelty to which the town subjects her.[46] It is the same with the dehumanization and objectification that takes place within Goffman's total institutions. Under the gaze of staff, inmates no longer have a recognized claim to control their self-presentation, including, most importantly, control over what can remain concealed and what revealed, over their bodies, and over their social relationships. As objects of treatment and supervision, the restraint called for by opacity ceases to play any role. Once free of that restraint, social cruelty, like at Winterbourne, almost always follows.

These examples, and others like them, suggest that opacity respect functions *inter alia* to protect us from social cruelty. But how does it do so? When we respect someone *as a person,* we yield to them specifically as *self-presenters,* as individuals who have a self-conscious perspective on both the world and their place in it, and a basic desire for recognition of that perspective by others similarly placed. Respect expresses the recognition that others require control over the division between inner and outer, over the body, and over the way they appear to others in public. As Thomas Nagel writes:

> One of the remarkable effects of a smoothly fitting public surface is that it protects one from the sense of exposure without having to be in any way dishonest or deceptive, just as clothing does not conceal the fact that one is naked underneath. The mere sense that the gaze of others, and their explicit reactions, are conventionally discouraged from penetrating this surface, in spite of their unstated awareness of much that lies beneath it, allows a sense of freedom to lead one's inner life as if it were invisible, even though it is not. It is enough that it is firmly excluded from direct public

view, and that only what one puts out into the public domain is a legitimate object of explicit response from others.[47]

The distance required by opacity respect serves to protect our three central interests by creating space for the self-presentation intrinsic to our sociable nature.

It is helpful here to draw a further contrast with the Kantian. For the Kantian, the respect that is at the heart of moral equality is a response to the absolute, intrinsic, and incommensurable value of rational agency; I am arguing, by contrast, that such respect is a response to our need, as sociable beings, for opacity. To deepen this contrast, and to illustrate how opacity respect, cruelty, and moral equality are interrelated, I will discuss three further examples. First, consider the wrongfulness of what we might call "invidious" discrimination, i.e., discrimination that involves demeaning or degrading members of a historically disadvantaged group (about which we will have much more to say in Chapter 3). In 1949, South Africa passed the first of several acts of parliament instituting a system of apartheid. Among these was a prohibition on interracial marriages. What makes discrimination of this kind wrong? The prohibition on mixed marriages explicitly targets nonwhite South Africans as appropriate objects of social contempt and public dishonor deserved in virtue of an indelible stigma. As we will see in much more detail in Chapter 3, such invidious discrimination is wrong because it is a humiliating attempt to undermine and fracture nonwhites' capacity to develop and maintain an integral sense of self.[48] What matters is not simply the denial of an opportunity to marry in accordance with one's choices (which one may never in fact want to take up), but its social meaning.[49] Opacity respect here plays an important role. In apartheid South Africa, nonwhites were not accorded any recognition of their need for self-presentation, or any recognition of their three central interests in developing and maintaining an integral sense of self. Instead, they were treated in accordance with an imposed, negatively tainted identity that served to legitimize their systematic oppression.[50]

Second, our account can help us to make sense of the moral complexities involved in helping those who are in need, such as the elderly. The elderly have, like everyone else, a deep concern for their physical appearance, their ability to make decisions for themselves, and their connections to communities of which they are a part (especially if they are retired). As we have seen, these are all aspects that (though often overlooked) are central to our sense of self, and hence our nature as self-presenting beings. But as we grow older our command over these three aspects of our lives inevitably diminishes. What does respect require in such circumstances? Even in cases where someone is in need, respect, as we have seen, requires us to treat another's weakness and vulnerability as opaque to us (even if we know and must take such vulnerability into account). But the elderly are especially vulnerable—think of Winterbourne—precisely because their access to the three social conditions becomes more tenuous with age. Ought we to continue treating them with opacity? In one sense, we clearly must. The frail are right to insist that we respect, we yield to, their demand to be treated "as a person, not as a decrepit old man." This does not mean, of course, that we *disregard* the frailty of their condition, but that we take such aspects of their condition into account while maintaining, as best we can, their secure and stable access to the three social conditions. This kind of balancing act, I believe, is at the heart of the virtue I have called acting with humanity. Someone who acts with humanity knows how to balance caring for someone who needs to be cared for while reinforcing their sense of self, knows when to pierce the veil of opacity and when to keep it in place. But to entirely disregard people's self-presentation—to aid them as if their own say in what remains inner and outer, what pertains to their bodies, and who they can see in their community does not matter—is often perceived (sometimes rightly) as cruelty.

I now turn to our third and final example. Think of how opacity respect operates in interactions among those of different social status. G. A. Cohen provides a useful example, which is worth quoting in full:

> All Souls College is an institution in which different people fulfill contrasting roles. One of those roles is the role of what is called a "Fellow," and another is the role of what is called a "scout," or, as he or she used to be known, in the embarrassingly recent past, a "staircase servant." The Fellows do academic work, and the scouts do menial work, cleaning the rooms, bringing the post, and so forth.

And scouts are regarded by Fellows in two contrasting ways, depending on who the Fellow is, and maybe also, sometimes, on
who the scout is.

Some Fellows regard scouts as, precisely, servants, that is, as
people who do serve others not as merely a matter of fact and circumstance, but as people whose *status* is such that it is *appropriate*
that their lot in life is to serve others. That sort of regard might
show itself, for example, in a certain brusqueness in the instruc-
tions as to the desired service that these Fellows give to scouts, and
in the nature of the response that scouts get when they serve well,
or badly.

But by some of the Fellows, at least some of the time, scouts are
regarded as equals, as people who, despite their low social status
(which is conferred partly by those who regard them in the *first*
sort of way) are as much deserving of respect as Fellows are themselves. In this way of regarding them, scouts merely *happen* to be
carrying out a service role—they are not thought of as people for
whom service is *appropriate*. Fellows show that they regard scouts
in that way when they pitch their requests to them nonbrusquely,
without conveying that, because of their *own* contrasting status,
they are *entitled* to the scouts' service. Of course, they are entitled
to that service in a certain sense: it is, after all, the job that the
scouts have contracted to perform. So one needs to specify in what
deeper sense the less egalitarian Fellows feel not unentitled to the
service, by contrast with the more egalitarian ones, who feel that
they are merely the lucky beneficiaries of that service.[51]

What might explain the intuition that the first set of Fellows do not respect the scouts as equals, whereas the second ones do? It is important
that both the egalitarian and the nonegalitarian Fellows accept the legitimacy of the hierarchy present in the example. The force of Cohen's
discussion presupposes our commitment to the idea that moral equality
doesn't proscribe all esteem-based or power-based hierarchy. The egalitarian Fellows' stance, that is, doesn't depend on the idea that the scout's
position deserves the same social esteem as the Fellow's or that the scout
ought to have the same contractually based power over the Fellow as the

Fellow has over the scout (as his employer). This means we cannot distinguish the attitudes and actions of the two on the basis that one wholeheartedly accepts the hierarchy while the other only does so *faute de mieux*.

Can the difference in regard be explained by the thought: "There but for the grace of God go I"? Do the egalitarian Fellows, in other words, treat the scouts as moral equals, as Cohen writes, "*because* they think their low status is an accident"? Interestingly, Cohen himself rejects this interpretation. Cohen argues that the explanatory arrow goes the other way around: "the egalitarian Fellows regard the low status of the scouts as a mere accident *because* they think they merit equal regard."[52] Indeed, the judgment that they occupy the role "by accident" *in the relevant sense* doesn't have anything to do with whether the scouts occupy their role as a result of luck ("accident") rather than choice. They would be entitled to the same regard *whether or not* they occupied that role by some choices they have made, or whether (counterfactually) they would occupy similar roles in any just society. And the judgment is also independent of the fairness or justice of the overall system that contains the role of scout. The egalitarian Fellow, we are to imagine, *shares* the judgment with his nonegalitarian counterpart that it is not unfair or otherwise unjust, all else equal, to employ scouts. Again, the egalitarian regard doesn't depend on a rejection of *all* esteem- and power-based hierarchies.

I think we do better by abandoning the idea of treating someone's lower status as an "accident." Speaking of it as an accident naturally leads to the thought (which Cohen himself, as we have seen, ends up rejecting) that the egalitarian regard hinges on an assessment of the scout's moral responsibility for being a scout.[53] A better explanation of the egalitarian regard in this case goes back to the idea that, in treating someone *as a scout,* we must also always treat them *as a person.* The nonegalitarian Fellow does not see the distinction. He disrespects the scout by treating his position *qua* scout as definitive of his person *tout court.* The scout is treated as *merely a scout,* rather than as a person *who has taken up* a contingent role in relation to you.

This moral failure, I want to argue, is best understood as a violation of opacity respect. To see this, consider that there are two complementary dispositions intrinsic to respecting someone's opacity. On one hand, when you treat someone opaquely (i.e., *qua* scout), you are disposed to treat any aspect of their person that is not relevant to the task at hand and which they do not present to you as a target for social interaction—such as their general virtues and accomplishments, their well-being and life plans—as opaque to you. But, on the other hand, you are *also* disposed to recognize that the individual has a life and person *independent* of their social role—a life in which they pursue life plans, projects, etc., *outside* of their role, and in which their accomplishments, virtues, etc., are not defined solely in terms of their role. The presence and importance of this life to the person concerned entails a coeval recognition of the importance of their interest in controlling the terms in which they appear to you as a scout, and hence of the importance of control over what to reveal and what to conceal. This is what motivates your yielding to the self *they* present—rather than the self *you* impose—as a target for social interaction.

The nonegalitarian Fellow strikes us as disrespectful because he fails to show any restraint with respect to the meaning that being *a scout* plays in the life of the *person*. By treating the scout's occupation as definitive of his character and his general position in relation to others ("people like him *deserve* to serve"), the Fellow fails to grant the scout any control over his self-presentation. We might say that he evaluates the scout's person—the aspects of his self-presentation that underlie all his social interactions, both inside and outside of College—in terms of his role rather than the other way around. In so doing, he treats him as bearing a stigma—as polluted and hence unfit for bearing any restraint in his dealings with him. The stigma marks him out for differential treatment not just by the Fellow in question but by everyone.[54] For the nonegalitarian, the scout's servile position would justify not only *his own* brusqueness and contempt but would also justify a similar regard by others of the same rank. So, in sum, there are two ways to violate opacity respect: one can either ignore the boundaries of the roles in which someone presents themselves to us, or one can treat the role as all there is.

But what is wrong with treating the scout in this way? It would not be informative at this point to say, "Treating the scout in this way is wrong because it is an affront to his dignity." That would just be a restatement of our conclusion. What we want to know is: In what exactly does dignity consist, and what, more importantly, are its grounds? We have already addressed how dignity-first accounts are ill-suited to provide a foundation for respect. Instead, we ought to recall the function that opacity respect plays. Opacity respect, I have suggested, protects us *(inter alia)* against social cruelty, against attempts to break or otherwise obliterate our capacity to develop and maintain an integral sense of self, and thereby makes it possible for us to enjoy the most important goods. In this case, the fact that there is a practice and history of domestic servitude (both voluntary and nonvoluntary) against which the interaction between the Fellows and scouts occurs is of significant importance. To mark this importance, imagine the same sort of brusqueness and contempt toward one's own lawyer (whose role, after all, is to *serve*). While it would be disrespectful and insulting, it would not be disrespectful in the same way as the relation between the Fellow and scout.[55] This is because of the symbolic and social meaning of the Fellow's attitudes and actions toward the scout.[56] In short, the Fellow's attitudes and actions acquire their inferiorizing force against a historical background that opened up domestic servants to pervasive humiliation at the hands of their superiors (recall the stigma of manual service). When the nonegalitarian Fellow treats the scout with contempt, he recklessly invokes that past, mobilizing a set of hierarchical societal norms to humiliate and attack the scout. This mobilization of hierarchy transforms the Fellow's action into a form of inferiorizing social cruelty that is absent in the interaction between client and lawyer.

The distinction between inferiorizing social cruelty and mere offense or insult is important. As in the case of the scout and the Fellow, an offense or insult becomes an instance of inferiorizing social cruelty, and hence an instance of treating as an inferior in the relevant sense, only if two conditions are met. First, the offense or insult must count as taking advantage of a significant differential in power, esteem, or social status. Because mere offense or insult doesn't normally count as inferiorizing in any of the senses mentioned (as it doesn't between the lawyer and his client), it does not meet a necessary condition for violating someone's status as a moral equal. Second, it must count as an attack on another's capacity to develop and maintain an integral sense of self understood as a structural ingredient of a flourishing life. An inferiorizing attack cannot therefore be *merely* offensive or insulting; it must also be an assault on another's very *capacity* to see themselves reflected in their projects and plans. An insult may temporarily shake one's sense of self, but if it is not correctly seen as an attack that is part of a systematic societal pattern whose effects reverberate throughout one's life and one's dealings with others (as with the mobilization of stigma in the case of the scout) or that forms part of an attempt to undermine one or more of the structural conditions for maintaining and developing one's integrity (as in torture), then it is not an instance of what I have called social cruelty. This has an important further implication. Recall that it is not enough for someone to feel as if their capacity to maintain and develop an integral sense of self has been attacked for it to be true. As I have already mentioned, and as will become important also later (in Chapter 3), whether something counts as inferiorizing social cruelty is an objective feature of the action. This implies that both the agent and the purported victim can be mistaken about whether an action is both inferiorizing and socially cruel. These two objective conditions can therefore also be used to distinguish mere insult and offense from, for example, invidious racial discrimination. As I will explore in much more detail in Chapter 3, invidious racial discrimination inferiorizes by stigmatizing and dehumanizing in a way that systematically undermines one of our structural interests—namely our interest in recognition of the society of which we are a part—in a way that mere interpersonal insult does not.

In closing this section, I want to discuss an important objection. Suppose now that the scout takes a very deferential attitude, especially toward the nonegalitarian Fellows, and that he does so because he conceives of himself as meriting that kind of treatment, as deserving no better. Imagine, that is, that the scout takes his servile position as definitive of who he is, and therefore as central to his self-conception. When the nonegalitarian Fellow treats him with contempt or disdain, we might therefore think that he *reinforces* rather than *undermines* or *attacks* his capacity to develop and maintain an integral sense of self (given the kind of self it is). Let us further imagine (as seems plausible) that the scout never consents to such treatment, precisely because it never enters his mind that being treated in this way would otherwise be impermissible (and hence require some special consent). To put it another way: This is not some game or play-act between the scout and the Fellow—defined and limited by an act of consent by both parties—but an ongoing social relationship defined by the hierarchical, deeply entrenched social conventions and expectations that make it possible.

This is true of, for example, Smerdyakov, the illegitimate son of Fyodor Pavlovich, who is described by Dostoevsky as an "abominable lackey." Smerdyakov's self-loathing leads him to internalize the cruelty directed toward him, and as a result he harbors profound but largely unconscious seas of resentment and anger, which finally burst forth in his own act of cruelty on his master and father. His precarious position and inner conflicts throughout lead him into situations and actions that are self-defeating and ultimately self-destructive; wildly awestruck and deferential one moment, suspicious and rageful the next, his servility is not a reflection of any deeper values, aspirations, or commitments, but a product of a deeply divided and fractured personality.

Alternatively, we might consider the Victorian ideal of femininity, the Angel in the House, described by Virginia Woolf in the following terms:

> She was intensely sympathetic. She was immensely charming. She was utterly unselfish. She excelled in the difficult arts of family life. She sacrificed herself daily. If there was chicken, she took the leg; if there was a draught she sat in it—in short she was so constituted that she never had a mind or a wish of her own, but preferred to sympathize always with the minds and wishes of others.[57]

Let us add to this picture of the Angel an abusive husband who treats her with contempt and disdain, as a child and servant to him; she does nothing to resist him because she does not feel that she deserves any better. As an Angel, she absorbs his disdain as her own. As before, our puzzle is that the husband's treatment seems to reinforce and mirror rather than undermine or attack her capacity to develop and maintain an integral sense of self (given the kind of self it is). So in what sense is his action cruel? And, if we don't conceive of it as cruel, in what sense is his treatment of her as an inferior wrong?

The reason such cases strike as cruel is that they are instances of taking advantage of another's vulnerability to humiliate and infantilize in such a way as to reinforce an *already fractured* sense of self. A sense of self is fractured when, as with Smerdyakov, deep and internal conflicts produce a pattern of life that is rudderless and self-destructive, or, as with the Angel, when it is self-*abnegating*: when, rather than playing the discussed constitutive role in the realization of the most important goods, it structurally undermines that role by undercutting one's capacity to see oneself reflected in one's values, projects, and commitments.[58] When asked to reflect on her attitudes, the Angel does not say, "my attitudes are a reflection of my perspective on the world, including its values, commitments, and concerns"; rather she says, "my values, projects, and concerns don't matter; only his do." Her selflessness is not in the devotion of a cause or role in which she sees her aspirations and plans reflected; rather, her selflessness is an act of self-*effacement* in which she abandons critical reflection on her aims, values, and commitments and how they contribute meaning to her life. Woolf's indictment of the Angel is revealing. Woolf is threatened by her presence, the "shadow of her wings"; the Angel whispers in her ear and, like a phantom, "guides her pen": " 'My dear, you are a young woman. You are writing about a book that has been written by a man. Be sympathetic; be tender; flatter; deceive; use all the arts and wiles of our sex. Never let anybody guess that you have a mind of your own. Above all, be pure.' " And so Woolf turns around and strangles her. "My excuse," Woolf writes, "would be that I acted in self-defence. Had I not killed her she would have killed me. She would have plucked the heart out of my writing."[59] The Angel threatens Woolf's integrity as a writer, her independence of mind and spirit, her ability to reflect and react in her own manner from her own perspective. The Angel, when internalized, undercuts the development and maintenance of an integral sense of self by structurally undercutting the ability to acquire self-understanding through self-reflection, to take pleasure in one's own mind and undertakings, to find recognition and love in one's own friends and lovers, and to develop one's own skills and accomplishments. It structurally undermines, that is, one's capacity to see oneself reflected in one's pursuits, commitments, and actions, and, in so doing, undermines the realization of some of the most important goods in a human life.[60] In taking advantage of that vulnerability, the husband, like Fyodor, recklessly and harmfully reinforces another's already fractured sense of self; as a result, the treatment counts as an attack in the relevant sense, and so is socially cruel.

CONSENT

What role does consent play in the overall account? Recall that our account of social cruelty includes a qualifier: if (genuine) consent is given to some action that would otherwise count as cruel, then it is no longer cruel. I gave the example of militaries, convents, and so on. *Volenti non fit injuria.* But there is also a deeper explanation for the role that consent plays. On the account defended here, consent—which is a normative power to make some otherwise impermissible actions permissible[61]— has an important instrumental value, namely to protect access to the conditions necessary for developing and maintaining an integral sense of self. Consider that consent has both negative and positive functions. Negatively, consent prevents social cruelty. When respected, it sets a limit to what others may do to us against our will. Positively, it functions to expand the possibilities for the development of our sense of self (and hence our engagement with the most important goods). To see the importance of this last point, imagine a world where there is opacity respect but no consent—no normative power to make otherwise impermissible actions permissible. Like the ethereal figures in Giacometti's *City Square,* this would be a world of extraordinary isolation. Consent is valuable in part because of the way it allows us to invite others behind the veil of opacity, to bring people in rather than just to keep people out.[62]

This provides another contrast to Kantian views. For the Kantian, we must respect the limits established by others' lack of consent because they are an essential expression of rational agency. To disrespect such limits would be to thwart their intrinsic dignity, to override the respect they are owed in virtue of their capacity for rational choice. The power of consent is therefore intrinsically valuable in the same way as our rational agency is. The Kantian, however, has trouble distinguishing among violations of consent. Drawing someone's hand without ever seeking consent (and, let us suppose, without their ever knowing) and raping someone without ever seeking consent (and, let us suppose, without their knowing), on this view, are both wrong *for the same reason*: they override the person's rational agency.[63] On my view, it is clear why drawing someone's hand is a much less serious violation—if it is a violation at all—than rape, since raping someone attacks the victim's central interests in control over how to use their body to express their sexuality (where sexual choice is central to one's sense of self, and hence to any flourishing life), whereas drawing one's hand does not.

VARIATION AND STATUS

So far, I have explained when and why treating as an inferior is wrong and delineated an account of opacity that could be used to explain the respect at the heart of our commitment to moral equality. In this section, I extend the account to explain in what sense we are equals in moral *status* and elaborate how it avoids the variation objection.

In making this argument, we first need to distinguish two senses of status that are sometimes confused. The first is the idea of status as one's position in a hierarchy; status in this sense indicates one's level of prestige or honor, or the prestige or honor associated with a position or office one occupies. This is the sense in which we speak of the high status or prestige of, say, a marquis or judge. Dignity-first accounts primarily appeal to this kind of status. All persons, on this view, possess psychological capacities that give us a dignity, raising us up "above all price" and hence above all mere things. Possession of these capacities marks us out as meriting the kind of respect, deference, and reverence owed to beings of supremely high rank.[64]

But there is a second, primarily legal, sense of status that does not presuppose a hierarchy of value, honor, or rank.[65] This is the idea of status as a bundle of rights constitutive of a distinctive legal position or office. The monarch, for example, has a status defined by a set of distinctive normative powers. But so does the bankrupt, whose status is defined by a set of disabilities. Other civil statuses include one's marital status, or the status of being an alien or a refugee. We can also speak of a *moral* status in the same way: just as we can speak of the set of legal rights constitutive of a particular *legal* status, we can speak of the set of moral rights constitutive of a particular *moral* status.

Our *status as moral equals,* I want to argue, is composed of the distinctive set of moral rights that protects us from being treated as inferior in the ways I have discussed. To see how rights enter the picture, return to our five paradigmatic ways of treating another as an inferior. I have argued that each of these five modes is wrongful when and because it strikes at one or more of the three fundamental interests at the root of our sociability, and hence at our capacity to develop and maintain an integral sense of self. Put another way: the individual interests underlying our sociability are so important that they ground a set of third-party duties not to treat with inferiorizing social cruelty and hence, as we have seen, also duties to respect the boundaries of individual consent and opacity. We can go further: because the duties are ultimately grounded in the individual interests of those who are the intended beneficiaries of our respect, they are "directed" duties, duties owed *to* those beneficiaries rather than duties owed to no one in particular.* By violating these duties, one therefore not only does wrong *in general* but

---

* A directed duty is a duty owed *to* someone such that, in violating it, one wrongs that individual. For example, by wrongfully breaking my promise to you, I violate a duty I have to you (but to no one else). A nondirected duty is owed to no one in particular. For example, I might have a duty not to swear in public, where this duty is not owed to anyone in particular. If this is the case, then in swearing, I do wrong, but I wrong no one in particular. The way of explaining the "direction" of the duties I have offered in the text is compatible with a wide variety of contemporary theories of rights, including Raz 1992; Kramer 1998; Sreenivasan 2010; Cruft 2013; and Wenar 2013. The only views with which it is incompatible are will theories that hold that a duty's direction is explained by who (if anyone) has some measure of control over the duty (including a normative power to release the dutyholder from his duty). This doesn't seem right to me, for someone acting in a cruel way would still wrong the victim, even if the victim did not have any normative control over that duty, even if, that is, the victim could not release the perpetrator from the duty. The most successful theories, I believe, explain this via some revised version of classical interest theories (as in the citations above), even when they import will-based considerations to parry other objections that are not germane to our topic here.

wrongs another *in particular.* And, because the presence of a directed duty necessarily signals the presence of a correlative claim-right,[66] we can put the points we have made in the language of rights: we each have moral rights against being treated as inferiors in the ways specified—and hence to the various forms of respect we have outlined— grounded ultimately in our interests in secure access to the three social conditions.

To treat *as an equal* is therefore to treat others as bearing a moral status conferred by possession of these rights, and to do so as a result of the importance of the interests underlying those rights. To treat as an equal is to recognize others as beings who have an interior life and a subjective perspective through which they present themselves to the world. It is to recognize the vulnerability to which such interiority exposes them, and hence to respect the social guise in which they present themselves to us. *Treating as an equal* is therefore a part of the broader virtue of treating others with *humanity,* the virtue displayed, as we saw in Chapter 1, by those who seek a reconciliation with others' particular perspective on the world by imaginatively projecting themselves into that perspective, and seeking an "accord and symphony" from within that perspective.

This shift in perspective also has an impact on how we understand the idea of moral equality itself. The point is best made as a response to an objection. The objector I have in mind wonders in what sense I have defended an account of moral *equality* at all. We possess the rights discussed. What does it add to say that we possess the rights *equally,* or that they are rights to *equal* status?[67] For all we have said, our claims to be treated as equals seems to resolve into the claim that we each ought to be treated in the way each of us deserves to be treated as a result of central interests we possess. There doesn't seem to be any essentially comparative element in the particular nature of the rights at all.

To answer this objection, we must return to the five paradigmatic modes and explain the sense in which each is, indeed, a mode of treating *as an inferior.* To treat as if an object, an irrational or irresponsible child, polluted, a tool, or an animal is to treat as *subordinate,* as either needing the control, power, and authority of one who knows how to use, tame, or cleanse, or, alternatively, as meriting exclusion, revulsion, destruction, or consumption by a superior. This is why synonyms for treating as inferior in the relevant sense include *demeaning* and *degrading,* which both refer to the relation between a superior that creates or reinforces another's inferiority. Insofar as they are protections against being treated as inferior (and hence relative to a superior), the rights constitutive of our status as moral equals are rights to equal treatment. This may sound strange, since here equality is defined in terms of an absence of a certain kind of inequality, rather than the other way around. But if I am right about the nature of our commitment, then this is how it should be. Our commitment is explained by a rejection of certain modes of inferiorizing treatment, not a celebration of some property or value that is equal in all of us, or a rejection of all hierarchies of power, social status, and esteem. We do not say: "What is wrong with being treated as an inferior is that we are all, in fact, equals in the possession of a set of capacities (or range properties) that bestow worth or dignity." Similarly, we do not say: "What is wrong with being treated as an inferior is that hierarchies in social status, power, and esteem are always wrong." Rather, we say: "Treating as an inferior is wrong when and because it is socially cruel (and hence harmful in the specific ways we have discussed); we therefore treat one another as equals in the relevant sense when we treat each other with humanity, recognizing the importance, for each one of us, of those central rights-generating interests against inferiorizing treatment grounded in our sociable nature." Our commitment to moral equality therefore is both *grounded in* and *constituted by* our rejection of inequality. It is for this reason that I have said, in the introduction to this book, that inequality is *prior* to equality.[68] It is prior, more precisely, in two senses. First, equal moral status is *constituted by* or *consists in* a bundle of rights against certain kinds of inferiorizing treatment (rather than the other way around), and, second, our commitment to moral equality is *explained by* or *grounded in* the rejection of inferiorizing treatment as socially cruel (rather than the other way around). In this light, it then becomes obvious why we do not have the same response to treating someone inappropriately as *superior* as its opposite—indeed, it seems strange to argue that we wrong another in treating them incorrectly as more worthy than they are in fact. There is a fundamental asymmetry in our allegiance to moral equality that a dignitarian view, which locates the wrong of treating another as inferior in the fact that they are of equal worth, cannot explain: isn't treatment as superior also a misrecognition of equal worth understood in a dignitarian way? In summary, rights to equal moral status are *noncomparative* with respect to their grounds—they are not grounded in, for example, a value-bestowing property or capacity that we all possess to an equal extent—but *comparative* with respect to their object, what they are rights *to*.

We can now come full circle. Recall that Kantian and Christian views faced the challenge from variation: on both views, respect is a response to a distinctive kind of honor, rank, or dignity bestowed on us by possession of a set of capacities. But some of us are more blurry images of God than others; some of us have a greater capacity to choose rationally than others. We are now in a position to see how my account surmounts this challenge. The view I have defended does not say: "You are owed respect because you have a distinctive kind of dignity, rank, or honor bestowed upon you in virtue of your possession of a capacity." Rather, respect, I have argued, is a response to our *vulnerability* rather than our *worth* as sociable beings. By never making any use of the idea of an absolute, interest-independent worth, or dignity, my account draws the sting from the variation challenge.

This may seem puzzling. I say that we have rights to equal status—which I have glossed as rights not to be treated as inferior in the ways discussed—if and only if we have a capacity to develop and maintain an integral sense of self. But our capacities to develop and maintain such integrity vary: some of us have strong, resilient, and highly fertile capacities to develop and maintain an integral sense of self while others only have weaker, fragile, and evanescent capacities. So don't I need to accept variation, too? Mustn't I say that our rights against being treated as an inferior—and hence to equal moral status in my terms—vary along with our capacities to develop and maintain an integral sense of self? In short, *yes*. My account answers the variation challenge by *embracing* it.

The key that allows me to do so in a way dignity-first views can't is that I do not yoke the possession of a capacity to the possession of worth or value. For dignity-first views, we are owed respect because we are worthy. The worth is what commands the respect (one might think of, say, a painting in the same way). This produces a problem because, if the capacities on which the worth supervenes vary, then the respect *qua* reverence persons are owed must vary as well: higher capacities, higher worth, greater respect. On my view, possession of a capacity to develop and maintain an integral sense of self does not give its possessor a higher worth. Rather, the possession of such a capacity makes us vulnerable to certain kinds of harm, and it is the rejection of these kinds of harm—namely, social cruelty—that triggers the need for a very specific kind of respect, which I have referred to as opacity respect (as a way of protecting people from the harm to which they are vulnerable). So, on my view, the third-party duties, and hence the character of the rights, will vary according to people's *vulnerability,* and hence according to the particular nature of their relationships to others, not according to their *worth.* But "variance" here should not be understood in terms of a scalar. There is no simple equation: less capacity, more vulnerable, "more" (opacity) respect. The respect that people are owed will vary in more complex ways than that, and my account of social cruelty helps us to explain why and how. Let me return to our example of the elderly to make the point.

For the Kantian, the degree to which we possess the underlying psychological capacities for rational choice are arrayed on a continuum. As we have seen, the Kantian claims that there is a threshold above which variation in such capacities ceases to matter in determining a being's dignity. Let us leave aside whether the Kantian has any plausible story to tell regarding why variation above the threshold ought to be disregarded. Above the threshold, we have dignity, and hence ought to be treated as ends-in-ourselves. Below the threshold, we lack dignity, and hence can be treated as mere means (except in cases in which treatment of such beings has an impact on those above the threshold). The account, as has often been noted, faces significant difficulties in providing a plausible response to borderline cases in which individuals, such as small children and the mentally ill or disabled, lack the rational capacities of normal persons—including *(inter alia)* capacities to respond reliably to reasons, to give informed consent, and so on. As I discussed in more detail in Chapter 1, the Kantian account seems implausible for two reasons. First, marking a particular threshold seems arbitrary: How can there be such a staggering cliff in value off which one falls as soon as one crosses the threshold in the wrong direction?* Second, what might justify putting the threshold *here* rather than *there*? At which point, exactly, does the child acquire dignity or the person with dementia lose it? Do those with various forms of mental disorder and disability disqualify on the Kantian view? What kinds of mental disorder and disability?

But can the account I have defended do any better? I believe it can, precisely because it embraces rather than seeks to avoid variation. The key lies in identifying the specific kinds of vulnerability to which children, the mentally ill, and the severely cognitively disabled are subject, and the ways in which attitudes like opacity respect are appropriate, given those vulnerabilities. Once again, there is no need to evaluate where exactly along some scale of worth these individuals lie. Rather, we focus on the way the vulnerabilities of such individuals shape their

---

* Some Kantians have tried to take the sting from this kind of objection in the following way (due to Allen Wood): "Of course we should respect rational nature *in* persons, and this means respecting the persons themselves. But my main argument here depends on saying that we should *also* respect rational nature *in the abstract,* which entails respecting fragments of it or necessary conditions of it, even where these are not found in fully rational beings or persons" (Wood 1998, p. 198). The argument turns on the thought that we ought to show respect to rational nature *itself,* i.e., to full or complete rational capacity, by showing respect to its constituents or other necessary conditions. This is an odd view. Take a painting that deserves our reverence and respect—say, the *Desmoiselles d'Avignon.* It is true that in respecting the painting *itself* we must also respect *its* constituent parts (e.g., the strokes of blue and pink and red that make it up). We can then generalize: for every painting that has the higher value that calls for our reverence (like the *Desmoiselles*), we must respect its constituent parts. And we can even extend the account one step further: we ought to respect great art as such (and hence independently of any instance of it). But why must we, in showing respect to great art, or to any one reverence-meriting painting in particular, respect the constituent parts of that painting taken not as tokens but as types? Why must we show the same reverence, in other words, to any stroke of blue and pink and red that we find even when it is found, say, in a mere sketch by no one in particular or, indeed, in a drawing that was never finished? What gives the painting the higher, incommensurable value that calls for our reverence is the arrangement of the strokes and their particular esthetic contribution to the whole. But then why shouldn't we treat "fragments and necessary conditions" of rational nature in the same way, i.e., as acquiring a dignity only when they work together to realize a fully rational nature? Why must we believe they grant their possessors dignity, like strokes of paint on paper, wherever they are found?

interests against particular kinds of harm. We then understand the rights as a function of those interests.

Let us take cases in which individuals lack the capacity to give informed consent across a wide range of decisions (regarding important life decisions, for example, where a lot is at stake either for them or for others), but *do* have the capacity to develop and maintain an integral sense of self. The capacity is reduced due to the limitations in their underlying psychological capacities, but it is not entirely absent. It takes no great imagination to see that children, the mentally ill, and those with severe cognitive disability are, as a result, very vulnerable not only to social cruelty but also to other forms of, for example, physical cruelty. This is in part due to their inability to understand the physical and social world adequately to coordinate their responses to it in coherent and consistent ways, and especially their inability to resist maltreatment. But it is also in part because they lack the shield of consent. As a result of their progressively weakening or only incipiently emerging competence, others must often—though, importantly, not always—decide for them. Yet, they clearly have an integral sense of self, a nascent or evanescent sense of who they are, what they stand for, and what their aims and values are. This is in turn what makes them liable to forms of social cruelty— and hence to treatment as inferior—that they otherwise would not have been liable to, and why they have special rights to opacity respect and against social cruelty that they would otherwise lack.

It is central to my account, however, that the specific duties and attitudes required of us will vary according to the particular nature of their vulnerability all the way through to and including cases in which beings entirely lack a capacity to develop and maintain a sense of self. The crucial element is *how* the account responds to variation. Take, for example, rights to opacity respect, which I argued are rooted in our interests in controlling the conditions in which we reveal and conceal elements of our inner life, controlling the terms of our social engagement with others, and controlling the use of our body. Consider, first, beings that entirely lack a capacity to develop and maintain a sense of self (including most if not all nonhuman animals). In those cases, it seems clear that opacity respect plays no role, since the beings in question lack the three central interests that opacity respect functions *(inter alia)* to protect.[69] It therefore follows, I have argued, that such beings lack the bundle of rights constitutive of equal moral status. (This does not imply, recall, that they therefore also lack *basic* moral status—whether they do or not will depend on whether they possess a conscious, evaluatively laden perspective on the world. And it also does not imply that we lack other kinds of reasons for treating them in certain ways, e.g., reasons deriving from our love or the love of others for them.)

But now consider borderline cases, where individuals have enough psychological capacity to develop and maintain a somewhat blurred or incomplete sense of self, but not enough for fully informed consent. In cases involving children and the mentally ill or disabled, opacity respect plays an important role, just as it did for the elderly discussed in the last section. To treat such persons as if they had no standing to demand opacity respect would be to treat them with what Strawson called an "objectivating" attitude, as persons who are "an object of social policy; as a subject for what, in a wide range of sense, might be called treatment; as something certainly to be taken account, perhaps precautionary account, of; to be managed or handled or cured or trained."[70] In so doing, we would be actively and recklessly undermining the integrity of their sense of self—in this case, their sense of self as participants in the give and take of everyday social life. But opacity respect will, at the same time, need to be tempered and selectively applied. This is because to treat another's self-presentation as definitive of the terms of our relationship to them would often be severely damaging. Imagine, for example, allowing a small child to drive a car, or someone in the middle to late stages of dementia to depart on a long trip unaided. As I said before, knowing when to pierce the veil of opacity will require acting with humanity. We will need to understand when we ought to err in the direction of their sociability and need for recognition—when, that is, their three central interests should predominate in our reflection—and when, and *how,* we need to disregard those interests in order to protect them from hurting themselves. The important point, however, is that our decisions with respect to them should be guided by the particular character of their social and physical vulnerability—by their variable interests as sociable beings—rather than by an independent assessment of their absolute worth or dignity, which requires determining whether they are above or below some (arbitrarily defined) threshold.

Another, related objection: What about those with a sense of self that is not easily fractured, those, that is, with a very strong sense of self? Do they *lack* rights against being treated as inferior? Recall that I said that we each have an interest in securing access to the three social conditions for the development and maintenance of an integral sense of self. But notice that these are interests possessed by even those with the most resilient and strong senses of self. Even Zora Neale Hurston's Janie Crawford—despite her strength and resilience—has a set of central interests in control over her body, over the terms of her social engagement, and over what remains inner and outer, which in turn ground a set of rights against inferiorizing treatment.[71] The racism and violence to which she is subject violates those rights (in addition to other rights against physical assault). But how can I explain, the objector wonders, the rights-grounding force of these central interests *in her case,* given that their satisfaction is, *ex hypothesi,* not necessary for the maintenance and development of her integrity?

In answering this objection, we need to distinguish the *general* relationship between the control interests identified and our capacity to develop and maintain an integral sense of self, and the specific fact that, *in this particular instance,* setting back her control interests will not fracture her integrity. It is important that the objector is not imagining a case of someone who has such a strong and impervious capacity that no limitation in control over the body, the terms of social engagement, and what is inner and outer could touch her integrity. Perhaps there could be such a being. But if there were, it would lack the essentially sociable nature that is typical of us as human. It would not be clear, as a result, what kinds of moral considerations would apply. Rather, the objector wonders how rights against inferiorizing treatment could still apply in *particular* cases in which the violation of the rights would not set back the interests on which, I have claimed, the rights are ultimately based. The fact that Janie Crawford is not the impervious being we have imagined marks an important difference, since it implies that, despite the strength of her sense of self, she is still vulnerable as a sociable being. While this particular attack did not break her sense of self, it might have.[72] So the fact that the attacks *threaten* the integrity of her sense of self precisely by thwarting those central control interests that are so important to it implies that they still violate her rights against inferiorizing treatment, even when the attempt fails.

PUNISHMENT

Once we raise the question of equal moral status, we also raise the question of what, if anything, could ever lead one to lose it. What of the great murderers and other perpetrators of systematic and widespread cruelty? Put in our terms, this question becomes: When, if ever, could one legitimately use inferiorizing social cruelty against another? Must one show opacity respect even vis-à-vis the greatest offenders? These are not easy questions for any theory of moral equality.[73] The question and its difficulty are best addressed via a discussion of punishment. Imprisonment, for example, always involves ritualized forms of humiliation—incarceration, stripping of clothes, uniforms, searching of bodies, the unrelenting gaze of staff, restricted social and public spaces, and often various forms of physical abuse. What do we say about these cases and others like them? Providing a complete answer would require a comprehensive theory of punishment, which would take us far beyond the scope of this book. But what we can say is how the account I have provided ought to frame any more comprehensive discussion.

I have identified a set of rights against inferiorizing social cruelty. Those rights compose a bundle that is constitutive of our equal moral status. But I have not provided any argument for saying they are absolute or unforfeitable.[74] I have left it open whether some or all of them, for example in extreme circumstances, might be permissibly overridden, infringed, or forfeited.[75] What I have established is that such rights protect something of basic and structural importance to a flourishing life. The rights are, as a result, very weighty and will be correspondingly resistant to being either permissibly overridden, infringed, or forfeited. So strong are these rights that they cast a shadow over all practices of punishment that work by attacking the capacity to develop and maintain an integral sense of self by stigmatizing, objectifying, instrumentalizing, infantilizing, or dehumanizing the punished. It strikes me as clear that they would outlaw the more extreme forms of inferiorizing social cruelty, such as torture, and other forms of cruel and degrading treatment. They would also, I believe, prohibit practices of solitary confinement, which strike at the root of our capacity to develop and maintain an integral sense of self.[76] But how far do rights to equal moral status go? What about, say, standard practices of incarceration? These are, as I have said, unmistakenly attempts to humiliate and humble prisoners by attacking all three of our central interests. This sets the task for any theory of punishment, since it requires such theories to explain how such weighty rights could either be forfeited, overridden, or infringed and under what circumstances.

Whatever the answer to these questions, we can pose a contrast with views that ground equal moral status in an account of human dignity. Insofar as such theories ground dignity in the absolute worth of a capacity for rational choice *apart from* its particular, contingent realization (as in Kantian and Christian theories), it becomes very unclear how one could ever forfeit one's own, or permissibly override or infringe another's, rights to equal moral status, since the whole point of such theories is to focus our attention on the absolute worth of the soul or will as it stands *beyond* the lives and choices and circumstances of any individual.[77] If the command to respect lies in the absolute worth of our rational capacities as untouched by the vicissitudes of empirical choice, contingency, and so on, then how could someone—through those very choices themselves—forfeit the demand to be respected, or, alternatively, how could the demand ever be overridden or infringed? The problem with such an intransigent view is that it collapses on the horns of a dilemma. It must either say that our rights to dignity do not permit, for example, *any* incarceration (and perhaps any punishment at all), or it must say that our rights to dignity are compatible with incarceration, but then allow that dignity does not provide any grounds for objection to the incarceration of the *innocent*. Because my view poses no strong discontinuity between the transcendental seat of our dignity and its empirical realization in a series of real-world choices, it avoids this problem. Of course, a theory of punishment constrained by my view must explain when and to what extent the bundle of rights to equal moral status can be forfeited, overridden, or infringed in cases of wrong-doing, but there is no conceptual or practical incoherence in supposing that this is possible.

CONCLUSION

I have argued that our commitment to moral equality can best be explained by considering when and why it is wrong to treat another as inferior. Underpinning our practices of treating each other as moral equals, I claimed, is a rejection of social cruelty as an attack on our capacity to develop and maintain an integral sense of self, and therefore on a structural element of a flourishing life. Once we put things in this light, we saw that there was no need to yoke an account of dignity or worth to a possession of a value-bestowing natural property that we possess to an equal extent. Armed with this account, I then turned to the reactive attitude that governs the domain of moral equality, namely respect, arguing that we respect others as persons when we respect the integrity of their sense of self, that is, when we respect their nature as self-presenting beings. And I concluded by noting the way the account draws the sting from the variation challenge.

In Chapter 3, I support this theory of moral equality, which I will refer to as the Negative Conception, by showing how it can be used to illuminate when and why discrimination is wrong. This will also give us the opportunity to provide a fuller characterization of the five modes of inferiorizing treatment I have identified in this chapter and will set the stage for Part II, in which I will discuss, among other things, the role of anti-discrimination norms in human rights law.

3

WHEN AND WHY IS
DISCRIMINATION WRONG?

IN THIS CHAPTER, I extend and deepen the Negative Conception by examining its implications for discrimination. There are at least three reasons to do so. First, as we will see in more detail below, the most promising moral theories of discrimination hold that discrimination is wrong when and because it fails to treat us as moral equals. Yet, few theorists of discrimination have examined in detail what the basis and justification for our commitment to moral equality is. Most theories of discrimination therefore lack determinacy and specificity. The theory of moral equality developed in Chapter 2 will help us to remedy this shortcoming. Second, there is a paucity of philosophical theories of discrimination, despite the importance of anti-discrimination norms in both domestic and international law and despite the fact that wrongful discrimination constitutes, as I have pointed out, a paradigmatic instance of treating others as inferior. As Benjamin Eidelson notes, "Since the idea of wrongful discrimination is expected to do so much work in our social and political lives, it is something of a philosophical embarrassment that so little has been done to explore or account for it."[1] Third, anti-discrimination norms are a central aspect of the international legal human rights system and the many tributary regional systems, such as the European Convention on Human Rights (ECHR) and the Inter-American Commission on Human Rights (IACHR).[2] In light of this fact, it is surprising that they are often overlooked in contemporary philosophical treatments of human rights. The account of wrongful discrimination I offer in this chapter will therefore also help to set the stage for the discussion of human rights to follow in Part II of this book.

The discussion to follow covers a lot of ground. It is therefore useful to provide the reader with a plan of the main claims in this chapter and their place in the overall argument. My discussion is divided into five sections. In the first, I define the concept of discrimination that I will employ throughout the chapter. In the second, I establish the importance of social meanings. More specifically, the second section defends four main claims. (1) I will argue against the view that direct and indirect discrimination is wrong only when, and because, it perpetuates broader patterns of stigma and second-class citizenship. (2) I will argue against the view that direct and indirect discrimination is wrong only when and because it reflects beliefs regarding the moral inferiority of those discriminated against or animus toward them. (3) Rather, direct and indirect discrimination can be wrong solely in virtue of the *social meaning* of the discriminatory acts or policies, and hence independently of broader societal effects and of the presence of faulty beliefs or animus toward particular groups. (4) I will argue that social meanings are objective properties of actions, express attitudes attributable to the agent, and can be a function of unconscious beliefs and desires.

But when and why are the social meanings of discriminatory acts and policies morally objectionable? The third section argues that they are morally objectionable when and because they express attitudes that are demeaning or disrespectful, in the sense that they undermine the equal moral status of those disadvantaged by them. The account therefore joins Deborah Hellman and Benjamin Eidelson in claiming that disrespectful or demeaning treatment is central to our understanding of wrongful discrimination. Where the account I defend—which I will call the Expressive Harm Account—goes beyond both views is in providing, rather than merely assuming, an account of moral equality that can explain what counts as demeaning and disrespectful action and why it is wrong.

The fourth section argues that, when conjoined with the Negative Conception of moral equality, the Expressive Harm Account can be used to make sense of both demeaning and disrespectful action. Doing so, however, requires a more fine-grained analysis of our five modes of inferiorizing treatment, namely stigmatization, dehumanization, infantilization, objectification, and instrumentalization, in particular contexts of discrimination. I first apply the Negative Conception to the stigmatization and dehumanization involved in racial discrimination; I then apply the Conception to the infantilization, objectification, and instrumentalization involved in various forms of sex discrimination. The aim of this section is to bring the analysis of social cruelty from Chapter 2 and the account of social meanings from earlier in the chapter to bear on paradigmatic instances of wrongful discrimination, and hence to show the fruitfulness of the Expressive Harm Account in reaching beyond current moral-equality-based views regarding the wrongfulness of discrimination.

The fifth section allows me to address two issues. First, one might wonder whether an account so focused on the attitudes expressed by actions could explain the moral wrongfulness of instances of objectionable *indirect* discrimination—discrimination, as we will see, where the discriminators have no conscious or unconscious bias or animus and do not intend to disadvantage members of a group as a result of their being members of that group. I argue that it can. The way it does so is by appealing to the idea of *indifference*. Second, examining the implications of the Expressive Harm Account for indirect discrimination allows me to clarify whether social meanings are *always* relevant to the explanation of the wrongfulness of discrimination. Can discrimination be wrong, for example, in the absence of conscious and unconscious prejudice, bias, animus, *and* culpable indifference? I will conclude that there are cases of structural injustice where none of these factors is present but where social meanings—and in particular the social meanings expressed by oppressive institutional patterns—are still essential. My conclusion is that all successful explanations of core cases of wrongful discrimination will include a reference to social meanings, and in particular to the meanings expressed by one or more of the five modes of inferiorizing treatment identified in Chapter 2.

Before moving on, it is important to clarify the relation between the moral theory of discrimination I offer in this chapter and the domain of discrimination *law*.[3] The theory I provide is intended to sketch a moral theory of discriminatory acts and policies. It is not, however, intended to provide a moral theory of discrimination *law*. From the fact that a discriminatory act or policy is morally wrongful according to the Expressive Harm Account, we cannot conclude, at least not without much further argument, that it ought to be legally regulated. Conversely, because some state or private conduct is justifiably subject to legal prohibition under the aegis of discrimination law does not imply that it is morally wrongful on the terms I set out here. I leave open, for example, whether discrimination law might justifiably be used to further ends that promote moral equality in the terms I describe, but where those ends are best promoted by legally regulating action that is morally neutral from the point of view of the Expressive Harm Account. That said, and as will become clear as we proceed, it would be a mistake to make the gap between the law and morality of discrimination too wide. At the heart of discrimination law is a concern with the morality and history of discrimination more broadly, and, if the account I provide is correct, also a concern with preserving relations of equality among all individuals, whatever their background, abilities, religion, race, sex, gender, or sexual orientation.

THE CONCEPT OF DISCRIMINATION

To fix ideas, I begin with a definition:

> *Discrimination:* A set of acts or policies X discriminates against (or in favor of) individual member(s) M of a group Y on the basis of a socially salient characteristic p iff M is comparatively[4] disadvantaged (or advantaged) by X in some dimension Z as a result, in whole or in part, of possessing p (or as a result, in whole or in part, of a mistaken belief that M possesses p).

I highlight three features of this definition. First, a characteristic is "socially salient" when it is, as Kasper Lippert-Rasmussen writes, "important to the structure of social interactions across a wide range of social contexts."[5] Membership of a group defined by race or sex is socially salient; membership of a reading group is not. This restriction is necessary to narrow the field of potentially wrongful discriminatory acts or policies; if we didn't include it (or a condition like it), then *any* act or policy that classifies, and in so doing disadvantages some at the expense of others, would count as discriminatory. The resulting theory would therefore lack specificity. For example, if we dropped the requirement of social salience, then a company policy that requires one to pay a fee to park in a certain place would count as discriminating against the group of people who would like to park there (compared to the group who doesn't). But why should we expect a moral theory of discrimination to tell us when and why such policies are wrongful (if they are)? Furthermore, interest in the morality of discrimination emerged along with a concern for the prospects and obstacles faced by historically disadvantaged groups marked out socially by a distinctive property or set of properties (so-called protected groups). Given this background, highlighting social salience allows us to track the moral urgency that accompanies any inquiry into discrimination.

Second, my definition is not moralized. Simply because an act or policy discriminates in the sense I have just outlined does not make it wrongful. For example, a regulation that allocates certain seats on public buses for senior citizens discriminates according to our guiding definition but is not wrongful. Similarly, as we will discuss in more detail below, an admissions practice at a historically black college in the United States that favors blacks over members of other groups discriminates, but does not do so wrongfully. I adopt a nonmoralized definition merely as a matter of convenience. If we adhered to a moralized definition of "discrimination," then we would need to come up with another term to identify the wider domain of cases that involve (direct and indirect) differential treatment of socially salient groups but that are *not* wrongful. My definitions make things simpler and clearer. We can ask, "What makes an instance of discrimination wrongful?" rather than "What makes an instance of differential treatment discriminatory, and hence wrongful?"[6]

We need, furthermore, to distinguish two different ways one might discriminate against (or in favor of) members of groups defined by socially salient characteristics.

Direct discrimination: A set of acts or policies X directly discriminates against (or in favor of) member(s) M of a group Y on the basis
of a socially salient characteristic *p* iff M is comparatively disadvantaged (or advantaged) by X in some dimension Z, and the expectation that M, as a result of a belief that M possesses *p,* would be
comparatively disadvantaged (advantaged) by X made a difference, in whole or in part, consciously or unconsciously, to the
outcome of the agent's / agents' or policymaker's / policymakers'
deliberation regarding X.

Indirect discrimination: A set of acts or policies X directly discriminates against (or in favor of) member(s) M of group Y on the basis
of *p* iff *Discrimination* but not *Direct Discrimination.*

According to these definitions, a policy that requires motorcyclists to
wear a helmet indirectly discriminates against Sikhs. The discrimination is only indirect because (let us assume) the policy's disadvanta-
geous effect on Sikhs did not make a difference, in whole or in part,
intentionally or unintentionally, consciously or unconsciously, to the
outcome of the deliberations leading to the policy. On the other hand,
a policy that imposes a "facially neutral" IQ requirement on hiring
and promotions directly discriminates against blacks if the comparative disadvantage that would be suffered by blacks as a result of the
policy made a difference to the outcome of the deliberations that
led to the policy (as was the case, we may assume, in *Griggs v. Duke
Power Co.**).[7]

---

* *Griggs v. Duke Power Co.,* 401 U.S. 424 (1971). Duke Power was a large energy company
in North Carolina that openly segregated its workforce. Black employees were confined
to performing the least desirable jobs—jobs involving manual work that occurred principally outdoors and that paid a very low rate—and were therefore not permitted to
transfer to other "white-collar" positions in the firm. After the passage of the 1964 federal Civil Rights Act, which prohibited racial discrimination, the company could no
longer openly segregate its workforce, and on the day the Act became effective, Duke
Power instituted several new qualifications necessary for jobs other than the field positions. Those qualifications included possession of a high school degree and a sufficiently high score on an IQ test. This had the predictable effect, due to the inadequacy
of the segregated educational system in North Carolina, of excluding the vast majority
of blacks from the better jobs and thereby perpetuating the company's segregated

My analyses of the concepts in play depart from conventional usage in the law. In the law, indirect discrimination is defined as a general policy or measure that, though couched in neutral terms, has a disproportionate or prejudicial impact on a protected group.[8] On this definition, a policy that was deliberately enacted in order to disadvantage a particular racial group by using a facially neutral criterion (such as an IQ test) counts as indirectly rather than directly discriminatory. This legal usage has a number of disadvantages for those interested in moral theories of discrimination. First, many often believe—incorrectly though intuitively—that indirect discrimination (on the conventional, legal definition) is less morally troubling than direct. But this is a mistake, evident once we consider cases like *Griggs,* in which a "facially neutral" criterion was deliberately used to track race (without appearing to do so). But why should such covert, intentional discrimination be any less morally wrongful (indeed, might it not be of graver moral concern precisely because it is covert)? Including such cases under the concept of *direct* discrimination, as I do, diminishes and corrects for the spurious effects of such intuitions and allows us to focus more carefully on cases of discrimination that are *genuinely* unintentional.[9]

A second reason to accept my definition rather than the conventional, legal definition is the following. Including the impact of *unconscious* bias on outcome-affecting deliberation in our definition of *direct* discrimination is useful because it allows us, when we turn to indirect discrimination, to focus more carefully on cases that are the result of *neither* conscious intention *nor* unconscious bias (and hence on instances of what we may call *truly* indirect discrimination). The issue of unconscious bias—of special relevance when discussing what counts as policies or acts that *express an attitude* held by the discriminator—will yield particularly interesting results in our overall analysis. The advantages of the definitions elaborated above will become more evident as we proceed.

---

workforce. The new qualifications strike us as objectionable because they cannot but be understood as a conscious and deliberate (though covert) attempt to exclude blacks by other means.

DISCRIMINATION AND SOCIAL MEANINGS

I begin our inquiry into the wrongfulness of discrimination with a paradigmatic case of racial discrimination, namely *Palmer v. Thompson,* decided in the United States in 1971.[10] In 1962, the mayor of Jackson, Mississippi, following federal desegregation legislation, decided to close down five public swimming pools (four of which had been white-only and one of which was black-only). The mayor closed down the pools to avoid desegregating them: "We will do all right this year at the swimming pools but if these [civil rights] agitators keep up their pressure, we would have five colored swimming pools because we are not going to have any intermingling."[11] The mayor feared that desegregating the pools would lead them to become de facto all-black because whites would no longer want to swim in them—and further believed, of course, that all-black pools were not worth maintaining while all-white ones were. This case is particularly relevant for our purposes because the freedom at stake, namely swimming, is relatively trivial; the opportunities available to blacks in Jackson—in this case opportunities to swim in public pools—were diminished to exactly the same extent as whites; and we might easily imagine that there were no further downstream effects on equality of socioeconomic opportunity more broadly considered. The closing of the pools is undoubtedly an act of morally wrongful discrimination. But why?

Some have been moved by the thought that direct and indirect discrimination is wrong just in case, and because, it perpetuates broader patterns of stigma and second-class citizenship, and hence harms Y *as a group.* Owen Fiss, for example, refers to the "group-disadvantaging principle," urging us to consider the societal consequences of particular discriminatory acts and policies. We can, for the moment, grant that such systematic propagation of stigma would be a sufficient ground for objecting to *Palmer,* and to many other policies or acts of discrimination. But, even if we grant that, there are still two questions to be answered. First, are such societal effects a *necessary* part of any explanation for the wrongfulness of core cases of discrimination? And, second, do they provide a complete account of the wrongfulness of the mayor's action in *Palmer*? I will argue that such societal effects are not necessary and that focusing solely on them would lead us to overlook the independent role of social meanings in explaining the wrongfulness of core cases of discrimination, including *Palmer*.

Suppose a restaurant in the desert will turn away any black person that enters. Only one black person, however, will enter and be rebuffed. Imagine also that once he has been turned away, he will die shortly thereafter in a car accident. The discrimination by the restaurant's owners, we are assuming, has no systematic societal effects, let alone any effect on the treatment of blacks *as a group*, and yet is clearly wrong. Indeed, we can go further: our judgment of the owner's exclusionary policy would persist even if the black man never found out the reasons for his exclusion, and even if we imagine that the owner would have been permitted to turn away the man for other, nonracial reasons.[12] Accounts that focus solely on societal effects, I submit, do not have the resources for explaining how such a policy could be wrong.

What the example demonstrates, I believe, is that we need to pay attention not only to the downstream impact on broader societal patterns of socioeconomic opportunity and status inequality but also to the moral character of what we might call the *relational nexus* between the discriminator and the discriminated against—between, that is, the City of Jackson and its black residents on one hand and the restaurant and the black man on the other. Without this interpersonal dimension, we lose sight of an important aspect of the wrong in *Palmer* and the desert restaurant and, indeed, of the wrongfulness of a central class of cases: a full explanation of the wrong in both cases must refer to the way those discriminated against have been wronged in particular, rather than as a mere byproduct of a broader group-disadvantaging consequence of the policy. Wrongful discrimination in these cases is more akin to a tort than to a maldistribution of resources or opportunities.[13]

Impressed by this kind of critique, many have argued that what explains the moral wrongfulness in cases like the desert restaurant and *Palmer* is the fact that the discriminatory acts reflect either a belief in the moral inferiority of the socially salient groups disadvantaged by the act or animus toward their members (whether or not such animus is triggered by a concomitant belief in their moral inferiority).[14] On this view, what matters, in addition to the downstream consequences of discriminatory acts on race relations, is the fact that the comparative disadvantage is suffered as a result of prejudice or animus. But here again, two questions need to be answered. First, while the presence of such attitudes might be, I will grant, sufficient to explain the wrongfulness of such acts, we still need to know: When and why are they relevant? Second, is the presence of such mental states necessary?

Let us take the second question first. Suppose the owner of a city restaurant has a policy of turning away blacks, not because of any racial hatred or beliefs in the inferiority of blacks but because he believes his discriminatory policy will make his business more profitable. In this variation of our example, we would still judge the policy to be wrongful even though the actor bears no objectionable animus or prejudice. And note, furthermore, that this judgment would persist even if we were to suppose that the overall effect of the policy were actually to stoke awareness of racism among customers and lead them into political action designed to stop it—even if we assume, that is, that the policy has *positive* societal effects on status and structural inequalities overall.[15] Our puzzle now becomes: Is there a unifying feature that is shared by city restaurant and by more standard cases of prejudice and animus that might help us to explain why they are all instances of the *same* wrong? If there is, then it would also help us to answer our first question about when and why mental states are important while at the same time explaining why the presence of such mental states is not necessary.

I believe there is. But to find it, we need to train our attention not on the mental states of the actors in isolation, or merely the broader societal consequences of a given act or policy, but on a given act or policy's *social meaning*.[16] In unpacking this aspect of the Expressive Harm Account, I will first discuss what social meanings are and what makes them important. In the next several sections, I will then turn to an explanation of how and when social meanings wrong not just groups (if they harm groups at all), but the particular individuals who are their targets.

To determine the social meaning of an act or policy, we need to look at the message the policy or act sends. And to determine what that message is, we need to consider the act or policy in light of the attitudes that it expresses against a wider social, cultural, political, economic background. Anderson and Pildes provide an instructive account of what is involved in "expressing an attitude": "An attitude to a person is a complex set of dispositions to perceive, have emotions, deliberate, and act in ways oriented to that person. . . . [T]o express an attitude through action is to act on reasons that attitude gives us."[17] My visit to you in the hospital might, for example, express my loyalty to and love for you, which gives it a certain social meaning against a particular sociocultural background. Note that attitudes, on this account, include not only beliefs but also emotions, desires, broader dispositions to act or react in various ways (including, importantly, failures to act or react in various ways), commitments, and even traits of character. For example, a racist disposition to judge young black teenagers taking drugs in inner cities more punitively and dismissively than white teenagers taking drugs in the suburbs counts as an attitude that can be expressed, for example, in a public policy response (inner-city blacks should be incarcerated; suburban whites should receive therapy).[18] Furthermore, an attitude can be expressed by an agent without being a direct reflection of a particular mental state. Anderson and Pildes give the example of the melancholy expressed by a musician in playing a piece, which does not imply, of course, that the musician herself was in a melancholic state of mind.

Making social meaning a function of the attitudes expressed by an action or policy has a number of advantages. First, it allows us to explain how wrongfully discriminatory policies or actions need not reflect any animus toward members of the affected group, express beliefs about their moral inferiority, or be a function solely of the particular societal consequences of an action or policy. Consider, for example, the city restaurant case mentioned above, in which the owner discriminates against blacks to increase profits. We can say, in this case, that the exclusion is wrong not only because it perpetuates the second-class status of blacks in that community (*if*, indeed, it perpetuates it) but also because it expresses a morally objectionable attitude of *indifference* to the weighty interests of blacks in protection from overtly negative racial classification.[19] Note here that the indifference is expressed—and hence, on my view, can be attributed to the agent—even though it is not based on prejudice, beliefs about inferiority, or animus, and even though the act or policy may have, in fact, no harmful downstream effects at all.[20]

Second, consider directly discriminatory policies that are not based on any beliefs about the moral inferiority of the excluded, or any animus toward them, but instead based on feelings of, say, race-, ethnicity-, or sex-based special connectedness. An employer, for example, might hire only whites because they feel more comfortable with them or feel that communication would be easier with them. Or someone might prefer not to be treated by a black doctor, not because of any animus toward blacks or beliefs about their inferiority but merely because they would feel more comfortable with a white doctor.[21] According to a social-meaning-based account, both discriminatory acts would be wrongful because they express an objectionable disregard for the stigma attached to the race-based exclusion. In this case, once again, the objection is to the way such disregard changes the social relation between the employer and those excluded (or, in the other case, between the doctor and the patient) rather than based solely on the broader societal effects of the exclusion or on the faulty character of the actor's mental states.

Third, consider an industry that is heavily male-dominated but it is unclear why. Initial inquiries reveal that the distribution of skill levels is roughly equivalent across males and females in various applicant pools and that just as many women apply as men. Upon receiving requests to clarify possible causes for the disproportion, the members of the industry board decide to do nothing. One might argue that the decision not to make further inquiries expresses, once again, an objectionable attitude of indifference. Note that a social-meaning account allows us to say this even if we assume the decision was not explained either by the board's beliefs about women's moral inferiority or by an intention to disadvantage women compared to men, and even though there may not turn out to be, in fact, anything objectionable about the hiring policy at all.

We have yet to explain *why* and *when* the social meaning of a discriminatory act counts as morally objectionable. We will turn to that explanation shortly. But before we do so, we must bring to light three further elements of a social-meaning-based account. First, social-meaning-based accounts say that social meaning is an objective property of an action. Whether or not some action counts as, say, *disrespectful* or *demeaning* or *empowering* or *celebratory* is not solely determined by whether participants—including both discriminators and those discriminated against—believe it is any of these things, but on whether the action really *is*. To be sure, the criteria for such a determination are set by normative standards whose application requires (I have claimed) essential reference to participants' attitudes (including beliefs and intentions) as well as to the social conventions and historical context of particular policies or actions, but the judgments are not reducible to any of them (singly or in combination). Put another way, any judgment regarding whether an action is, say, *demeaning* requires a normatively governed interpretation of the action in a particular historical, social, cultural, and political context, but the judgment cannot be read off from what individual participants themselves believe they are doing. Here's an analogy: a good interpretation of the meaning of a work of art makes reference to the context in which the artwork was produced[22] but cannot be reduced to either the meaning assigned to it by the artist or any member of the public (singly or in combination). In the same way, a particular policy might be disrespectful or demeaning or empowering or celebratory even though those affected may not feel demeaned or disrespected or empowered or celebrated. Whether or not people feel demeaned, etc., might provide good evidence that the actions really are demeaning, etc., but the fact that they feel this way is not sufficient. Discriminators may be mistaken about the attitudes expressed by their actions and so can be mistaken about whether those actions really are demeaning, etc., just as those discriminated against can be mistaken about the very same thing.

The second element of social-meaning-based accounts can be probed via an objection. One might wonder: Why must social meanings be a function of the attitudes in light of which actions are performed? Can't the social meaning of an action be determined solely by, for example, social conventions, and hence independently of whatever attitudes the actors display in acting?[23] Racist jokes that are the product of sincere and nonculpable ignorance provide an example. Suppose someone recites a racist limerick about a man from Lahore. But suppose that the person believes that Lahore is a fictional city, useful for a rhyme but referring to no particular socially salient group. And further imagine that the person was not culpable in their ignorance: there is no (moral) sense in which they should have known better. If one took the view that social conventions can determine social meanings, then the recitation would be, say, demeaning (though, we might also say, the reciter is blameless in demeaning others by the utterance). If, on the other hand, we took the view that social meanings must reflect attitudes (in the broad sense just described) that can be correctly *attributed* to the actors—as I am suggesting we should—then the recitation would not be demeaning. I submit that the question is somewhat difficult to answer, but my sense is that the latter view has the upper hand here: I see no reason to believe that the interpersonal relation between the ignorant reciter and Pakistanis has changed once the joke has been told. To be sure, a Pakistani who was witness to the limerick would be reminded of the racism he or she faces in the society of which they are a part, but they would have no reason to feel they have been disrespected or demeaned (even blamelessly) by the reciter himself. Of course, things would be otherwise if the reciter was insincere in their ignorance, or culpable for not checking whether Lahore was in fact a fictional place, or (as we will discuss in more detail in a moment) held unconscious racist beliefs, but that is not the case we are imagining.

An important caveat: saying that the recitation does not carry a negative social meaning does not make its recitation *permissible*. We can still say that the recitation is morally impermissible if, for example, it has the effect of further propagating the racist beliefs in those who hear it.[24] The recitation by the actor we have imagined, then, would be classed as a case of *blameless wrongdoing*: though impermissible, he was not culpable for failing to know the facts that made the recitation impermissible, so he is not to blame for it.[25] An analogy might be useful in making this point: When I unwittingly put arsenic instead of sugar in your tea, what I do is impermissible, but not because of the social meaning of the act, but solely because my action kills you without justification. Unwittingly putting arsenic in your tea is therefore an instance, like the racist joke, of blameless wrongdoing. As we have already discussed above, this distinction between an action whose wrongfulness derives from the social meaning of a particular harm or deprivation, and an action whose wrongfulness derives solely from the meaning-independent features of the action (such as the death in one case and the propagation of racist beliefs in the other), is essential. If, for example, we focused only on the meaning-independent deprivation in *Palmer*—namely the loss of opportunities to swim in public pools—we would be unable to explain in what sense, if any, the closing is wrong.

This analysis may seem to rest on a mistake. Imagine a racist landlord turns away a couple because they are black.[26] But suppose that, had the landlord made further inquiries (which we imagine he did not), it would have been permissible to turn away the couple for other reasons (say because they had pets). What do we say in this case? Is turning away the black couple permissible or impermissible? The action clearly has an objectionably racist social meaning.[27] And yet, *ex hypothesi,* it would have been permissible to turn away the couple for other reasons. There is a simple solution: we ought to say that the action under the description "turning away the couple" is permissible, but the action under the description "turning away the couple because they are black" is impermissible. This allows us to claim that the landowner has wronged the couple but that he is under no duty to give them the flat.[28] As in *Palmer,* the impermissibility is a function of the expressive wrong, and hence of the action's social meaning, rather than its meaning-independent character as a turning away.

This leads us to the third feature of expressive, social-meaning-based views, namely how they handle cases of unconscious bias. As a variation of the racist joke case, imagine that the reciter unconsciously harbors racist beliefs that unwittingly shape his deliberation regarding the recitation: he (consciously) believes that Lahore is an imaginary city, but (unconsciously) knows that it is a city in Pakistan, and (unconsciously) sets on telling the joke because of its racist import (while consciously not being aware that this fact about his unconscious beliefs has shaped his deliberation). The influence on action of such unconscious beliefs is a staple of the psychological literature.[29] This case requires a different treatment than the case of sincere and nonculpable treatment just considered. Does a social-meaning account have the resources to account for this difference? I believe it does. The key lies in the broader idea of an attitude at the heart of expressive accounts. When the reciter tells the joke, we can say that he is (albeit unconsciously) expressing a racist attitude; the racist attitude expressed, in turn, shapes the social meaning of the action, thus making it, for example, demeaning. We might also say that, because the reciter has no control or awareness of his unconscious beliefs, and consciously disavows such views, he is not morally blameworthy for his wrongdoing.[30] This case, then, could also be described as a case of blameless wrongdoing. Notice, however, that it is very different in nature from the first racist joke case. This is because, in this case but not the first, a successful explanation of its wrongfulness must make reference to its social meaning. The recitation is wrong not simply because it has downstream societal effects (if it does) but because it expresses an objectionable set of attitudes attributable to, though not avowed by, the reciter. In this case but not the first, Pakistanis would be right to think that, though the reciter is blameless, the recitation changes the character of the moral relation between them. The joke has revealed, we might say, aspects of the reciter's attitudes that, though unwitting and disavowed, are still part of him. If we believed that social meanings could be determined by social conventions independently of the attitudes attributable to the agent, then we would be unable to explain the moral difference between the first and second racist joke cases.

The account easily generalizes. Suppose you are a paramedic called to the scene of an explosion in a downtown square. Bodies are strewn across the square, and, in the heat of the moment, you do everything in your ability to save as many as you can. Closed-circuit television footage after the event reveals something shocking. Though blacks were 50 percent of those injured, blacks number only 10 percent among those you saved. The footage reveals that, in many cases, you have saved whites who were farther away. You hold no prejudice or animus toward blacks, and you have long supported progressive racial policies. Assuming you had no reason to believe that you harbored unconsciously racist beliefs, it strikes me that you are not culpable. Like the racist joke examples, this is a case of blameless wrongdoing. This does not mean, however, that your unconscious attitudes play no role in explaining the wrongfulness of your actions. Your actions express those attitudes, which in turn affect the social meaning of your action. The blacks affected would be right to say that your actions were wrong not simply because they raised unfairly the chances that they would die but also because they expressed the view that black lives were worth less than white ones. This expressive wrong, though blameless, changes the character and meaning of your having reduced the chances that any black person present will survive, just as it changes the character of the racist joke that was told as a result of unconscious bias.

DEMEANING AND DISRESPECTING

So far we have argued that social meanings are essential to explaining the wrongfulness of a central class of cases of direct discrimination, both where there are further downstream effects (e.g., *Palmer*) and where there are not (e.g., desert restaurant), and both in the presence of objectionable mental states including animus or beliefs about moral inferiority (e.g., *Palmer*), and in their absence (e.g., city restaurant). We have argued that social meanings are a function of the attitudes expressed by an action, and that such attitudes can also change the social meaning of an action when they are unconscious (e.g., unwitting paramedic). But we have yet to give an account of *why* and *when* the social meanings of discriminatory acts are, in fact, morally objectionable. This is what I will do in the rest of this chapter.

The Expressive Harm Account is a variant of what I will call a moral-equality-based account. According to moral-equality-based views, discriminatory treatment is wrong when and because it fails to treat those affected in some appropriate sense as moral equals. There are currently two main moral-equality-based accounts of discrimination. *Disrespect-based views* claim that discrimination is wrong when and because it fails to accord us the *respect we are due as persons*.[31] *Demeaning-based views* claim that discrimination is wrong when and because the treatment *demeans*.[32] But what is it to disrespect someone as a person? And what is it to demean?

According to Benjamin Eidelson, whose *Discrimination and Disrespect* is the most fully worked out exemplar among disrespect-based views, "to respect a person's equal value relative to other persons one must value her interests equally with those of other persons, absent good reason for discounting them."[33] The argument must therefore turn on what Eidelson means by weighing interests equally. Eidelson writes, "The point of the respect requirement . . . is to insist on the need to justify partiality on any given basis. That is the upshot of saying that people have, as beings of equal value, a presumptive claim to equal consideration."[34] To demonstrate his thesis, he gives the example of an employer that selects a white person over a person of Arab descent for promotion because he gives the person of Arab descent's welfare less concern on account of her race. Because "race has no salience with respect to . . . the correlative concern one owes," the employer's discriminatory decision is disrespectful and hence wrong. But notice that none of the normative work is done by the idea of equal worth itself. All the work, instead, is done by the thought that race is not a good reason to treat people differently. But we are not told *why* (and indeed when) race is irrelevant (compare a historically black college or an affirmative action program). Crucially, we are not told when and why differentiating among people in accordance with their race disrespects their equal moral worth. Eidelson writes, "But this is a question we should be content to beg. There is simply no reason to think that Fatima's race *does* warrant discounting her reasons."[35] This is striking: what we were looking for was some account of the considerations—grounded in the idea of equal moral worth—that might explain why and when selection according to race is disrespectful; the idea that discriminatory treatment is disrespectful unless it is justified, or, as Eidelson puts it, the idea that "one must value . . . interests equally . . . , absent good reason for discounting them" doesn't deliver that conclusion. It simply passes the buck to some independent account of the "relevant reasons."

The emptiness of the "respect requirement" becomes evident when we consider a more controversial case of wrongful discrimination. Recently, the UK government has sought to restrict the access of European Union (EU) migrants, in their first four years of residence, to in-work benefits to which Britons are entitled.[36] According to Eidelson's account, we therefore ought to ask: Does restricting access to in-work benefits fail to accord recent EU migrants with the respect they are due as persons? Using the "respect requirement," Eidelson's answer should be that it does if and only if recent EU migrants' interests are treated with equal weight as the interests of Britons, "absent good reason for discounting them." This account of respect leaves us empty-handed, since it merely reframes what we are looking for: Is there, or is there not, a justification to treat the interests of recent EU migrants differently? And, crucially for a moral-equality-based account, how does the idea of equal moral worth help us to decide?

As a paradigm of a demeaning-based account, let me turn to Deborah Hellman's *When Is Discrimination Wrong?* According to Hellman, "To demean is to treat another as not fully human or of not equal worth."[37] Hellman's account therefore resolves into her account of persons' equal moral worth, and so on answering two questions. First, in what sense and why are we equal in worth? And second: What kinds of constraints on discrimination does this commitment properly understood set? Surprisingly, however, Hellman doesn't provide an answer to either question. She assumes that we already have some intuitive grasp of what makes something a violation of another's equal moral status, and hence demeaning. But how might it help us in less clear-cut cases? How might we determine, as with Eidelson, whether a policy that permits access to in-work benefits for British workers but not for EU migrants working in Britain in their first four years of residence demeans? Put another way: Does the social meaning of the UK policy carry the message that EU migrants are "less worthy of respect and concern" *in the relevant sense?* The policy is, after all, directly discriminatory: the policy puts EU migrants at a comparative disadvantage—a disadvantage that was both foreseen and intended by the policymakers, and hence played a role in determining the character of the policy. Answering this question by pointing to an uninterpreted notion of equal moral worth can't help us until we know why we have it and what respecting people's equal moral worth requires of us.

I conclude that both accounts are seriously underdetermined.[38] To make sense of the idea of disrespecting or demeaning another, we need an account of moral equality that is never provided.

A FRESH START: THE EXPRESSIVE HARM ACCOUNT

So far I have defended a theory of the wrongfulness of discrimination that points to the central importance of objectionable social meanings. Social meanings, I argued, can make discrimination wrong, even in the absence of further societal effects, beliefs, or conative states such as aversion alone. I then suggested that social meanings make discriminatory acts wrong when they send a message of moral inferiority, but concluded that two recent attempts to fill out such moral-equality-based accounts were underdetermined. How do we move beyond this impasse? As we have seen in Chapters 1 and 2, we need to explain what shape our commitment to moral equality takes before we can understand why an act (such as an act of discrimination) counts as treating someone as an inferior *in the relevant sense*. Recall, for example, that treating another as an inferior—for example, as an employee or a private—is not always wrong. In the rest of this chapter, I argue that the Negative Conception from Chapter 2 can provide an appealing solution, and, in particular, an appealing account of what it is to demean and disrespect someone in the relevant sense. It allows us, that is, to traverse the same terrain traveled by Hellman and Eidelson with a fresh perspective.

If we are to make greater headway than the two moral-equality-based views we have just considered, we must be able to do two things. First, we must be able to explain how paradigmatic instances of wrongful discrimination count as treating as an inferior in the relevant sense, and hence can be understood in terms of our five modes of inferiorizing treatment, namely stigmatization, dehumanization, infantilization, objectification, and instrumentalization. Second, we must be able to explain when and why the presence of each of these modes of treatment makes discriminatory acts wrong, and do so in a way that doesn't presuppose an already worked out view about moral equality. I will not say that to demean in one of our five ways is wrong when and because it is to treat as a moral unequal. Rather, I will say that to demean by dehumanizing, stigmatizing, infantilizing, objectifying, or instrumentalizing is *a way of* treating another as an inferior in the relevant sense; it then remains to be explained when and why doing so is wrong.

Recall, furthermore, that I eschew any attempt to explain this commitment by appeal to our equal moral *worth*. I will not try to show that to demean in any of the ways identified is to fail to respond correctly to the incommensurable, absolute, and unconditional worth, or dignity, of our humanity (as embodied, for example, in our capacity for rational choice). Rather, I will argue that demeaning by stigmatizing (or dehumanizing or ...) is wrong when and because it is an attempt to fracture the victim's capacity to develop and maintain an integral sense of self, and so risks undermining one of the structural conditions for a flourishing life. This will allow us, in addition, to expand and deepen the discussion of each of these notions beyond what I presented in Chapter 2. I begin with stigmatization and dehumanization and then turn to infantilization, objectification, and instrumentalization.

Stigma and Dehumanization in Racial Discrimination

To set the stage for this discussion, and to isolate the issue we are concerned with, let us return to *Palmer v. Thompson,* which will also allow us to tie together the strands of the account of social meanings offered above. Recall that the mayor closed down the pools in Jackson, Mississippi, to avoid desegregating them. This, we concluded, was an act of morally wrongful discrimination. Above, I argued that the case trains our attention on the *message sent* to blacks about their status in Mississippi. But what, exactly, is this message?

To understand the social meaning of the closure, we must look at wider cultural and social patterns in the United States at the time. In the 1920s and 1930s, recently gender-desegregated public pools, especially in the hot South, had become, as one commentator puts it, "leisure resorts," replete with sun decks, grassy areas, and artificial sand beaches.[39] Crowded with families, they were at the center of public social life. And, of course, they were all white. In some bigger cities (as in Jackson), there were public swimming pools for blacks, but they were badly funded, often dilapidated, and much smaller in size. Desegregation swept away, in just a few years, the culture of the public swimming pool, as hundreds of pools were closed in just the same way as the ones in Jackson. In its place came the myriad private, residents-only, "community" swimming pools we see across the United States today. So why were whites so willing to give up a central aspect of their social life rather than to see it desegregated? According to Jeff Wiltse, part of the explanation lies in fears that blacks harbor communicable diseases that will easily be transmitted in water and changing rooms.[40] But the main explanation is another one. Recall that the pools had recently been *gender*-desegregated. Wiltse writes, "Most whites did not want black men interacting with white women at such an intimate and crowded public space."[41] Dominant here is the image of the sensual, hypersexualized black man and the vulnerable, precious white woman who needs protection. In the background is the fear of rape by black men, and Emmett Till, the fourteen-year-old black boy who, in 1955, was famously lynched for speaking on friendly terms with a white female shopkeeper.[42]

I want to argue that the attitudes expressed by the closures are demeaning because they treat blacks as bearers of a dehumanizing stigma, as polluted and animalistic, and hence as outside the give and take of "civilized" life. But why is such treatment wrong? The moral wrongness of such attitudes, it might be thought, is easily explained by pointing to the way in which they willfully misrepresent a series of self-evident facts. But this can't be the whole story. What if the whites involved sincerely believed these things to be true of blacks? Yes, one might say, but such beliefs, although sincerely held, failed adequately to take into account the relevant evidence regarding disease and character traits among different races. The explanation seems to make the dehumanizing, stigmatizing attitudes wrong solely because of their faulty epistemic status. But can the wrong here really be explained as a mere violation of epistemic norms governing the gathering of evidence and the formation of beliefs? Much more seems to be at stake.

Rather, the stigmatizing, dehumanizing attitude is wrong, I want to suggest, when and because it is an attack on the victim's capacity to develop and maintain a sense of self. In Chapter 2, I argued that we are, at root, sociable beings who have a central interest in social recognition. We each develop an integral sense of self in dialogue and interaction with others similarly engaged. We are constantly involved in the presentation of a self to a world of other selves. But our capacity to develop and maintain a sense of self will not—without unusual strength and resilience—have any stability or integrity without receiving some positive echo in the societies of which we are a part. It is for these reasons that rigid, systematically imposed, and negatively tainted identities pervasively undermine our sense of ourselves *as* self-presenters, as beings who need some degree of control over the terms in which we appear to others in public. As Frantz Fanon writes,

> And already I am being dissected under white eyes, the only real eyes. I am *fixed*. . . . I am laid bare. I feel, I see in those white faces that it is not a new man who has come in, but a new kind of man, a new genus. Why, it's a Negro! . . . Shame. Shame and self-contempt. Nausea. When people like me, they tell me it is in spite of my color. When they dislike me, they point out that it is not because of my color. Either way, I am locked into the infernal circle.[43]

Such stigmatization is, in turn, deepened and reinforced when the imposed identity denies wholesale the very interiority and capacity for self-presentation on which, paradoxically, the attack depends. The stigmatization then becomes dehumanization—the treatment of another "like an animal," as in the image of the black man as a hypersexualized brute. And, as the passage highlights, stigmatization has a further predictable effect on our ability to maintain and develop an integral sense of self. The attitudes that express and reinforce the stigma will ultimately be echoed in our own self-conception, and so infect the way we interact with others, both intimately and publicly.[44] At the extreme, such stigmatized identities, when fully internalized, finally undermine our ability to access and realize the most important goods—recall, for example, Smerdyakov and the Angel in the House.[45]

It might be objected that this emphasis on the social-relational aspect of discriminatory practices downplays or somehow overlooks what *really* makes such discrimination wrong. In paradigmatic cases of discrimination, one might believe that what *really* matters is the arbitrary physical violence, denial of liberty, or economic deprivation that comes along with discriminatory practices, not the thwarting of an interest in social recognition, let alone a denial of opacity respect. This kind of objection is equivalent to arguments that what really makes torture wrong, ultimately, is the pain suffered by the victim. Once again, I have no doubt that the wrongness of discrimination in part stems from the way particular discriminatory acts deprive their bearers of liberty, or expose them to violence, or subject them to economic deprivation. My point is rather that the character, and hence the wrongness, of these deprivations cannot be understood *without* the social-relational dimension (as is the case, I have argued, also with torture). The social-relational dimension gives the deprivation of liberty, or exposure to violence (or other comparative disadvantage), a new and different form. The social meaning of a comparative disadvantage is now also an act of demeaning: no longer, as it were, merely a raising of the arm but a salute; no longer removing someone's scarf without permission but removing a Muslim woman's *niqab* without permission.

In each of these cases, the social meaning is not merely an aggravating feature of an action that would be wrong independently—let alone solely a reflection of the faulty character or virtue of the agent—but fundamentally changes the nature of the action itself. This is why I have focused on *Palmer,* which turns on the deprivation of a relatively trivial opportunity or liberty, and so trains our attention on the social meaning of the deprivation rather than on the deprivation as such. This is also why I have focused on cases, like the racist landlord, in which the deprivation would in fact be permissible were it not for its objectionable social meaning, and on the paramedic case, whose wrongfulness is a function of neither malice nor vice in the paramedic.

Notice, by comparison, that even the idea of an arbitrary deprivation cannot be enough to account for the wrongfulness of these cases of discrimination. Imagine, for example, that the mayor had closed the pools, not out of any racist animus, but simply because he found swimming unseemly. In this case, the closure would have been arbitrary, and it would have denied the opportunity to swim in pools to all residents of Jackson, but it wouldn't have been wrongful, let alone wrongfully discriminatory in the senses we have been trying to identify. Social meaning is essential.

With this account in hand, the epistemic status of the beliefs that trigger the stigmatizing, dehumanizing attitudes becomes relevant in a new and perhaps unexpected way. Above I argued that whether the beliefs are held sincerely, or whether they are adequately responsive to evidence, cannot on its own explain their moral significance. The faulty epistemic status of these beliefs, however, can play a more indirect, yet still crucial, moral role. The faulty epistemic status of the beliefs is morally relevant because of the way it *reinforces* the social meaning of the actions that are rationalized in terms of those beliefs. The fact that the beliefs are, for example, not responsive to widely available evidence, or very resistant to challenge, makes the stigmatizing, dehumanizing attitudes instances of contempt. The resistance to fact sends the following message: "We really don't care what the facts about people like you are. You are objects of disdain and disgust *whatever the facts.*"

So far we have focused on cases in which victims of wrongful discrimination were aware of the social meaning of a particular act. But, reflecting back on cases like the desert restaurant and the racist landlord, we might wonder what implications the account has for variants in which the persons discriminated against do not know that they have been discriminated against. In these cases, how can the social meaning be objectionable, in my account, if it doesn't carry any psychological or material harm to the individual?[46]

Answering this question allows me to highlight a feature of the Expressive Harm Account. When the racist landlord sends away the couple but the couple does not know that they have been sent away because they are black, they have been harmed in two ways: first, they have been denied an opportunity that they otherwise would have had;[47] second, their interests in social recognition, and hence in being free of the stigma associated with being black, have also been set back. The latter claim will strike us as doubtful only if we have an implausibly narrow understanding of harm, in which one must suffer some psychological or physical damage for something to count as harm.[48] But if, as I do here, we take harm to be a setback to interests, then it strikes me as clear that their interests in recognition have been set back even if they don't know that they have. An analogy is useful. When your friend betrays you, it seems clear that you have been harmed even if you don't know it. The reason is that your interests in not being betrayed have been set back; your life is now, all else equal, less flourishing than it would have been had your friend not betrayed you.[49] When you find out, you are crushed by the recognition of the harm that has been (already) done to you; your psychological pain is a *response* to the harm, not constitutive of it.[50] But if this is plausible in the case of the betrayal, then it strikes me as just as plausible in the case of the racist landlord or the desert restaurant. It is important to remember that, on the view I have defended, what makes a particular act or policy of discrimination wrong (if it is wrong) doesn't require that the act or policy have any broader societal consequences. It is enough if it negatively impacts what I have called the relational nexus between the discriminator and the discriminated against. But notice also that my view doesn't imply that the landlord's racism is somehow "intrinsically" wrong.[51] It doesn't imply that, for example, it violates a *sui generis* moral entitlement to be respected in a certain way; it is wrong when and because it stigmatizes and hence sets back central interests that we all have in social recognition—in *real* recognition, we might say, not the mere appearance of recognition. With respect to a view regarding the intrinsic wrongness of racism, we can always wonder: "Yes, but in what way, exactly, does racism disrespect us, and why does such respect matter?" As we have seen, the account will most likely bottom out ultimately in an (implausible) account of what is required by dignity, or in some other, incomplete account of moral equality.

Reverse Discrimination

What are the implications of the Expressive Harm Account for the question of so-called reverse discrimination? Take, for example, historically black colleges in the United States, such as Morehouse. Such colleges operate a discriminatory admissions policy that explicitly limits the numbers of nonblacks who are admitted. These policies comparatively disadvantage whites (and members of other minorities) because they are white. Are such policies wrongfully discriminatory? (Imagine, for comparison, that the University of California at Berkeley excluded nonwhites in the same way that Morehouse excludes nonblacks.) There are two points to make in this context. First, there is no plausible sense in which the policy objectionably stigmatizes, infantilizes, objectifies, instrumentalizes, or dehumanizes whites. Morehouse appeals to students, for example, by distinguishing itself as a place where, as its website puts it, "after being ignored, stereotyped or marginalized, it's about finally finding that 'home' . . . where you are the heart, soul and hope of the community. And where you are not alone."[52] The aim is to provide, in short, a top-class education that, at the same time, tries to extend and promote solidarity among blacks as blacks, and to secure a platform for overcoming oppression and disadvantage through excellence; it is not plausibly seen as reflecting or perpetuating or expressing the view that whites are "polluted" or otherwise worthy of disdain or contempt. A whites-only equivalent, on the other hand, could not but be perceived as trying to do exactly that.

One might wonder: But what about a black-owned café that shuts its doors to whites because the owners perceive whites to be evil or inherently exploitative? Would such a policy be wrongfully discriminatory on my view? The policy, we imagine, is designed to show contempt and disdain for whites. Imagine that you are a white member of the local community. The policy cannot but be understood to express a message about you and others like you to those within your community, an attempt to stigmatize and hence to wound. Under this description, it would therefore be an instance of wrongful direct discrimination. But note that the policy would not be as wrongful as the reverse. The policy does not reinforce, perpetuate, deepen, or mobilize racialized patterns of stigma; its effort to exclude can therefore only ever be incomplete. Notice, for example, that for the example to have force, the excluded white must be a member of the community. If he or she were not, then the attack as an attack would look even more remote. Though it would still be wrongful *qua* attempt, the social conventions are not stable or widespread enough to set back your central interests in very deep or pervasive ways on an (objective) understanding of what those interests are and an (objective) understanding of what the social meaning of the action ultimately is. The Expressive Harm Account therefore creates a space for the possibility of wrongful reverse discrimination in theory while clarifying how rare it would be, given current conditions, in practice.

Infantilization, Objectification, and Instrumentalization in Sex Discrimination

Thus far I have discussed racial discrimination. In this section, we expand the Expressive Harm Account to encompass sex discrimination, which is the other paradigmatic instance of wrongful discrimination.

It might be thought that we could simply generalize our discussion of stigmatization and dehumanization to include discriminatory acts toward women as well. However, while there are many instances of sex discrimination that involve treating women as bearing a stigma—think of attitudes toward menstruation, childbirth, prostitution, and pregnancy, or broader patterns of misogyny[53]—to stop there would be to overlook how sex discrimination operates across a much wider domain of human activity. A fuller account of sex discrimination requires an expansion of the analysis and its categories, but one that is united by our underlying concern with inferiorizing treatment, and hence with the idea of demeaning. The key categories that we need to reconstruct are, I will argue, the categories of infantilization, objectification, and instrumentalization.

Infantilization

A significant swathe of the discrimination experienced by women ultimately derives from and otherwise contributes to the gendered division of labor. Whatever the origins of this division of labor and its particular reflection in the modern family, it is hard to doubt that cultural and ideological practices have a large role in both justifying and propagating it, and in shaping its particular character. The association of women with the intimate sphere, with the body, with reproduction and mothering, and men's association with what Arendt called "appearance," with the public, the sphere of speech, action, and reasoned deliberation, is reproduced and justified by a network of conscious and unconscious assumptions, beliefs, emotions, experiences, and desires.[54] It is also hard to doubt that such practices might be changed—as they already have been in pockets around the world—to mitigate or even eliminate such discrimination. To be sure, the prospects of a general transformation may be a long way off and require painful adaptations and reforms, but it would be very difficult to argue that such change would be impossible.[55]

Perhaps the most fundamental cultural and ideological belief that has sustained and reproduced the gendered division of labor, and women's particular place within it, is the belief in women's physical and psychological weakness, and their consequent need for men's protection and tutelage, especially within the institution of marriage; and, closely related, the idea that women's qualities and very being are but a derivative and paler reflection of men's. Referring to the story of Genesis and to Aristotle, Simone de Beauvoir writes, "Humanity is male, and man defines woman, not in herself, but in relation to himself."[56] And again: "But what singularly defines the situation of woman is that being, like all humans, a freedom, she discovers and chooses herself in a world where men force her to assume herself as Other: an attempt is made to freeze her as an object and doom her to immanence [to a static, passive, inert, animal role, as opposed to an active, dynamic, free, and rational creativity]."[57] This infantilizing ideology has had far-reaching legal, political, economic, social, and cultural consequences. Wendy Williams recounts how women figure in Blackstone's late eighteenth-century commentaries on the common law:

> Just before the American Revolution, Blackstone, in the course of his comprehensive commentary on the common law, set forth the fiction that informed and guided the treatment of married women in the English law courts. When a woman married, her legal identity merged into that of her husband; she was civilly dead. She couldn't sue, be sued, enter into contracts, make wills, keep her own earnings, control her own property. She could not even protect her own physical integrity—her husband had the right to chastise her (although only with a switch no bigger than his thumb), restrain her freedom, and impose sexual intercourse upon her against her will.[58]

To be sure, these practices and their justificatory baggage are no longer widely endorsed, but they have congealed in institutions and societal patterns—such as marriage, employment practices, legal entitlements to public benefits, interpersonal relations—that reproduce, in a new form, their essential structure.[59] We live in the shadow of this history. According to Okin,

> [Marriage and the family today] constitute the pivot of a societal system of gender that renders women vulnerable to dependency,

exploitation, and abuse. When we look seriously at the distribution between husbands and wives of such critical social goods as work (paid and unpaid), power, prestige, self-esteem, opportunities for self-development, and both physical and economic security, we find socially constructed inequalities between them, right down the list.[60]

This history and these consequences are at once reflected in and contribute to the wrongfulness of much sex-based discrimination. Our task is to explain how. In this section and the next, I focus on direct sex-based discrimination. I then turn to indirect discrimination more broadly, and to the objection that theories of discrimination cannot account for structural injustice.

It is evident that one of the sources of objection to these practices is their evident unfairness. But we must be careful in stating what form this unfairness takes. It is tempting to say that the practices that reproduce and reflect the gendered division of labor are unfair because they are ultimately based on a set of *arbitrary* distinctions between women and men. These distinctions are arbitrary because they are false: women are not merely pale reflections of men; they do not, as the profoundly influential Aristotelian theory holds, have a deliberative faculty that lacks the authority of the male equivalent; they are not, by nature, fit to be ruled by men. But, as in the case of the stigmatizing, dehumanizing beliefs regarding blacks discussed above, the wrong cannot be solely explained in virtue of the mere falsity of the beliefs themselves. The wrong here is not analogous to the wrong that might be exhibited by a distribution of prizes that rests on false beliefs about the relative merits of the winners. What matters are the wider attitudes toward women of which the beliefs are a part, and, more specifically, as we will see in a moment, the message sent to women as a result of policies adopted and justified by those attitudes.

The unfairness, furthermore—and once again analogously to the racial cases discussed above—cannot be solely explained as an instance of maldistribution. Being denied a position on the basis that one is a woman, for example, is wrong for a very different reason than being denied a position because one doesn't belong to the owner's family; while both employment decisions are instances of unfairness, and so, we might argue, a violation of norms of equality of opportunity, the former is demeaning in a way that the latter is not.*

To highlight how the social meaning matters over and above the maldistribution and the epistemic character of beliefs and believers, I will discuss a landmark case of sex-based discrimination, namely *Muller v. Oregon*,[61] decided by the US Supreme Court in 1908. This case upheld an Oregon law prohibiting female (but not male) bakers from working more than 10 hours a day. The case is relevant for us because laws restricting working hours for *both* men and women strikes us today as a *legitimate* and perhaps *morally mandatory* way of equaling the bargaining power of workers who are liable to exploitation (in a way that did not strike the *Lochner* Court, *except* in the case of women[62]). We do not, I will assume, have any justice-based objection to a restriction in working hours *as such*. So, in one way and holding other factors of the legislation constant,[63] it is the men who are put at a relevant disadvantage, since they are denied a moral entitlement that women are granted. The source of our objection to the discrimination in this case does not, therefore, reside in the fact that women are denied a work-based benefit or opportunity available to men.

Similarly, our objection cannot reside merely in the generic paternalism of the legislation. In *Holden v. Hardy* (1898), for example, the Court upheld maximum-hours legislation for (male) miners, arguing, among other things, that long hours in the mines had devastating effects on miners' health.[64] But, if we have no objection to such legislation, then why not come to the same judgment with respect to the Oregon law restricting working hours for women, especially given the copious empirical detail that Brandeis and his sister-in-law provided regarding the effect of long hours on women? Why, in other words, not

---

* It is relevant here that no jurisdiction of which I'm aware prosecutes nepotism as a violation of anti-discrimination norms. This is easily explained: the focus on only "protected groups" such as racial, ethnic, and religious minorities; women; the disabled; and LGBTQ communities is due to an underlying concern with stigma, dehumanization, infantilization, instrumentalization, and objectification, and hence to a concern, ultimately, with the treatment of others as inferior. Nepotism, while unfair, lacks this quality. If I am right about discrimination and its connection with moral equality, then this exclusion is warranted.

conclude that there is nothing wrong with *Muller* just as there is nothing wrong with *Holden?* Pointing to generic paternalism (or, indeed, to the unequal bargaining power between employees and workers) seems, on its own, insufficient to differentiate the two.

The key resides in the social meaning of the Court's decision and its rationale, and therefore in the message sent by the legislation against a wider background of beliefs about the role of women in the family and their dependence on men. As we will see, it is the particular *form* that the paternalism takes in these cases that is troubling, rather than paternalism *as such*. In his opinion for the Court, Justice Brewer writes:

> History discloses the fact that woman has always been dependent upon man. . . . Education was long denied her, and while now the doors of the schoolroom are opened and her opportunities for acquiring knowledge are great, yet, even with that and the consequent increase of capacity for business affairs, it is still true that, in the struggle for subsistence, she is not an equal competitor with her brother. Though limitations upon personal and contractual rights may be removed by legislation, there is that in her disposition and habits of life which will operate against a full assertion of [her] rights. She will still be where some legislation to protect her seems necessary. . . . [L]ooking at it from the viewpoint of the effort to maintain an independent position in life, she is not upon an equality. Differentiated by these matters from the other sex, she is properly placed in a class by herself, and legislation designed for her protection may be sustained, even when like legislation is not necessary for men, and could not be sustained. It is impossible to close one's eyes to the fact that she still looks to her brother and depends upon him. . . . [S]he is so constituted that she will rest upon and look to him for protection.[65]

Justice Brewer claims that the very same facts with respect to inequalities in adverse working conditions, bargaining power, and so on, ought to have a different role in the Court's reasoning when the persons concerned are women. This is because women are, by nature, ultimately dependent on men for their own protection (and hence on the all-male

Court and legislature), and, again by nature, and despite receiving the "education long denied her," less able to resist exploitation than men. Hence, protective legislation concerning women does not have to meet the same demanding standards as protective legislation designed for men. This is an instance of the infantilization at the heart of the gendered division of labor.

Infantilization, however, is not always wrong. It is not wrong, for example, vis-à-vis children. It might be thought that all we need to say in response is: "But women are not children." But, as we have seen, the wrongfulness of infantilization cannot be explained by a mere appeal to the epistemic faults of those who believe that women *are* relevantly like children. We have also seen that the objection cannot reside merely in the fact that it deepens the unfairness of a distribution of socioeconomic opportunities, or that it is an instance of generic paternalism. So what makes the infantilization of women objectionable?

I want to argue that infantilization undercuts the authority of women to speak for themselves; infantilizing practices send the message that women do not have the standing to define the terms of their social, and in this case economic, engagement with others without the intermediation of men. Infantilization is, like stigmatization, therefore a violation of opacity respect: a rigid, systematically imposed, negatively tainted identity that denies women the capacity to shape the terms in which they are to be seen by others.[66] If we assume that the workplace is one of the central places in which such self-presentation and its recognition becomes important, then the kind of infantilization expressed by the Oregon law and the Court's opinion in *Muller* is particularly troubling. Recall Beauvoir: "an attempt is made to freeze her as an object and doom her to immanence." According to Beauvoir, human beings all strive to transcend their embodied, finite existence through projects; at the center of human freedom is therefore activity and creativity in a world of others; this is close to what I have referred to as the power to present ourselves to others and our consequent need for recognition of that power. By systematically imposing a rigid, negatively tainted identity as both dependent, inferior, and destined by nature to inhibit the realm of the body, namely the private sphere, women are "frozen" as (passive) objects rather than (active) agents; the capacity for self-presentation is, as it were, stilled. Infantilization, in this sense, then also becomes a form of *objectification*. As MacKinnon writes, "men's power over women means that the way men see women defines who women can be."[67] If I am right that the power to shape the terms of our social engagement with others and the need for recognition of this power—especially in the workplace—are empirically necessary conditions for the development and maintenance of an integral sense of self, then infantilization is an attack on that capacity, and hence an instance of social cruelty. The attack has further consequences, as we have seen in Chapter 2, if and when it is internalized: like the Angel in the House, the abdication of one's independence not only opens one up to cruelty and violence but also requires abdicating the investment of one's self in the realization of the most important goods in a human life. It is for these reasons that demeaning by infantilizing is wrong, not because of a failure to bow down before the absolute, incommensurable, and unconditional worth of our capacity to act according to the moral law.

The background, as in the case with race, is relevant here. Consider that, after the *Muller* decision, a raft of protective legislation directed toward women was passed, including legislation that barred women from certain professions (most famously, from being lawyers or barmaids without the permission of an elder male family member).[68] It is also relevant that this raft of legislation was passed during a period in which women were not permitted to vote (women attained the right to vote in the United States only in 1920). The message, in each case, was the same: women's deliberative, rational capacities are stunted when compared with men's; women require men's supervision and control to attain what they need to live a good life. It is men who control the terms in which women will present themselves to others. And here the regnant attitudes toward the facts, as in the racial case, also play an important role. Whereas the Court in *Muller* was attuned to the facts regarding women's health and safety at work, they were not at all concerned to verify the facts regarding women's inferior capacity to reason and deliberate or their capacity to attain a flourishing life without the supervision or control of men.[69] The facts and their significance were ascertained, as it were, by nature. These oversights send the message, as before, that "we don't care what the facts are; women require supervision and control by men whatever their rational capacities."

The comprehensiveness of these policies and their justifying apparatus is important to distinguish the paternalistic attitudes expressed in cases like *Holden* from those expressed in cases like *Muller*. In *Holden*, the Court was intent on limiting the scope of the protection by pointing to the great importance of miners' liberty interest in contracting on their own terms, but argued that this case was exceptional in view of the very great harms, and in view of the weak bargaining position of workers vis-à-vis employers. There was no sense that the weak bargaining position was a result of anything other than their relative poverty, and no question of the value of men's being able to choose independently across a range of other occupations. In *Muller*, while the Court did recognize the importance of woman's liberty interest in contracting her own labor, it discounted it relative to men's on the basis not of the facts regarding women's particular bargaining position or the structural circumstances in which they made those decisions, but on the basis of her inferior ability to "assert her rights" in *any* position—an ability that was deemed inferior not with respect to a particular set of *employers* in a given, exceptional set of conditions but vis-à-vis men *in general*. And when the Court points out that her "effort to maintain an independent position in life" is inferior to men's, this is not to conclude that something should be done to remedy her condition, but rather to *reinforce* it. On the other hand, when the Court, in *Holden*, remarked that miners and their employers do not "stand upon an equality" and that "the proprietors lay down the rules and the laborers are practically constrained to obey them," they conclude that "self-interest is often an unsafe guide, and the legislature may properly interpose its authority."[70] In the former case, an inequality of position justifies an attempt to maintain and perpetuate a hierarchy; in the latter, it justifies the interposition of a public authority to *dismantle* it, thus increasing the control of working men over their environment. The social meaning of *Muller*, I conclude, serves therefore to attack women's authority to set the terms of their engagement with others in a way that *Holden* does not attack men's.

So far I have argued that sex-based (direct) discrimination—such as in *Muller*—is wrong when and because it demeans women by infantilizing and hence objectifying. I then went on to argue that the wrongness of such infantilization *qua* objectification cannot be explained solely by reference to the downstream societal effects on inequality of socioeconomic opportunity, by generic concerns with paternalism, or by reference to the mere epistemic faultiness of the beliefs sustaining it. We must pay attention, as in the race-based cases discussed above, to the dimension of social meaning. I then argued that infantilization *qua* objectification is wrong when and because it systematically undercuts women's power to shape the terms of their social engagement with others, and hence represents an attack on their capacity to develop and maintain an integral sense of self. The epistemic faultiness of infantilizing believers then acquires a different meaning: it is not, I argued, any mere epistemic irresponsibility that explains the wrongness of the actions that express those beliefs. Rather, the imperviousness of the underlying beliefs to empirical verification—indeed, the insensitivity to any empirical evidence at all—sends the message that these facts don't really matter. All that matters is the fate assigned to women as objects by men as knowers.

Although I won't do so here, it should be clear that the account can be extended to cover other cases of direct sex-based discrimination that invoke the same structure of infantilizing attitudes described above. It should also be clear that the account could be extended to cover direct sex-based discrimination that reflects unconscious bias (as we did for race-based direct discrimination above). For example, consider (oft-replicated) studies of implicit gender bias that show that an identical curriculum vitae (CV)—say, a CV intended for an academic faculty hiring in the STEM subjects (science, technology, engineering, and mathematics)[71]—will be evaluated differently according to whether the CV bears a female or a male name. Insofar as such implicit gender biases are in part explained by unconscious beliefs regarding women's natural inferiority in reasoning and deliberative capacity, their insecure place in the world of work, and so on, and therefore reflect the same attitudes that gave rise, historically, to the gendered division of labor, they will be objectionable for the very same reasons we have already discussed: they not only put women at an unfair socioeconomic disadvantage with respect to men but also, at the same time, send a demeaning, infantilizing message. One might, at this point, wonder what the implications of the account offered have for *indirect* forms of discrimination, in which gender and race play no role, conscious or unconscious, in the deliberations leading to a particular course of action or policy. We will turn to that question shortly, but first we need to consider another important aspect of wrongful, direct sex-based direct discrimination— an aspect that might not, at first glance, seem to involve any infantilizing, stigmatizing, or dehumanizing attitudes, yet still strikes us as wrongfully inferiorizing. This aspect of sex-based discrimination is most evident when we consider why sexual harassment is an instance of sex-based discrimination in the workplace. This is the topic to which we turn in the next section.

Objectification and Instrumentalization

The term "sexual harassment" was coined in the mid-1970s to refer, broadly, to unwelcome sexual attention in the workplace that serves to intimidate, coerce, or humiliate women. The issue was, from the beginning, taken up as an issue of sex-based *discrimination*. It may not be immediately clear why. If direct discrimination is, as I have defined it, any set of acts or policies that comparatively disadvantages a member of a socially salient group as a result of their being a member of that group, and where the expectation that the individual would be so disadvantaged makes a difference in whole or in part, consciously or unconsciously, to the outcomes of an agent's deliberation, then how does a particular act of sexual harassment count? Under what conditions can we interpret unwelcome sexual attention as disadvantaging a woman *because she is a woman* (rather than disadvantaging because the attention is unwanted *simpliciter*)? (And how do our answers to these questions bear on female-male, male-male, and female-female cases of harassment?) In this section, I use the Expressive Harm Account to answer these questions.

I begin with a paradigmatic example of what is often referred to (especially in the law) as "hostile environment" sexual harassment, namely

Robinson v. Jacksonville Shipyards.[72] In 1991, Lois Robinson reported a case of sexual harassment at a Jacksonville shipyard, where she worked as a welder. Numerous men at the shipyards—a heavily male industry where Robinson was among only a small number of female workers (6 women and 846 men were employed as skilled craft workers at the shipyard in 1986, and the company had never employed women in supervisory jobs like foreman, coordinator, leaderman, or quarterman)—routinely engaged in verbal and sexually charged taunting directed at Robinson (e.g., "women are only fit company for something that howls"). Pornographic images, including some that were intended to look like Robinson herself, were festooned across the locker-room and dry-dock areas. "Eat me" was spray painted across her work station when she went for a drink, and when Robinson complained, a "Men Only" sign was painted on the side of a trailer. This is a clear case of unwanted sexual attention that serves to intimidate, humiliate, and coerce.

But why is this an instance of sex-based *discrimination* rather than a case of generic bullying or unwanted sexual attention *simpliciter?* It seems incontrovertible here that the shipyard workers targeted Robinson *as a woman,* mobilizing the gender-based hierarchy present at the shipyard and in the wider society not only to exclude Robinson but also, as we will see in a moment, to *silence* her. The posting of pornographic images and the verbal taunting cannot but be understood as an attempt to make Robinson feel as if she were, in their eyes, an object fit only for their sexual control, unworthy of being treated with respect as a colleague. The harassment sends the message: "You are not welcome here *as a woman;* do not forget that this is a man's world in which you count only as an object of our sexual perusal; here the only authority that counts is a male one." What is here invoked and reinforced are the same patriarchal norms that have sustained the gendered division of labor: women are objects of what Beauvoir called immanence—destined to be inert, passive, and restrained to the body and the private, intimate sphere. Men are subjects of transcendence, who seek to develop themselves through projects, control, and mastery of their surroundings. In settings like Jacksonville shipyards, unwanted sexual attention is not simply, as it were, unwanted sexual attention *simpliciter,* or a mere assertion of power or authority as may occur in any hierarchical work setting, but an assertion of dominance whose effect is to humiliate, coerce, and intimidate *through the mobilization of norms governing a gendered structure of power.* Sexual harassment of this kind is therefore, I conclude, an instance of sex-based discrimination.[73]

But what makes sexual harassment of this kind wrong? It is wrong, once again, not merely because and insofar as it causally reproduces or perpetuates patriarchy, or broader structures of socioeconomic inequality. Even if we imagined that the act or policy did not have such downstream societal effects, we would still object (recall the race- and sex-based cases already mentioned above). It is also not merely wrong because it is ultimately based on an inaccurate view of what women are really like (as if the shipyard workers had merely gotten their facts about women wrong), let alone because it picks out women on the basis of a "morally arbitrary" characteristic—a characteristic that is, on one reading, merely the product of (bad?) brute luck (and: Would it have made a difference had Robinson been a woman by choice?). The idea of infantilization or stigmatization doesn't seem to get it quite right either, since there was no question of protection or paternalism, or, arguably, the imposition of a "polluted" identity. I want to argue that discriminatory sexual harassment of this kind is wrong when and because it takes the form of a special kind of *objectification.* I first discuss what objectification is and when it is wrong, and then turn back to *Robinson.*

Objectification involves the treatment of persons as things. But what is it to treat a person as a thing, and when and why is such treatment wrong? (Especially since, after all, we are *also* things? We are not freely floating intelligences, like Kant's angels.)[74] In response to the first question, I begin with Martha Nussbaum's insightful analysis of objectification as involving one or more of the following seven features:

1. Instrumentality: The objectifier treats the object as a tool of his or her purposes.
2. Denial of autonomy: The objectifier treats the object as lacking in autonomy and self-determination.
3. Inertness: The objectifier treats the object as lacking in agency, and perhaps also in activity.

4. Fungibility: The objectifier treats the object as interchangeable (a) with other objects of the same type, and / or (b) with objects of other types.
5. Violability: The objectifier treats the object as lacking in boundary integrity, as something that it is permissible to break up, smash, break into.
6. Ownership: The objectifier treats the object as something that is owned by another, can be bought or sold, etc.
7. Denial of subjectivity: The objectifier treats the object as something whose experience and feelings (if any) need not be taken into account.

Nussbaum's powerful insight, defended by appeal to preponderantly sexual examples (around which most of the literature on objectification has centered), is threefold. First, none of these seven features is individually necessary for objectification, and one or more may be, depending on context, sufficient. Second, it is possible to objectify another person without wronging them. For example, you might use someone to shield against the wind—and hence as you might use an umbrella—without wronging them. Third, and most importantly, *no subset of these seven features is necessary or sufficient to make objectification wrong.* One can think, in other words, of *permissible* instances of objectification in which one or more of *any of these seven features* are present (and perhaps all together), and one can think of *impermissible* instances of objectification that involve nonoverlapping proper subsets of each of these conditions. The rugby transfer market provides an instructive example.[75] The rugby transfer market can plausibly be construed as involving at least six, if not all seven, of Nussbaum's conditions. Players in the transfer market are treated by owners of a club as owned by them (players are often traded from one club to another); as fungible (two players might be considered of equivalent value); as lacking in subjectivity (the experiences and feelings of players are not taken as relevant, only their skills, etc.); as lacking in autonomy (players can be traded against their will); as instruments (a player is valued insofar as he or she wins games for the team); and as violable (by fielding a player, you treat him or her as legitimately subject to being "broken" and "smashed up"). The only condition that seems to be missing is *Inertness*, and, even there, we might think that when a large player is fielded to add weight to a scrum, they are treated in their "passive" rather than "active" capacity, as bulwarks rather than playmakers.

For our purposes, the most interesting examples are sexual ones. Nussbaum calls our attention to D. H. Lawrence's *The Rainbow* and to Tom Brangwen's self-immolating, consuming desire for his wife, Lydia. Nussbaum describes how Tom resigns both his autonomy and his subjectivity. She writes: "The power of sexuality is most authentically experienced, in [Lawrence's] view, when the parties put aside their conscious choice-making, and even their inner life of self-consciousness and articulate thought, and permit themselves to be, in a sense, object-like, natural forces meeting one another with what he likes to call 'blood knowledge.'"[76] In the presence of Lydia's "kernel of darkness," Tom yields his self-containment and self-sufficiency. He becomes passive, inert, in his surrender of agency. Both are also in a sense fungible, since both become objects of a nameless, primal desire. The boundaries between self and other become porous, and Tom longs to be "destroyed" and "burnt away" by Lydia. Nussbaum has described a kind of sexual objectification in which most, if not all, of the conditions of objectification are satisfied, and yet we have no moral objection. Indeed, the loss of definite boundaries—of autonomy, subjectivity, control, individuality, inviolability, self-ownership—are a hallmark, in this case, of a profound mutual trust.

This is important for our analysis of objectification because it suggests, if Nussbaum is right, that the wrongness of objectification, including sexual objectification, cannot reside in the mere presence of one or more of the seven conditions. It must reside in some wrong-making property possessed by some but not all instances of objectification, and that cannot be reduced to any of the seven conditions (singly or in combination). For the desired criterion, Nussbaum invokes Kant's idea of treating someone's humanity as an end-in-itself.[77] So, for example, in discussing Lawrence's *The Rainbow*, she claims that the loss of boundaries, etc., is morally unobjectionable because it occurs in circumstances of equality and mutual respect.[78] But by now we have seen that, while this may be correct, it is radically underspecified: What does mutual respect and equality, exactly, require? In what sense do Lydia and Tom (and, we might add, the owner and the players) treat one another as equals? In what sense do they respect one another? The problem with the end-in-itself formulation, as I argued in Chapter 1, is the following. If it is taken to mean taking into account a being's evaluative perspective on the world, then it only gives us the idea that a being has a *basic* moral standing rather than an *equal* moral standing. And if it is taken as referring to a much more substantive account of equal moral worth, such as the idea that our capacity for rational choice has absolute, incommensurable, and unconditional value, then it is implausible.

Even the more intuitive idea of instrumentalization, of treating someone as a "mere means" or "mere object," doesn't seem either necessary or sufficient for wrongfully treating as inferior. It is not sufficient: What do we say, for example, about a torturer who would have treated someone even worse had it not been for their humanity? Because the torturer holds back, the victim cannot be said to have been treated as a *mere* means, and yet this counts as a clear case of treating as an inferior.[79] It is not necessary. First, a gangster might treat the waiter as a vending machine (and be willing to kill him at a moment's notice should something go wrong). But as long as he pays for his coffee and walks out, there is nothing to object to.[80] Second, there are many cases of wrongfully treating another as an inferior that don't seem to involve any instrumentalization. Our case of sexual harassment is one. If someone isn't treated as a means to anything, then they can't be treated as a *mere* means. But in what sense is Robinson treated as a means? A means to what? The men have no "use" for her at all, hence their antagonism and attempt to exclude her. (The rugby players seem to be treated as "means" to a much greater extent than Robinson.) The idea that the men treat her as a means to discharge their misogyny, or as a means to exclude her, seems stretched to the breaking point; any purposive action would thereby count as using as a means, which would make the category "instrumentalization" empty.

One might think that what sets the dividing line between the permissible and impermissible cases of objectification is the fact of consent *simpliciter* (consent here understood as the criterion that sets apart cases that do and do not involve treating as mere means). In the rugby case, the players consent to being tradable and smashed up in a way that Robinson did not consent to her treatment at the shipyards. But there is a problem with this view: lack of consent to objectification *simpliciter* is not sufficient to make objectification wrong. For example, consider drawing someone's portrait without their consent. The portraitist uses someone's body in this case as both a mere means and as a mere object, but is it wrong for that reason? (And if it is, what makes it a wrong *of a different kind* than, say, sexual harassment or rape while unconscious?) To make sense of the moral differences in these cases, we need an account of our interests against rape and sexual harassment when compared with our interests in not being drawn—an account that mere appeal to the importance of consent (or being treated as a mere means) cannot give us, but an account of what is central to our capacity to develop and maintain an integral sense of self (in this case, control over our sexuality) can.[81] To put it another way: Consent operates as a normative power to change an *already existing* distribution of rights, but it cannot itself establish the existence of those rights in the first place. (Why, for example, do we take the fact that your neighbor does not consent to your having a dinner party in the garden as irrelevant to whether you have a permission to do so?) So we need to know why we have moral rights against being sexually harassed (or smashed up in the case of the rugby players) that we lack against being drawn, before we can know how consent can operate to change the permissions and duties. Our account of the connection between control over our own sexuality (and the violability of our bodies in the case of rugby) and our ability to realize the most important goods provides the missing link.

This raises the question of whether lack of consent is *necessary* for objectification to be wrong. Can there, in other words, be cases in which we consent to objectification but where objectification is still morally objectionable? Imagine, *per impossibile,* that the owners of the Jacksonville shipyards had requested Robinson to sign a form consenting to her sexual harassment on the job (just as the rugby players consent to being "smashed up" and traded), and suppose she had accepted (in full knowledge of the facts and in the absence of duress). Is there a moral difference between the two cases? If so, where do we locate it? Recall that on my account, if we genuinely authorize someone to attack our capacity to develop and maintain an integral sense of self, then the resulting actions are not cruel and hence not instances of treating as an inferior in the relevant sense. But what counts as *genuine* authorization, an authorization that succeeds in waiving or transferring a right? The rugby players waive their rights to not being traded, smashed up, and so on, as a result of a contract. Why couldn't Robinson waive her rights to be treated without being sexual harassed, thus making what would otherwise be an instance of cruelty no longer such an instance?

It strikes me that the contract in the hypothetical is problematic for two reasons. First, we object to the terms and conditions on the grounds that the sexual harassment is not essential, in any sense, to the role of a shipyard worker (in the way that getting traded and smashed up is to the role of a rugby player). Setting the terms and conditions in this way therefore strikes us as exploitative and coercive. But this cannot be definitive, since it begs the question: Why should the practice of rugby be permissible in the first place? And: What if sexual harassment were essential to being a shipyard worker? Would that make it morally unproblematic?

The second reason we object refers back to our account of what is necessary to develop and maintain an integral sense of self, and to its connection to the realization of the most important goods. We can easily imagine how a rugby player is invested in his or her role *as* a rugby player, and hence in being smashed up and traded and so on. But we have trouble making sense of a woman (or a man) being invested in her (his) identity as shipyard-worker-and-object-of-sexual-harassment; we have trouble seeing how the job offer can serve as anything but an attempt to undermine her (his) capacity to develop and maintain an integral sense of self, or alternatively, as anything other than an attempt to reinforce an already broken sense of self (recall our discussion of the Angel in the House and the servile lackey from Chapter 2).[82] In this sense, the fact that sexual harassment is nonessential to being a shipyard worker matters insofar as it changes the social meaning of the contractual offer. This is why we may even balk at the very supposition required by the hypothetical: What woman or man (who wasn't under severe pressure or who didn't possess an already fractured sense of self) would ever consent to such treatment? And what kind of employer would ever take advantage of that vulnerability? Isn't the very offer of the contract humiliating, a further attempt to put Robinson in her place? For these reasons, I conclude that the contract offer is, as a result, exploitative and coercive in a way that it isn't vis-à-vis the rugby players.*

These points are also relevant to our assessment of prostitution. Again, we ask, is it intelligible that a woman (or man) taking up prostitution under current conditions could see it as anything other than an objectifying practice that serves to attack the integrity of her (his) sense of self, or to reinforce an already fractured sense of self? Here it is relevant that current forms of prostitution involve (often gendered) forms of coercion, intimidation, and humiliation of a kind that cannot but be understood as cruel. On this basis, it seems hard to deny that the vast majority of those who solicit or employ prostitutes are complicit in the structural exploitation, coercion, and humiliation that underlies the practice as it currently operates. But while this is the *reality* of prostitution, we can *conceive* of forms of prostitution that would not involve any of those things (in a way that, I submit, it is nearly impossible to conceive of similarly unobjectionable practices of sexual harassment). Our objection to prostitution should therefore be to the cruelty of current practices, not to the (objectifying) sale of sex *per se*. (Similar things might be said about strip clubs and pornography.)

Note that we are not discussing whether prostitution (strip clubs, pornography) should be *illegal*, which raises a further set of issues. We are asking whether it is *morally* permissible to offer a prostitution (strip

---

* It might be thought that we could deal with cases of this sort solely by appealing to the *third-party* effects on women in general—the downstream societal effects on the norms supporting patriarchy. To be sure, this could be *part* of the explanation of our moral objection to the contract, but it couldn't be the whole story for at least two reasons. First, on its own, it leaves unexplained the wrong done to Robinson; indeed, its structure presupposes that Robinson *succeeds* in waiving her rights. We could therefore blame Robinson (in addition to the men) for taking up the contract, for, as it were, letting other women down by increasing the general force of patriarchy. Second, as we have already seen with the other cases we have discussed, our objection to the contract remains even if we suppose that the contract has *no* further societal effects (recall, e.g., the desert restaurant).

club, pornography) contract (whatever its legality), whether such contracts wrong those who consent to them, and whether consent to such a contract should waive any rights not to be treated in what would otherwise be a cruel way. So our assessment of prostitution is compatible with the view that it would be difficult and perhaps infeasible to implement a real-world system permitting (and, say, regulating) prostitution that would prevent (or at any rate seriously limit) cruelty.*

We should therefore resist the Kantian temptation. But then what criteria should we use to distinguish permissible and impermissible objectification? My answer is the same as it has been for all the other modes of treating as inferior I have discussed. Objectification is wrong when and because it uses our vulnerability to attack our capacity to develop and maintain an integral sense of self. Let us return to *Robinson* to see the account at work. Using Nussbaum's criteria for identifying objectification, the harassment to which Robinson was subject satisfies, most importantly, denial of subjectivity, inertness, fungibility, and denial of autonomy. In mobilizing a gendered, hierarchical trope—men as exerting sexual control over women, who are considered passive, inert, and subject to the unilateral demands of male sexuality and desire—the men at the Jacksonville shipyards attempt to silence Robinson as a coworker, thus denying her subjectivity and autonomy. She is "put in her place," made to feel fungible and lacking in individuality. These denials are wrong because they cannot but be understood as attacks on her capacity to develop and maintain an integral sense of self in the

---

* This possibility also leaves untouched whether and to what extent permitting prostitution (pornography, strip clubs) would have other, objectionable downstream causal effects on women in general. Does permitting prostitution (strip clubs, pornography) make dismantling structures of patriarchy—including the gendered division of labor—more difficult in general? Answering this question would require a causal analysis that is far beyond the purview of this book. The important thing to note is that the answer to it would not address whether prostitution (strip club, pornography) contracts wrong the women (and men) who take them up. For the idea that pornography (and, we might add, prostitution and strip clubs), as social practices, might not merely *cause* the subordination and silencing of women in general, but themselves legitimate and hence *authorize* the subordination and silencing of women in general, see Langton 1993; Hornsby and Langton 1998. I am convinced by the powerful replies to this kind of argument given by Jennifer Saul (2006a, 2006b) and by Leslie Green (1998, 2000).

workplace. This is all accomplished via a denial of opacity respect: by invoking the patriarchal trope mentioned above within the shipyard's gendered structure of power, the men attempt to claim for themselves her power of self-presentation; an attempt is made, therefore, to "fix" (recall Beauvoir) or silence Robinson. She is denied a place on which to stand and set the terms of her social engagement with her coworkers as coworkers.[83]

The account can be generalized to other cases of sexual harassment, which, although they may not be as severe, will still count as wrong when and because they satisfy the criteria I have just adumbrated.[84] The account, furthermore, has the added advantage that it can easily be applied to *non*sexual, sex-based harassment, explaining the sense in which it, too, is a form of wrongful discrimination. A good example is *Hall v. Gus Construction Company*,[85] in which male construction workers refused women colleagues' rights to use the toilet, urinated in their gas tanks, and taunted them for being women in a male industry. This kind of harassment is a wrongful instance of sex-based discrimination for the reasons given above with respect to *Robinson,* even though sexual attention plays no part in it.

I conclude our analysis of objectification, sexual harassment, and sex-based discrimination by reflecting (albeit briefly) on its implications for other forms of harassment (for example, female-female, male-male, male-intersex harassment, etc.). If I am right about the morality of sexual harassment as an instance of discrimination, then these further cases, as long as they turn on and reproduce heterosexual or cisgender dominance in much the same way as male-female sexual harassment does, will be susceptible to a similar analysis. But what about cases of harassment that do not involve either heterosexual, sex, or cisgender dominance? They, too, can be wrongful when and because they constitute an attack on another's capacity to develop and maintain an integral sense of self.[86] But because they do not attack another in the relevant sense *via a mobilization of gender hierarchy or heterosexual dominance,* they do not count as discriminatory in the relevant sense.[87] I also believe, though it would take us very far afield to demonstrate this in any detail, that, precisely because they do not operate via cisgender-, sex- or hetero-based hierarchies, the threshold for counting as an attack on another's capacity to develop and maintain an integral sense of self will be higher.[88] The fact that paradigmatic cases of male-female, hetero-homosexual, cisgender-transgender harassment operate via structures of gender and hetero-sexual hierarchy make such instances more insidious and threatening than, for example, cases of sexual harassment that do not fall into these categories (all else equal). Cases of sex, gender, and sexual orientation harassment, furthermore, will also have the effect of deepening and perpetuating wider patterns of hierarchy, economic disadvantage, and bias throughout a society in a way that other kinds of harassment will not. For both these reasons, I conclude, male-female, hetero-homosexual, and cisgender-transgender harassment are different, if not in kind, then at least in degree, from other kinds of harassment.

INDIRECT DISCRIMINATION

So far, we have provided an account of what makes various forms of direct discrimination wrong, focusing on what I have called the relational nexus between the discriminator and the discriminated against. In doing so, I have been careful to distinguish our objections to the inter-personal, relational context in which violations of anti-discrimination norms occur, and our objections to the broader societal consequences of wrongfully discriminatory acts or policies. I have also claimed that such societal consequences—though very important wrong-making features of many central cases of discrimination—are not necessary for the wrongfulness of many others. We now face the question: Are there cases in which such societal consequences are the *only* wrong-making feature of a particular set of discriminatory acts or policies? To illustrate, consider the cases of sexual harassment we have just discussed. In *Robinson,* we have focused on the way in which the men used gendered tropes and structures to wrong Robinson. But surely there is another wrong-making feature of the discrimination, namely that it *also* serves to propagate and deepen gender hierarchies in the society at large, just as, we might say, closing down the pools deepened the stigma, exclusion, and racism to which all blacks were subject not only in Jackson,

Mississippi, but across the United States. Are there cases in which discriminatory acts and policies have such unjust societal consequences, but where social meanings play no part in explaining their wrongfulness?

It might be thought that *all* cases of wrongful indirect discrimination must be identified solely in terms of broader societal consequences, since, by definition, the comparative disadvantage of the affected members of the group not only was not intended by discriminators but also played no (even unconscious) role in the deliberation of the discriminators. If it played no such role, then how could the discriminators express, through their attitudes, any objectionable social meanings, let alone demean those subject to the discrimination? The question reflects an overly narrow conception of what kinds of attitudes can be expressed in action. Recall that an action or policy can express a morally objectionable *disregard* or *indifference* toward the members of a particular group. I gave the example above of an industry board that, though they know that women are disproportionately disadvantaged by a certain employment procedure, do nothing to investigate why. Let us further imagine that they don't intend for women to be disadvantaged, and that women's being disadvantaged by the policy played no role in their deliberation (we might suppose that they wouldn't change their procedures if women started to be hired at a higher rate). Even in this case, we might still believe that the policy expresses an attitude of indifference. In cases like this, indirect discrimination can wrong the women affected by sending the message that their relative exclusion is treated as irrelevant (and, of course, it can also be wrong insofar as it propagates unfair patterns of disadvantage).

A good real-world example is the landmark ECHR case *Ostrava*,[89] which is also useful for drawing out some of the nuance of the Expressive Harm Account. We will then be in a better position to evaluate cases of, as it were, *pure* indirect discrimination, which do not turn on an evaluation of the attitudes expressed by a set of acts or policies, but solely on their downstream societal consequences. And we will then also be in a better position to evaluate an important objection to the whole account, namely that it misses the injustice of *structural* inequalities that are not expressed in individual acts or policies. In 2000, eighteen

Roma applicants brought suit under the ECHR, alleging violation of Article 14 (setting out the ECHR's anti-discrimination rights). The case involved discrimination in the provision of primary education. Roma children in the Czech Republic were selected for special needs education at a much higher rate than non-Roma children. In 1999, 56 percent of special school children were of Roma background, which meant that Roma children were twenty-seven times more likely to be placed in special schools than non-Roma children. The Court found no evidence of an intent to disadvantage the Roma children because they were Roma. All children across the country—and hence also in areas where there was a small or nonexistent Roma population—were subject to the same methods of psychological and pedagogical assessment for special needs. According to the state parties, the disparate outcome was the result of low intellectual capacity measured with the aid of standard psychological tests used in educational psychology centers. There was no irregularity found with respect to the administration of these tests. The adequacy of the tests, however, was questioned by some of the submissions to the Court, who wondered whether the special linguistic and cultural circumstances of the Roma were taken into account in designing the tests. According to one such submission,

> the assessment of Roma children in the Ostrava region did not take into account the language and culture of the children, or their prior learning experiences, or their unfamiliarity with the demands of the testing situation. Single rather than multiple sources of evidence were used. Testing was done in one sitting, not over time. Evidence was not obtained in realistic or authentic settings where children could demonstrate their skills. Undue emphasis was placed on individually administered, standardised tests normed on other populations.[90]

The fact that similar tests were used across the country for sorting children into special education, coupled with the fact that there were no administrative irregularities (let us assume this was true), makes this, let us suppose, a case of *indirect* discrimination: the disadvantage to which the Roma community were subject as a result of the tests played no role, in whole or in part, consciously or unconsciously, in the deliberations governing the testing policy.[91] That does not, however, exculpate the state parties, because we can ask: Does the *indifference* to the disadvantage that would be suffered by the Roma itself send an objectionable message of inferiority?

According to the Expressive Harm Account, to answer this question we need to look at the social meaning of the policy against the cultural, historical, social, and political background of the Czech Republic. The Roma have been subject to a long history of persecution and persistent exclusion in the Czech lands going back at least four centuries.[92] Just in 1972, for example, fear of a dramatic rise in the Roma population led to a program of forced sterilization that continued well into the 1990s. In 1999, and despite international condemnation, the city of Ústí nad Labem built a seventy-foot-tall concrete "noise barrier" to separate a poorer community housing a majority of Romani people.[93] Against this background, I submit, the Czech educational policy cannot but be understood as a form of indifference that serves to further stigmatize and deepen the exclusion, daily injustice, and economic deprivation to which the Roma are subject. It is therefore wrongful both because of the particular harm it does to those Romani families whose children are stigmatized and excluded from receiving a standard education and because of its broader societal effects on attitudes toward the Roma and on wider patterns of socioeconomic opportunity.

Even if we accept the possibility of extending the account of social meanings along these lines, we are still left wondering whether there can be cases of indirect discrimination that are wrongful solely because of their societal effects, and hence in the absence of an objectionable relational nexus. I believe there can be, but that such instances will not be core cases of wrongful discrimination; they are the exceptions that prove the rule. Such cases will have in common the following features: (a) there is an objectionably harmful downstream effect on a historically disadvantaged, socially salient group, (b) the effect was not foreseen by the actor, and (c) the actor was not culpable for failing to foresee the harmful downstream effect (i.e., there was no indifference or disregard for the interests of those harmed). We have already encountered one such case, namely the first racist joke example. In the first variant of that example, the actor's recitation was, I argued, impermissible due to the downstream effects on the Pakistanis within earshot of the joke and due to the more general propagation of racist stigma. I also argued, however, that the reciter was not blameworthy given his nonculpable ignorance that Lahore is a city in Pakistan. We might imagine others. Suppose, for example, that a police force expects all graduating cadets to wear hats. The policy does not, however, take into account that there might be Sikhs among its ranks. Suppose that there have never been any Sikhs in the community or in the police force and that this year saw the first enrollment of a Sikh. We might argue that the makers and enforcers of the policy are nonculpably unaware of the comparative disadvantage suffered by the new cadet. In this case, the policy would be considered wrongful because of the exclusion, even though no one is to blame for it. These, and other similar cases, are peripheral because they turn on a contingency, namely nonculpable ignorance, that is unlikely to last very long in practice: once the disadvantage comes to light (as it inevitably will), the case immediately develops a relational nexus that becomes subject to evaluation in terms of social meanings. For example, if the police force, upon finding out about the Sikh cadet, were to continue the policy without making an exception, the force would now be expressing a stigmatizing attitude of disregard and no longer nonculpably ignorant.

One might wonder whether there are other, less peripheral cases where it is only societal effects that matter, and where nonculpable ignorance does not play such a fleeting role (if any role at all). The question gathers some edge when we consider this possibility in light of the following objection to theories of discrimination in general. According to Iris Marion Young,

> considering discrimination the only or primary injustice that women or people of color suffer . . . focuses attention on the wrong issues. Discrimination is primarily an agent-oriented, fault-oriented concept. Thus it tends to focus attention on the perpetrator and a particular action or policy, rather than on victims and their situation. . . . In its focus on individual agents, the concept of discrimination obscures and even tends to deny the structural and institutional framework of oppression. . . . One misses how the

weight of society's institutions and people's assumptions, habits, and behavior toward others are directed at reproducing the material and ideological conditions that make life easier for, provide greater real opportunities to, and establish the priority of the point of view of white heterosexual men.[94]

The objection might seem to hit with special force, since I, too, have treated discrimination as an "agent-oriented, fault-oriented" concept (hence the emphasis on what I have called the relational nexus). Must an account like this "deny the structural and institutional framework of oppression"? In a later work, Young continues the theme, arguing that many (though not all) injustices arise from the operation of "structures," which are "produced and reproduced by large numbers of people acting according to normally accepted rules and practices," but where the harms produced by such compliance are so diffuse that they "cannot be traced [morally] to particular contributors to the practice."[95] A hypothetical example, due to Derek Parfit,[96] can be used to bring out the force of Young's objection. We will then draw the analogy to more real-world contexts. Suppose that someone is wired to a torture machine connected to fifty million switches. If none of the switches is flipped, then no current runs through the machine. If fifty million switches are flipped, the person will be in severe pain. But no one switch makes a discernible difference to the pain experienced by the person connected to the machine, no matter how many switches have been flipped previously. It is only the combined effect of the switches that makes a difference. Imagine that each switch is operated by a single individual, and that each person knows that, by flipping the switch, they contribute (infinitesimally) to the torture. And also assume that the switches are also connected to each person's house lights, so there is no way for them to turn on their house lights without sending the charge through to the tortured person, and no way to avoid doing so without collectively organizing to rewire the electricity network.

For our purposes, I will take oppression to include, among other things, racially and sexually marked patterns of socioeconomic inequality and the kinds of stigma, infantilization, objectification, and dehumanization that we have already identified. Young argues that much of this oppression (she refers by way of example to the situation of women and blacks in the United States) is caused by myriad individual actions, adjustments, choices, deliberations, and patterns of institutionalized and uninstitutionalized behavior that are not objectionable on their own and yet together do great harm (we might call such sets of acts "structures" and leave it open how much they determine and are determined by practices or institutions rather than looser patterns of behavior). So, for Young, we are, like Parfit's harmless torturers, manning the switches of oppression (indeed, it is compatible with this picture that the oppressed themselves also play a role in this reproduction).

I think this is an important insight, but I don't believe that it (a) impugns the account I have offered of the concept of discrimination itself, (b) undermines my social-meaning-, moral-equality-based account of why and when discrimination is wrongful, or (c) presents us with a case in which only societal effects matter in the absence of a relational nexus. First, let us consider my account of the concept of discrimination. Young's account of structural injustice vis-à-vis members of a particular disadvantaged group[97] can be easily cast as an instance of indirect discrimination. The diffuse production of oppression, if Young is right, is, in our terms, a form of indirect discrimination because (a) members of some socially salient group(s) are comparatively disadvantaged and (b) the comparative disadvantage plays no role, conscious or unconscious, in whole or in part, to the outcome of any individual's deliberation; while the agents may be aware of how, in the aggregate, particular actions, decisions, or patterns have an impact, they do not believe that their particular contribution makes any real difference, and so they will simply disregard such facts in deciding what to do. Furthermore, in many if not most cases, the individuals concerned will not even have a very clear picture of how their actions, decisions, and patterns contribute to the oppressive result, and so the facts about how such smaller-scale actions, decisions, and patterns combine will never become part of the agent's (conscious or unconscious) awareness.[98] As Young writes, "usually we enact these [oppression-producing] conventions and practices in a habitual way, without explicit reflection on the wider implications of what we are doing, having in the foreground of our consciousness and intention [only] those immediate goals we want to achieve."[99]

So it seems straightforward to extend our account of what counts as discrimination to cover structural oppression. But how do we explain the sense in which it is wrongful? Must we assume, as Young suggests, that no one is culpable for structural oppression, and hence abandon our concern with the relational nexus (which is an "agent- and fault-oriented" concept)?* Must we therefore focus solely on the effects of particular patterns of action, behavior, and disposition on oppression and leave aside the issue of social meaning? I want to argue that Young is too hasty in exculpating those who together sustain and reinforce structures of oppression. To see this, return to Parfit's harmless torturers. It strikes me as absurd to argue that no one is morally culpable for the torture in Parfit's example—indeed, that is the whole point of the example. But if this is true in that example, then it must also be true in the case of Young's structural oppression, which works, I have argued, in exactly the same way. But how do we account for the nature of this wrong, given that no one's actions, decisions, or patterns of behavior

---

* Young writes: "The lesson I think we should take from my objections . . . is that responsibility in relation to structural injustice should not be thought of as an attenuated form of responsibility as complicity. . . . What we should seek is not variation on a weaker form of liability, but rather a different conception of responsibility altogether . . . we should not be judged morally or legally blameworthy or at fault" (Young 2011, pp. 103–104, 107). This different conception of responsibility is forward-looking and more akin to the responsibilities or duties attached to a role, such as a lifeguard. But this raises a further question for Young: Why do we have an obligation to take up the role of "lifeguard" for the oppression in our society? One response Young might give is to say that we have a natural duty of justice to do what we can to fight injustice, and that this duty requires us to take action with respect to structural injustice. This is not the response that Young in fact gives (presumably because it would apply to any individual, anywhere, and so not pick out, say, Americans). Instead, what triggers the role responsibility, for Young, is our *causal* relation to the oppression, rather than our *culpability* for it. This is puzzling; if the role responsibility is solely triggered by one's causal relation to the outcome, then what, if not some kind of liability (perhaps strict), accounts for why it would be wrong for us *not* to assume it? Suppose that my jacket gets caught in the steering wheel of a boat on which I am out with friends, which causes the boat to run aground. If I bear no (backwards-looking) moral responsibility for the fact that my jacket has gotten caught, then why should I have a special forward-looking responsibility to, say, pay entirely for the damages? If I bear no (backwards-looking) moral responsibility for making the boat sink (suppose, for ex-

make any (noticeable) difference to the oppression—just as no one person's switch makes any (noticeable) difference to the pain felt by the man? I want to claim, with Christopher Kutz, that we ought to think of each person as playing their part in the larger *set* of acts that together oppresses (or tortures).[100] To the degree to which they know, have reasonable alternatives, and yet still do nothing in response, they are complicit in the oppression of the group (as they are complicit in the suffering of the man), and hence share moral responsibility both for its occurrence and its continuance. In our terms, each individual's failure to seek a collective solution would count as sending an objectionable message of indifference, and that is part of what makes the set of acts wrong (by changing the social meaning of the oppression and harm it causes). Note that this is true even if people do not know exactly *how* their small-scale actions, decisions, or patterns of behavior combine to create oppressive conditions; as long as they know *that* such small-scale actions, decisions, and patterns have such effects—which more often than not will be institutionally mediated—and that there are reasonable alternatives, their indifference becomes (at least *pro tanto*) objectionable.[101] Disregard for these downstream inferiorizing effects therefore counts, on this view, as a way of objectionably treating

---

ample, that I could not have known that it would run aground), then why should I have a special forward-looking responsibility to, say, compensate those who have been harmed by it? What makes my causal role in the event morally significant? As I explain in the text, for such remedial obligations to be triggered (absent an independent argument for imposing strict liability that Young never provides), one must at least be culpable for *negligence* (failing to take into account risks that one should have taken into account) or *recklessness* (showing practical indifference or contempt for the risks one was conscious of imposing) toward the harmful outcome to which one has causally contributed (e.g., *inter alia,* it must be true that one could reasonably have avoided it). So I affirm in the text what Young denies: backwards-looking responsibility *does* matter in explaining why we have remedial duties to fight oppression (in addition to whatever natural duties of justice, or indeed of reciprocity, we may also have). It is also important to emphasize that focusing this way on culpability does not imply that we must then think that the best way to rectify the wrongs is to *compensate* in a narrow, tort-like sense. I take it for granted that the best way to address racial and gender injustice is not through "reparations," for example, but through structural reform. My argument is just that those who perpetuate the diffuse harms have special and more stringent obligations to engage in structural reform as a direct result of wrongfully reproducing injustice, rather than merely being causally implicated in it. I thank Jude Browne for helpful discussion.

another as an inferior, and hence as demeaning. The relational nexus can therefore matter even in cases of structural oppression.

A real-world example is useful to illustrate the analysis and its implications for the question regarding the role of societal effects with which we started. Rates of incarceration in the United States are staggering. In the past forty years, the US rate of incarceration has increased by *500 percent* and is around *seven times* greater than that of France, Spain, or Canada. But perhaps more staggering is the fact that blacks are 13 percent of the general population but now form over 50 percent of the prison population. Blacks are incarcerated at a rate six times higher than that of whites; one in three black men are likely to be imprisoned over a lifetime.[102] This has large knock-on effects on racial disparities broadly, given the implications for work, family, mental health, and criminality that being a convict carries, especially in the United States (consider, to name but one example, that the children of convicts are much more likely to be convicts at some point in their lives as well).[103] What explains this ballooning of the prison population and its disproportionate impact on blacks? The answer is clear: the 1980s "war on drugs" and associated calls for "getting tough on crime."[104] Let us suppose, contrary to the facts,[105] that this is not the result either of any direct discrimination in the criminal justice system or of any direct discrimination in the policymaking process that led to the "war on drugs." This requires us to imagine that there was no unconscious or conscious bias in policing, sentencing, and so on, and no direct discrimination in the policymaking process. On this bending of the facts, the higher rates of incarceration for blacks would be entirely due to the punitiveness of the system and to higher rates of drug-related crime among blacks.

Using our analysis, the higher rates of black incarceration would, *ex hypothesi,* be instances of indirect discrimination in the criminal justice system (taken as a set of acts and policies). Now suppose that the American public reflects on these facts and concludes, "No individual bears any responsibility for exhibiting (conscious or unconscious) bias or prejudice or otherwise intending to disadvantage blacks because they are black, so there is no special problem of racial injustice to address." Leaving aside the punitiveness of the system for the moment, this raises the further question: What then explains the racial disparities in rates of drug-related crime? Any analysis that does not take into account the effects of past oppression on, for example, patterns of black poverty, ghettoization, and family life would be radically insufficient. But past oppression isn't communicated to the present, and reproduced across generations, by magic. The effects of past oppression can comprehensively shape the structure of people's sense of self; their small-scale interactions, exchanges, and decisions; and wider patterns of rules, opportunities, and expectations in such a way as to entrench racially structured disparities *even in the absence of any current (conscious or unconscious) direct discrimination.* We have already analyzed, for example, the way stigma, when internalized, can affect the way individuals understand themselves and their own prospects, and how others treat them in turn.[106] But this is only one mechanism for transmission. Another is more obvious: historically important forms of socioeconomic and cultural disadvantage are inherited by the next generation, and social class of origin is an important predictor of one's general prospects and opportunities (and hence also one's liability, in our case, to criminality).[107] So we have a clear example of the diffuse reproduction of oppression highlighted by Young.

In the face of these commonly known facts, the response—"there is no direct discrimination *now,* so there is no problem of racial injustice to rectify"—communicates a message of indifference that cannot but be understood as stigmatizing. As Anthony Thompson notes in a wide-ranging study of the effects of mass incarceration on "reentry" into society, "elected officials have built electoral platforms on the backs of communities of color, waging wars on crime and drugs with little consideration of, or concern for, the communities that would suffer the greatest casualties."[108] To make this clearer, let us turn to the other side of our explanation for high rates of black incarceration (again limiting ourselves to our counterfactual), namely the punitiveness of the "war on drugs." Suppose that, as is true in reality, the policy is not effective. While crime rates in general drop, there is little evidence that this is due to the punitive policy; drug use and drug-related deaths increase, and there continue to be high rates of recidivism with respect to drug-related offenses.[109] Glenn Loury surmises that, were one in three white males destined to be incarcerated under a policy that is as ineffective as the "war on drugs" has been, this would almost certainly be considered a national emergency.[110] If the counterfactual Loury imagines were true, this would constitute evidence of, at the very least, unconscious bias in the policymaking system. But what if the counterfactual were *false* (as I am assuming for the sake of argument)? Against the background of historical oppression and its current diffuse reproduction, the fact that the policy triggers no moral concern would still, I submit, send the stigmatizing, dehumanizing message that blacks are the bearers of an ineradicable, morally deserved "polluted" or "spoiled" identity: black lives don't matter. I conclude that, once again, the relational nexus is important in accounting for the wrongness of *indirect* discrimination, even where the discrimination occurs via structures reproduced by diffuse means, and even in the absence of conscious and unconscious bias, malice, or prejudice.

So we do not yet have a core case of indirect discrimination where it is *only* societal effects that matter, or, for that matter, a case in which structural oppression inculpates no one. The fact that it is so difficult to come up with genuine versions of such examples serves to strengthen the point I am trying to make: the relational nexus and the inferiorizing social meanings expressed by it are essential to the wrongfulness of core cases of *both* direct and indirect discrimination.

Before we can conclude, however, we have to consider one final case that will significantly complicate our picture. In our discussion of structural injustice thus far, we have assumed that if a relational nexus expresses objectionably inferiorizing social meanings, then those that express those meanings via their actions (and inactions) must be culpable (for indifference, malice, and so on). But this is false in at least two types of cases. First, recall our discussion of unconscious bias. In those examples (for example, the paramedic), the actors involved express objectionably inferiorizing social meanings but, I argued, are blameless for them. Like the case of the Sikhs, these cases will be peripheral because, once it becomes known that we harbor unconscious biases of particular kinds, we have a duty to take steps to extinguish their effects. If we don't, then that counts as *(pro tanto)* objectionable indifference, and so becomes culpable.

The second type of case is more interesting, and we will spend the rest of this section discussing it. In this type, (a) no one is individually to blame (even as complicit in a larger set of acts), (b) objectionably inferiorizing social meanings matter in explaining its wrongness, but, unlike in the cases of unconscious bias just discussed, (c) the blameless-ness in (a) survives becoming aware of all the relevant consequences and social meanings of one's actions. Discussing such cases in more detail will allow us to draw out the truth of Young's account of structural in-justice, while showing at the same time how exceptional they really are in practice. They will also allow us to show how important inferiorizing social meanings are and how few cases of wrongful discrimination turn solely on broader societal effects.

I will develop the argument via a last variation on our incarceration example, which will require us to bend the facts even further. Imagine now that the US population has taken good-faith steps to address racial disparities not only in the broader society and economy (including, for example, greater investment in developing the human capital in under-privileged neighborhoods and expanding access to good-quality edu-cation) but also in incarceration (including, for example, reducing mandatory sentence requirements for low-level drug offenses, reclassi-fying some drug-related offenses from felonies to misdemeanors, step-ping up prevention efforts in underprivileged neighborhoods, and creating a public body whose mandate it is to find new solutions and monitor the success of those already implemented).[111] And suppose that, as before, there is no (conscious or unconscious) direct discrimina-tion in policing, sentencing, and so on, and that current reform efforts cannot be faulted for falling short of what could be done (given our current knowledge about the efficacy and feasibility of various possible reform strategies). Yet, we imagine, racial disparities, while less marked than before, still remain significant. In these circumstances, there is no objectionable indifference: the US public at large can no longer be charged with an objectionable, stigmatizing disregard. However, there is still indirect discrimination: blacks suffer comparative disadvantage *qua* blacks.

Is the discrimination wrongful? I believe that it is, but that ex-plaining its wrongfulness still requires an appeal to social meanings. When racial disparities are directly traceable to previous wrongs that *were* a product of conscious and unconscious bias, prejudice, malice, and indifference, both the disparities and people's experience of them will continue to infect the tenor of social relationships throughout the society (even in the absence of *current* conscious or unconscious bias, prejudice, malice, or indifference). As Glenn Loury notes with respect to mass incarceration, the "historical resonance between the stigma of race and the stigma of imprisonment serves to keep alive in our public culture the subordinating social meanings that have always been associated with blackness."[112] Even if the original social meanings are not transmitted by any present actions or policies in isolation, they are transmitted via the very disparities themselves and by the patterns of class, behavior, self-presentation, and stigmatization that in part explain *them*. Like a fossil in which the embodied presence of the imprinting animal has long gone, the institutions and daily life of our imagined society bear the trace of the social meanings that marked its past. While there is nothing morally objectionable about the relational nexus among any of the relevant participants *now* (given the good-faith efforts of its present population), social meanings still matter because of the way they continue to determine the structure of the society and its social life. So in blamelessly reproducing the disparities the society also reproduces, at one remove, the social meanings that originally gave rise to them. This is the truth, I believe, in Young's account of structural injustice, but it is noteworthy how far we have had to bend the facts to get there.

Looking back to our theory of moral equality, we are now in a position to ask: Does this idealized society exhibit any cruelty? And here we can say: yes, it does, but it is not the cruelty exhibited by a relational nexus among a particular set of agents (as it was in *Palmer, Ostrava, Robinson,* and so on), but by a set of structural patterns and institutions. Such cases instantiate what I will call *structural* rather than *interpersonal* social cruelty: victims of wrongful indirect discrimination are treated by institutions, practices, and less formal patterns of interaction as inferiors in the relevant sense, even though no one is blameworthy for such treatment; even though those structures are reproduced in the absence of anyone's conscious or unconscious indifference, bias, prejudice, or malice; and even though the society is committed, in good faith, to eliminating the injustice. That is the tragedy of what we might call *truly* structural injustice: institutions, patterns of behavior, and daily life carry social meanings that are inescapable though no longer desired, consciously or unconsciously, by anyone.

In this section, we have examined the wrongfulness of indirect discrimination and asked whether there are any cases of indirect discrimination that are wrongful solely because of their societal effects (and hence not in virtue of the objectionable social meanings they express). We concluded that, while they do exist, they are peripheral. Core cases of wrongful indirect discrimination can be understood either as communicating objectionably stigmatizing, dehumanizing, infantilizing, instrumentalizing, or objectifying messages of *indifference* or *disregard* to those comparatively disadvantaged (as in the male-dominated industry example, the *Ostrava* case, and the first variant of the incarceration example), or as echoing past inferiorizing social messages even in the absence of current malice, prejudice, bias, or indifference (such as our second incarceration example). Along the way, I also answered an important objection to any account of wrongful discrimination, namely that it cannot account for structural injustice vis-à-vis historically disadvantaged groups. I argued that this objection overlooks both how individuals can be complicit in the diffuse production of discriminatory acts that together send inferiorizing messages to those disadvantaged by them, and how much social meanings would still matter even when no one is to blame for indifference, disregard, prejudice, or malice. The Expressive Harm Account, I conclude, provides a powerful framework for reflecting on the wrongfulness of both direct and indirect discrimination, and hence also on forms of structural injustice involving historically disadvantaged groups.

PART II

HUMAN RIGHTS

4

THE CONCEPT OF HUMAN RIGHTS: THE BROAD VIEW

THE CURRENT DEBATE in philosophy about the concept of (moral)[1] human rights is split between two camps. Orthodox theorists claim that human rights are those individual moral rights that we possess merely in virtue of our humanity.[2] Political views contend that human rights are those individual moral rights (or morally urgent interests)[3] whose violation (primarily) by states makes sovereignty-overriding interference or other forms of international action (including kinds of action that are *not* sovereignty-overriding, such as international assistance) permissible if not required.[4]

In this chapter, I will argue that both views face insurmountable challenges and that, even if we overlook these challenges, the debate between the two camps risks dissolving into a mere verbal disagreement. I will suggest a path for moving beyond this stalemate by defending what I will call the "Broad View" about the concept of human rights. Along the way, I will also reject a central assumption that is shared by both views (and that in part explains how the debate has ended up). This assumption is that there is a *single* overarching practice of human rights. The primary task of a philosophical theory of human rights should therefore be to reconstruct its moral core, derive a "master list" of human rights from that core, and then to use that list as a critical standard to reform and improve the practice. Tasioulas (who defends an Orthodox view) is a good representative of this assumption: "[Our aim is] to identify the core or focal concept, the basic normative idea that enables us to make the best sense of what we pre-reflectively identify as the ... practice of human rights."[5] Similarly, according to Raz (who defends a Political view), "The ethical doctrine of human rights should articulate standards by which the practice of human rights can be judged, standards which will indicate what human rights we have."[6] Call this the Single Practice Assumption.

Once we adopt the Broad View and abandon the Single Practice Assumption, we will be in a position to conclude that we also ought to reject the search for a philosophically grounded master list of moral human rights by which the practice as a whole can be judged. The search for a master list of human rights that will both reveal the moral unity underlying *all* of human rights practice and serve as a standard for its criticism is chimerical. But this is not to say that more contextually focused *conceptions* of moral human rights cannot be developed. The chapter ends by showing how context can matter in developing particular conceptions of human rights. Chapter 5 will then elaborate a particular conception of such rights for a specific context, namely international law.

DESIDERATA

All Political and Orthodox views begin in the same way, namely by drawing a distinction between the *concept* (or idea or nature) of human rights and their *content, scope,* and *grounds.* Roughly, the *concept* of human rights is meant to identify what human rights are, and an account of their *content, scope,* and *grounds* is meant to tell us what rights we have, who has them, and why we have them. For both of the going approaches, the task of identifying the concept is taken to be primary. To specify what human rights we *have,* we need to know what human rights *are* first.

How do we decide who has the better view? There are four desiderata that any theory of moral human rights should satisfy.[7] First, human rights theories must demarcate and explain the sense in which human rights are a proper subset of the set of all moral rights *simpliciter*. If they are unable to do so, then talk of human rights is redundant; one might just as well talk about moral rights. (Call this the Subclass Desideratum.) Second, human rights theories must be sufficiently faithful to the human rights culture that has emerged since 1945 and that is captured in the main human rights instruments, such as the Universal Declaration of Human Rights (UDHR) and the International Covenant on Civil and Political Rights (ICCPR). By "sufficiently faithful," I mean that human rights theories must not interpret human rights to be something so alien to the dominant practices that it would count as changing the subject. The desideratum is explained by our goal: in interpreting what human rights are, philosophers take themselves to be engaged in a collective project of identification, critique, and defense that is shared with practitioners.[8] (Call this the Fidelity Desideratum.) Third, human rights theories must be able to explain why we have *good normative reason* to be *un*faithful to human rights practices in cases in which any given human rights theory diverges from the culture's self-understanding. The rationale for this desideratum should be clear: the ultimate goal of a human rights theory is not descriptive and explanatory but normative and critical. Our human rights theory should therefore give us good (though not necessarily exhaustive) reasons to depart from current practices where it would improve things to do so. (Call this the Normativity Desideratum.) Fourth, human rights theories should be reasonably determinate. They should, that is, provide a set of standards that are informative enough to aid us in evaluating and improving human rights practices (including, but not limited to, the system of international human rights law). This desideratum follows directly from a general worry that human rights talk is excessively loose and free-flowing. (Call this the Determinacy Desideratum.) As I will now seek to argue, I do not believe that either the Orthodox or Political view alone can successfully meet all four. To meet all four, we must adopt the Broad View, which subsumes both as distinct applications of a broader concept adapted for different contexts.

AGAINST ORTHODOX VIEWS

There are many and diverse criticisms of Orthodox views. In this section, I will focus on two that I believe to be decisive, the first one directed at James Griffin's theory of human rights and the second at John Tasioulas's. Although I cannot show that any Orthodox view must fail in the same way, I hope to provide some progress to that conclusion by directing my criticism at two of the foremost Orthodox theories currently available.

Recall that for all Orthodox theorists, human rights are those moral rights that we possess merely in virtue of our humanity. To meet the Subclass Desideratum, therefore, Orthodox views must explain what it means to possess a moral right "solely in virtue of our humanity." Griffin attempts to solve the subclass problem by appealing to those moral rights that are *necessary for the protection of normative agency*. But what counts as "normative agency" in the relevant sense? There is a danger here. If Griffin identifies "normative agency" as a fully realized capacity "to choose one's own path through life," as he sometimes seems to, then *all* moral rights could be construed as contributing to such a life.[9] For example, do we have a human right that others' promises to us are kept (given that promise-keeping is important to one's capacity to pursue our conception of a worthwhile life)? A human right that others not cheat on their taxes (given how important tax-paying is to the functioning of the public services on which we depend)?[10] A human right that others not steal from us (given how important the stability of external property relations is to our "path through life")? A human right to a proportionate prison sentence (given how important the curtailment of our freedom of movement is to one's exercise of agency)?[11] Interpreted in such an expansive manner, the account would fail the Subclass Desideratum.

As a result, Griffin often emphasizes that the moral rights must be *necessary* to the protection of agency.[12] But what does "necessary" mean in this context? Suppose we take "necessary" as delimiting those moral rights such that, without them, we could not live a worthwhile life as agents. But then the resulting human rights theory would be implausibly narrow; even slaves, or those who have been tortured, can still live worthwhile lives as agents. Simply being tortured or enslaved doesn't render one's life worthless. Similarly, being tortured or enslaved doesn't (in most cases) make us incapable of exercising *any* agency; it just makes it much harder.[13]

Griffin is alive to these concerns and tries to address them by appealing instead to the idea of a "minimum." He writes: "[Human rights] are protections of that somewhat austere state, a characteristically human life, not of a good or happy or perfected or flourishing human life. . . . There is a minimalist character to human rights. . . . The element of austerity, that reference to a minimum, must not be lost."[14] Welfare rights, for example, secure "minimum provision"; other rights secure a "minimum" of health, education, information. As we have already noted, agency is not, however, an intrinsically "minimalist" concept, especially if one includes, as Griffin does, protections for its realization and exercise. So from what normative source does Griffin draw the standard for how "minimal" the protection afforded by a given right should be? What, in other words, determines the threshold above which a protection of agency ceases to be a human right? Griffin writes: "For one thing, it seems that the more austere notion is what the tradition of human rights supports. For another, it seems to be the proper stipulation to make. If we had rights to all that is needed for a good or happy life, then the language of rights would become redundant."[15] Griffin appeals here both to what we have called the Fidelity and Subclass Desiderata: we ought to append a "minimalist" rider to the demand to protect the exercise and realization of agency because it tracks the way human rights are conceived by practitioners and solves the Subclass Desideratum. Although arguable—consider how "maximalist" the International Covenant on Economic, Social and Cultural Rights (ICESCR)[16] is, for example—let us grant the assumption. With the Normativity Desideratum in mind, we now wonder: Do we have *good normative reason* to tailor our human rights theory to practice in this way? Why are practitioners (or those in the longer human rights tradition) *correct* to think of human rights as "minimal" protections? (Or, alternatively, if practitioners are not using the term properly, what normative reason do they have to reorient uses of the term in ways suggested by

Griffin?) Griffin's account, I am suggesting, does not have the resources to provide us with an answer. And it is doubtful, even if he were to explain why we have good normative reason to think of human rights as *minimal* protections, whether the theory would be able to meet the Determinacy Desideratum. What criteria should we use to draw the "minimum" threshold in a determinate place?[17]

Perhaps Griffin could turn here to what he calls "practicalities," namely the requirement that for something to be a human right it must not only be grounded in some aspect of agency but also reflect a "socially manageable claim[] on others."[18] On this interpretation, human rights claims must be "minimal" because otherwise they would impose an "unmanageable" range of moral duties on third parties. And one might understand "unmanageable" here as "unfeasible." If there were a human right to more than a minimum, then it would impose moral duties on others to secure the object of the right so onerous that they would be unfeasible. The problem here is that Griffin accepts that we can have a range of "manageable" or "feasible" moral duties grounded in correlative rights that *don't* count as human rights. We have, for example, a range of promise-keeping duties, justice-based distributive duties to others to secure more than a minimum of welfare, and justice-based corrective duties to pass proportionate sentences. All of these duties, furthermore, are "directed" to a respective rights-bearer, such that someone who has had a promise broken without excuse, someone who has been denied their fair share, and someone who has been unfairly sentenced can all properly say that they have been *wronged*. So why couldn't all of these rights plausibly count as *human* rights? In the response envisaged here, Griffin must be able to say that these can't be *human* rights because they are "socially unmanageable" or "infeasible." But this doesn't seem to be the case with any of the moral duties correlating with the rights just mentioned. And, given that any genuine moral right correlates with some duties, the response will fail comprehensively for all moral rights. The "practicalities" defense, in short, does not succeed in meeting the Subclass Desideratum.

As noted by Tasioulas, Griffin's account also fails to explain why *only* personhood interests should count in generating human rights claims. Why shouldn't interests in, for example, "accomplishment, knowledge, friendship, and the avoidance of pain"[19] also be sufficient (under the right circumstances) to ground third-party duties? Put in our terms, the restriction to personhood interests cannot satisfy the Normativity Desideratum. Take, for example, Griffin's exclusion of the severely mentally disabled and children from the scope of human rights.[20] What normative reasons do we have to exclude children and the disabled? The potential gain in determinacy is purchased at the price of arbitrariness.

Tasioulas's Orthodox account attempts to go beyond Griffin in two main ways: first, his account appeals to a much wider array of interests as grounds for human rights claims; second, his account puts much more emphasis on the directed duties that are triggered by any purported human right. The former aids Tasioulas in meeting the Normativity and Fidelity Desiderata. The latter is necessary to specify more carefully what can count as a rights-grounding interest in the first place, and therefore helps Tasioulas to satisfy both the Determinacy and Subclass Desiderata. Tasioulas's account is therefore well-placed to become the champion among Orthodox theories. Is it successful?

I will argue that Tasioulas's view does not satisfy the Subclass Desideratum. Recall that Griffin attempted to meet the Subclass Desideratum through a *content*-based restriction that was meant to qualify and explain which moral rights we have "merely in virtue of our humanity." Griffin claimed that those moral rights we have in virtue of our humanity are those we have in virtue of our agency. Given Tasioulas's more pluralistic account of the grounds for human rights, he cannot do this. Instead, he appeals to the idea that human rights are *general* rather than *special* moral rights. According to Tasioulas, "the possession of a human right cannot be conditional on some conduct or achievement of the right-holder, a relationship to which they belong, or their membership of a particular community or group."[21] But what about justly convicted criminals? They lose the right to free movement and association, and in many cases, also the right to political participation, to hold office, and so on in virtue of their previous conduct. Does that mean that their human rights have been violated? Or that rights to freedom of association, free movement, political participation, and so on, don't count as human rights since they are held conditionally on the basis of things one has done (or not done)? On this restriction, the only human rights there would be are the rights that could not legitimately be stripped from justly convicted criminals. However short the list is, it is far shorter than the list envisaged by Tasioulas or by any human rights movement. The suggestion risks purchasing the Subclass Desideratum at the price of the Fidelity Desideratum. But there is also the problem of the Normativity Desideratum: What normative reason do we have for thinking that human rights are limited to those rights that prisoners[22] cannot lose?

There is also the problem that the right to a fair trial, the right to vote, and the right to education, for example, also seem conditional, not on what one has done, but on whether one is subject to the legal authority of a political community (in the first two cases) and on whether one can benefit from an education (in the other). One holds a right to a fair trial only if one is relevantly subject to a legal authority, just as one holds a right to vote only if one is a member, in some relevant sense, of a political community. Similarly, one has a right to education only if one can benefit from it. These rights, therefore, don't appear to be rights that we have "merely in virtue of our humanity."

Tasioulas's solution is to fold the condition into the statement of the right: one has a general right to [vote *only if* one is a member of the political community in question];[23] one has a general right to [an education *only if* one can benefit]. One could apply, of course, the same strategy to the right to freedom of movement one has a general right to [free movement *only if* one has not been justly convicted of a crime of kind *x*]. The conditionalized general rights are possessed by all human beings (even those who have committed crimes or do not belong to a political community or cannot benefit from education), and so can be human rights.

The trouble is that this maneuver won't satisfy the Subclass Desideratum. The reason is that *any* moral right can be converted into a general right, including any *special* right, by folding its factual precondition into the statement of the right. For example, the special right that others keep their noncontractual promises to us (barring exceptional circumstances) can also be stated as a general right: we have a general right that [others keep their noncontractual promises to us *only if* they have actually made a promise to us and *only if* exceptional circumstances do not hold]. When we include the conditions in the content of the right, the right becomes fully general: even people who have not had any promises made to them have the (general) right that [others keep their promises to them *should they ever make such a promise*]. The right is held by people who have no special relations or history. Similarly, any *derived* moral right, such as my right to vote in Italian elections, can also be restated as a fully general right, and hence, on this account, a human right: one has a (general) right to [vote in Italian elections only if one is an Italian citizen]. All (genuine) moral rights, using this strategy, can be converted into general rights. The advantage is that Tasioulas can then deal with the prisoner, fair trial, and education counterexamples. The disadvantage is that he then fails to meet the Subclass Desideratum.

A potential response is to impose conditions on the *kinds* of antecedents that can be folded into the statement of the right. In response to a similar objection by Nicholas Wolterstorff, Tasioulas does just that.[24] To deal with the objection from derived rights (such as the right to vote in Italian elections), Tasioulas bans the use of proper names. And to deal with the fair trial and education objections, he requires that "the conditions specifying the duties [and hence the rights which are their basis] must refer to circumstances that are not unduly remote for all human beings given the sociohistorical conditions to which the existence of the right has been indexed."[25] But what about the promising counterexample? What about the right to a proportionate sentence? And what about other moral rights that also look to be entirely general, such as the moral right not to be insulted? All of those rights could easily be conditionalized, none of them uses proper names, and their corresponding duties do not refer to circumstances that are unduly remote.

Tasioulas could say (as he seems tempted to say)[26] that these are indeed human rights on a correct understanding of what human rights are. But this would be a difficult bullet to bite. It would undermine at a stroke one of the main advantages of an Orthodox view, namely its fidelity to the human rights movement (especially when compared with Political views, to which we turn in a moment). No human rights practitioner takes such an expansive view. We might try to add further conditions on admissible conditionals until we have a view that looks about right. It is unclear to me, however, whether any such general criteria could *exclude* things like promises or taxes or insults but *include* fair trials and education. But there is another problem. How do the stipulated conditions on admissible conditionals meet the Normativity Desideratum? What *normative reason* do we have to accept them? The addition of further conditions would seem *ad hoc*.

I conclude that the going Orthodox approaches to human rights are insufficient on their own to satisfy the four desiderata. While there may be other Orthodox views that can respond to these objections and meet all four desiderata, the two most promising ones, I have argued, cannot.

AGAINST POLITICAL VIEWS

Political views are tailor-made to satisfy the Subclass Desideratum, and hence do well where Orthodox views do poorly. The way they do so is by jettisoning the idea that human rights are those moral rights human beings possess *in virtue of their humanity*. Instead, they say that human rights are those moral rights that *have a certain function in international affairs*. As we have seen, Political views vary in the kinds of functions believed to be definitive of human rights. In this section, I will press a criticism that affects all subvariants, namely that they fail the Fidelity and Normativity Desiderata. By making the conditions for the existence of a human right depend too much on shifting contingencies, they depart significantly from the aims and purposes of an important aspect of current human rights culture.[27] And they provide no good normative reasons to do so. What is gained by satisfying the Subclass Desideratum is lost with respect to the Fidelity and Normativity Desiderata.

Imagine someone is tortured in Pakistan. And imagine that any criticism or other international action (whether sovereignty-overriding or not) would severely destabilize the region such that it would not be justified. According to the Political view, while there is certainly a moral right that has been violated, it is not a *human* right. But now imagine that international circumstances change enough that international action (whether sovereignty-overriding or not) becomes justifiable. Has the person tortured acquired a human right in the process—a right that they previously lacked? Can we gain and lose our human rights in virtue of shifting international circumstances?[28]

Political views therefore are a far cry from the way claims are pursued within human rights organizations, which are mostly concerned with bringing to light severe abuses in other states *whatever* the international circumstances supporting a particular course of action.[29] And they don't even seem to track the usage of human rights law within the UN system (where one might think a Political view would find the most traction). In human rights law, whether something counts as a human rights violation, and the kinds of remedies that are available for such violations, are two different things.[30]

Political theorists have a ready response to this objection.[31] They can claim that the existence conditions for a human right vary not with the *all-things-considered* reasons for undertaking international action, but only with *pro tanto* reasons for such action. On this clarification, there can be *pro tanto* reasons to take international action with respect to the torture victim even if current international circumstances make it all-things-considered unjustified to do so. The objection to this common move comes in the form of a dilemma. The dilemma is raised when we consider what kinds of considerations we need to take into account in determining whether there is in fact a *pro tanto* reason to take some specific form of international action. The point is easiest to see with an intervention-based variant (I will generalize the point immediately thereafter). On such a view, human rights are those moral rights whose violation would give third parties a *pro tanto* reason to intervene militarily. We face a number of questions: Holding constant the harm involved in the violation of a given moral right, under what circumstances do we have such a *pro tanto* reason to intervene? What kinds of countervailing considerations can override or outweigh the reason? How strong is the reason? We now confront a choice. Do we answer these questions by identifying what a "normal" set of circumstances for such intervention would be? Or do we identify the strength, weight, and presence of the reasons with more idealized circumstances?

Suppose we take the former route (this is the first horn of our dilemma). On this route, we begin by listing the most common consequences of military intervention, given what we generally know about the current international situation, the degree of support that can be expected for intervention among general populations, and so on. In this way, we abstract from any particular situation that we may face here and now. And then we ask: Would we have an *all-things-considered* reason to intervene militarily in the typical situation envisaged in the first step, in light of the violation of some moral right (or set of moral rights) *x?* If we answer yes, then the moral right (or set of rights) in question is a human right. It is a human right because the moral right's violation would warrant an intervention *under normal circumstances.* While the warrant is only provisional—it could be overridden or outweighed by more specific knowledge of any actual conflict—it is sufficient to ground the existence of a human right.

The problem is that this line of response faces the same difficulty as the first-cut, all-things-considered variant. Why should the human rights we have vary with what count as "normal" circumstances? For example, military interventions can become much more difficult with subtle shifts in the international balance of power (consider how different the prospects for military intervention seem after the 2003 invasion of Iraq, for example). Do we say that before the shift (before 2003), individuals in Pakistan had one set of human rights, and after 2003 they have another? Once again, such a move would be wildly at variance with practitioners' self-understanding. What normative reason could there be to accept it? What it gains in meeting the Determinacy and Subclass Desiderata, it loses with respect to the Fidelity and Normativity Desiderata.

This horn of the dilemma is just as difficult to surmount for an international-action (rather than military-intervention) version of the Political view. For there too we wonder: What are the "normal" circumstances that would warrant international action of type *x?* And there too we worry that this leaves human rights too dependent on the shifting sands that determine what count as "normal circumstances."

There is pressure to take the second route, namely to idealize the circumstances against which we determine the presence, weight, and strength of the *pro tanto* reasons. And here the Political view faces the second horn of our dilemma. Rather than point to "normal" circumstances, the idealizing interpretation abstracts further from the things that we know about military intervention. It claims: There is a *pro tanto* reason sufficient to ground the existence of a human right as long as there would be all-things-considered reason to intervene militarily in *ideal* circumstances. To avoid the charge of contingency, the interpretation imagines what we might call a *frictionless* case, namely a case in which, say, military intervention was both costless and sure to succeed. Would we intervene in that case (again, given some specified violation of a moral right)? If so, then there is *some* reason to intervene, and this is sufficient to say that there is a *pro tanto* reason to intervene, and hence that the moral right is a *human* right. The danger here is that the view would then fail the Subclass Desideratum. If it were really true that military intervention were both costless and sure to succeed, then, absent countervailing considerations, the violation of *any* moral right would warrant such intervention. The verdict seems to hinge on what, exactly, we mean by "costless" and "sure to succeed." Notice that the more realistic we make the costs and prospects of military intervention, the more the contingency objection begins to bite. And the less realistic we make them, the more the Subclass Desideratum impinges. This is a set of simultaneous equations with no solution. Any amount of contingency will seem to make the existence of a human right depend on the wrong kind of thing, and any elimination of such contingency will make human rights indistinguishable from moral rights.

Notice further that the second horn of the dilemma impales international-action variants with greater force than intervention ones. Because the range of legitimate remedial actions that can ground a human rights claim will be much less costly and disruptive than a military intervention (converging, at the limit, to mere criticism), the international-action variant will fail the Subclass Desideratum much more quickly than its interventionist cousin. After all, one might reasonably think that *any* violation of a moral right would give us *pro tanto* reason to criticize the violation publicly *especially* if such criticism is sure to succeed in preventing or stopping the violation and has no other costs. And even if the Subclass Desideratum would be satisfied—by isolating, for example, only morally more significant rights—it would fail to satisfy the Normativity Desideratum: of what use would the (long) list of claims that give us *pro tanto* reason to subject violators to international criticism be, given the diversity of concerns that practitioners within human rights organizations, international institutions, and states have?

(More on this point below.) I conclude that Political views also cannot, on their own, meet all four desiderata.

A MERELY VERBAL DISAGREEMENT

Even if we assume that my criticisms of both views do not succeed, there is a further problem: debates between Political and Orthodox views have a tendency to resolve into merely verbal disputes. In this section, I illustrate how this happens. In the rest of the chapter, I provide a solution.

Imagine a proponent of the Orthodox view argues that there is a human right to education. The Orthodox theorist claims that this is because a moral right to education is possessed by each human being in virtue of their humanity alone.[32] The proponent of the Political view joins the discussion, claiming that the Orthodox view says something false. There is *no* human right to education. This is because a violation of a moral right to education does not (even *pro tanto*) justify sovereignty-interfering action by third parties. Are they really disagreeing? Or is this just a verbal dispute?

We can use what Chalmers calls the "method of elimination" to test whether this disagreement is merely verbal.[33] The idea is to eliminate use of the key term—"human right"—and see whether any substantive dispute remains. The Orthodox theorist, let us suppose, claims that (a) there is an individual moral right to education that generates third-party duties on modern states to supply a basic minimum of education to each citizen, (b) this right is ultimately grounded in universal human interests in being able to live one's life free from deceit and domination by others, and hence is held "in virtue of our humanity," and (c) violations of the moral right to education would not justify, in current circumstances, foreign, sovereignty-overriding interference (or other international action) to secure it. It strikes me that the Political theorist could happily *agree* with propositions (a)–(c). The only thing that the two parties would be disagreeing about, I conclude, is whether to *call* that moral right a human right. This suggests, therefore, that they are engaged in a merely verbal dispute.

THE BROAD VIEW

Is there a way out of this impasse? To sketch a way out, I proceed in two steps. First, I provide an articulation of the concept that is broad and ecumenical and that captures what is best in both the Orthodox view (the focus on moral rights) and the Political view (the focus on the moral and political significance of human rights claims) while avoiding the worst in each one (the Contingency and Subclass objections). Second, I will distinguish more clearly the *concept* of human rights and particular *interpretations* of that concept, and demonstrate how doing so allows us to abandon the Single Practice Assumption and to account for the broad and diverse range of usages in contemporary human rights practices. I end by arguing that the Broad View satisfies all four of the desiderata with which we started.

The Concept

According to the Broad View, human rights are not those moral rights *possessed* in virtue of our humanity, but those moral rights whose systematic violation ought to be of universal moral, legal, and political *concern*. Any violation[34] of a moral right that ought to garner universal moral, legal, and political concern is a human right.

It is worth highlighting four main features of the Broad construal of the concept. First, the concept is intended to have very wide scope, encompassing most contemporary usage. On the Broad construal, it is enough for a protest group, for example, to sincerely believe that the systematic moral rights violations they raise and reforms they pursue under the banner of human rights ought to garner universal moral, political, and legal concern for their claims to count as a *conceptually correct*—though not necessarily *substantively valid*—use of the term. It is a further question whether the systematic moral rights violations they believe ought to garner such concern *really are* moral rights violations and *really do* merit universal, concern just as it is a further question what *counts* as the relevant kind of universal concern. And, with a sideways look toward Political views, it is also a further question whether any specific remedial or corrective action is warranted given some set of systematic violations.

Second, the Broad construal is not so broad as to be meaningless. The Broad View tries to capture the distinctiveness of human rights claims in all their diversity (on which, see more below). On the Broad View, the most distinctive aspect of human rights is the idea that the morally most urgent claims of individuals and minorities are taken to be matters of *universal* rather than only of local moral, legal, and political concern. (As we will see below, what counts as relevantly "universal" and relevantly "moral," "legal," and "political" and what counts as the rights' correlated duties will vary by context.) This basic feature of human rights was central to the American and French revolutions and their accompanying declarations, and connects those revolutions with the spread of liberal constitutionalism throughout the globe (including its near obliteration in the years leading up to the end of the Second World War).

Third, notice that the Broad construal does not isolate the subclass of human rights from the class of moral rights *simpliciter* via a reference to a property shared (equally) by all human beings, such as their humanity, or dignity, or normative agency. For all I have said, there could be moral rights that are possessed by nonhumans[35] (or, indeed, the severely handicapped or children[36]) or by collectives.[37] As long as the systematic violation of those moral rights ought to be of universal moral, legal, and political concern, then they are not conceptually disqualified before the discussion ever gets started. This feature, as I will discuss in more detail below, prevents further useless verbal disagreements.

Fourth, the Broad View does not isolate human rights, as Political views do, in virtue of a unique political function or role they play in international affairs, such as "human rights are moral rights whose systematic violation would *pro tanto* justify humanitarian intervention, or sanctions, or diplomatic intervention," or some other remedial action. Rather, it isolates them by reference to their moral *significance* for some (yet to be specified) moral, legal, or political context. Because it does not yoke the existence of a human right to the justification for some remedial action *as a matter of conceptual necessity*, it does not fall prey to the contingency objection. Notice, for example, that the Broad View allows for someone to *specify* (as the relevant form of universal moral, legal, and political concern) that they are only interested in those human rights whose systematic violation would trigger some form of intervention; what it bars them from saying is that this is all there is to the concept of a human right, or that these are the only human rights that are genuinely human rights, or that people who focus on other types of universal moral, legal, and political concern are necessarily misguided. As a result, a Political view stated as a specification of the Broad View no longer faces the contingency objection; a proponent of such a view can always say, "Just because the human rights I am interested in are those that trigger some form of intervention doesn't mean that we can't have human rights in other senses, too."

The Broad View, furthermore, leaves entirely open, as a result, who the duty-bearers can be as well as the particular remedial actions that ought (normally) to follow particular violations. As a conceptual matter, the Broad View allows for the primary duty-bearers to be not only states but also transnational corporations, nongovernmental organizations, paramilitaries, guerrillas, and indeed even nonaligned individuals. As long as the systematic violations in which each of these duty-bearers are engaged (are perceived to) merit universal moral, legal, and political concern, then the use counts as conceptually correct.[38] So-called interactional accounts of human rights are therefore *not* excluded on conceptual grounds (as they are according to the Political view).[39]

Similarly, the Broad View does not exclude Orthodox views as long as they allow for other specifications of universal concern to count as legitimate interpretations of the concept of human rights and as long as they specify both what type of universal concern they envision and how that particular kind of universal concern allows them to meet the four desiderata (especially the Subclass Desideratum). An Orthodox view developed as an interpretation of the Broad concept might, for example, say that the human rights are those *basic* moral rights that we possess in virtue of our humanity and whose enjoyment is a necessary precondition for the enjoyment of any other moral right and then argue why a right's being basic merits some specific kind of universal concern.[40]

The Broad View therefore subsumes both Orthodox and Political views, explaining each as a special interpretation of the overarching concept. We now face two questions: How can a view as broad as this meet any of the desiderata mentioned above? And: How does the Broad View avoid merely verbal disagreements? I will spend the rest of this chapter answering these questions.

The Diversity That Stands between Concept and Conception

The key to the Broad View lies in the way it conceives of the *relation* between concept and conception.[41] One natural way to proceed would be to list all the moral rights and correlated duties whose systematic violation would merit universal moral, legal, and political concern. Call a list generated in this way the "Extended List." (For the moment, I will assume that such a list could, in fact, be drawn up, even though I will soon question that very assumption.) The Extended List would constitute the endpoint of a fully fledged human rights theory that accepts the Broad construal of the concept, and be a competitor to similar lists generated by Political and Orthodox views (in their fullest articulations). It would be an attempt to specify the list of human rights and their correlated duties that underlies and justifies human rights practice as a single, coherent whole. I will argue that is *not* the way in which a defender of the Broad View ought to articulate a conception of human rights. Seeing how it would fail will help motivate our rejection of the Single Practice Assumption, which, of course, the Extended List approach also accepts.

While the Extended List approach would satisfy the Subclass and Fidelity Desiderata, it would straightforwardly fail the Determinacy and Normativity Desiderata. The Extended List would satisfy the Fidelity Desideratum because it would capture a central feature of all human rights claims, namely their universal and peremptory status. And it would also satisfy the Subclass Desideratum by isolating a subclass of all moral rights and their correlated duties, namely those moral rights and correlated duties whose systematic violation merits universal moral, legal, and political concern. Take the violation of promissory rights. Barring exceptional circumstances, such violations are not morally significant enough to warrant universal moral, legal, and political concern (on any plausible construal of "universal" and "moral, political, and legal concern"). Systematic violations by states of individuals' right to bodily integrity, on the other hand, clearly do.

But there would be insurmountable problems with a conception developed along the lines of the Extended List. First, notice that the Extended List is severely indeterminate. What particular duties and duty-bearers, for example, ought to be associated with the List? Should, for example, the List be taken to correlate with duties owed by states, by public, nonstate actors, or by any individual anywhere? How stringent are the duties? To whom are they owed? In the absence of some more determinate conception of "universal moral, political, and legal concern" that can help us to answer these questions, it will be impossible to know what follows from one's acceptance of the List, and so what, in practice, the List would commit us to.

The Extended List would also fail the Normativity Desideratum. Imagine one has in hand a determinate version of the Extended List. What normative relevance would it have? Suppose we were called to the House of Lords with a freshly printed copy of our List. Of what use would it be to judges deciding whether to allow the indefinite detainment of foreign nationals suspected of terrorism on national soil (or, alternatively, judges deciding whether the European Convention on Human Rights [ECHR] ought to be applied extraterritorially to those detained by UK forces in Afghanistan)? How would the List help them determine a morally informed reading of the content and scope of the right to a fair trial according to the Convention? What moral rights and correlated duties, that is, warrant the *specific kind* of universal moral, legal, and political concern triggered by a Law Lords' ruling under the Human Rights Act? Knowing that there are moral rights and correlated duties that ought to merit some kind of (unspecified) universal moral, legal, and political concern would be irrelevant to their decision.

Or imagine we went to Human Rights Watch with our list. Human Rights Watch wants to know whether to mount a monitoring effort to track homophobia in South Africa. Once again: What good would it do to know those are moral rights and correlated duties that merit some kind of (unspecified) universal concern? What Human Rights Watch wants to know is whether moral rights to engage in homosexual relations warrant a global monitoring campaign designed to pressure governments and individuals into action. This is the same sort of skepticism that motivated a (wrongheaded) move away from the Orthodox to the Political view.

As a way of deriving a conception of human rights, the Extended List is a nonstarter. How can we do better? The solution begins by abandoning the Single Practice Assumption. Both Political and Orthodox views (and the Extended List approach) assume that there is an underlying moral unity to human rights practice, such that one can derive a single, unified list of moral rights that can be used to criticize any particular human rights practice. But why assume that there is any such master list there to be discovered? And why assume that practitioners—including the UN High Commissioner, the Justice on the European Court of Human Rights, the South African or German judge, activists in Amnesty International, domestic movements across Latin America, sub-Saharan Africa, and Asia—must all be implicitly appealing to such a unified list by using the term "human rights"? Why not instead be faithful to the multiplicity? That is what the Broad View tries to do.

The way it does so is by treating "human rights" as a context-sensitive term such as "tall," or "every bottle" in the expression "every bottle was empty." "Tall" has a general linguistic meaning that doesn't vary across contexts, namely *having a maximal degree of height above some threshold*. But the *content* of particular uses of "tall"—and hence the property picked out by a particular use of the term—will vary according to the context. So when I say that "Michael Jordan [who is six feet, six inches tall] is short," I might be saying something true. The expression is true when I am speaking *about basketball players*. It is false when speaking *about men in general*. The term "tall" does not, that is, refer to any property until the parameter determining the specific threshold above which one counts as tall has been settled—either explicitly by interlocutors (for example, when one participant in a conversation clarifies the reference class they intend for their usage of "tall," say, *basketball players*) or implicitly by the conversational context (for example, when the participants are at a basketball game, discussing the players).[42] Similarly, the expression "every bottle is empty" may be true in a conversation at a dinner party, but false in the cellars of Möet et Chandon. In the latter case, the parameter that sets the domain of the quantifier is set implicitly by either the conversational context (we are in the cellars) or explicitly by the interlocutors themselves ("no, no, I meant every bottle *in the cellar* not every bottle *in this room*"), just as in the case of "tall."

I want to say the same about the expression "human rights."[43] While the term has a general linguistic meaning that doesn't vary across contexts (i.e., "moral rights whose systematic violation merits universal moral, political, and legal concern"), the term's specific content varies with the context referred to by the speaker, which determines what *kind* of universal moral, legal, and political concern is at stake. Put another way, there is no single, master list of human rights and correlated duties against which one can evaluate expressions of the general form "*y* has a human right to *x*" just as there is no all-purpose threshold above which someone counts as tall. As we will see in a moment, this context-sensitivity enables the Broad View to meet both the Determinacy and Normativity Desiderata in a way that the Extended List approach alone could not. (Call this the Context-Sensitive way of developing conceptions of human rights within the Broad View—or CSBV for short.)

To determine which particular specification of universal moral, political, and legal concern is appropriate for a given context, the CSBV theorist begins by asking: given the uses to which human rights are put in a certain context *x,* what moral rights and correlated duties would warrant the *specific kind* of universal moral, legal, and political concern relevant for that context? To answer this question, the CSBV theorist needs to provide an interpretation of the kind of universal moral, legal, and political concern at stake in the particular context he or she is interested in. This lower-level, and hence *mediating,* concept of human rights *for context* x helps to give shape and determinacy to the overall account, and is equivalent to explicitly fixing the domain for the quantifier "every" in "every bottle" or fixing the reference class and threshold for a gradable adjective like "tall."

For example, imagine you are a philosophically minded human rights activist within Amnesty International. You want to know what human rights violations should define the main aims of Amnesty's advocacy. You resist the temptation to answer: "Just the ones in the UDHR" since you want to be able to evaluate whether the UDHR lists all (and only) the human rights we actually have or otherwise contributes to their realization. It would be a mistake (as we have seen) to make this evaluation by trying to find only those moral rights and correlated duties that we possess merely in virtue of our humanity. Instead, we ask: "Which systematic violations of moral rights ought to garner universal moral, legal, and political concern?" You realize, however, that there will be no determinate, truth-evaluable answer to this question until we have specified exactly what *kind* of universal concern we have in mind.

The CSBV then says: "Don't look for a single, general-purpose type of universal moral, legal, and political concern that will be adequate for *all* contexts in which human rights are invoked (as the Extended List approach did). Rather, accept the great diversity in the kinds of universal concern relevant to different contexts. With this in mind, begin by asking yourself what the point and purpose of Amnesty is; begin, that is, by giving an account of the role that human rights claims are meant to play in the particular practice you are interested in. What uses does Amnesty's invocation of human rights serve?" To this question, we might then respond: "Human rights advocacy of the type pursued by Amnesty aims to protect individuals against standard state-authorized (and often also state-enforced) threats to liberty, especially (but not exclusively) in civil and political domains." A fuller interpretation would refer to the history of Amnesty, and in particular to Amnesty's aim to be "nonaligned": human rights were meant to be "above politics," and hence not identified with the particular aims of any one liberal democracy or communist state, Islamic regime, or more straightforwardly authoritarian regime.[44] Amnesty aims therefore to protect all individuals against the abuse of political power, wherever it occurs; hence the importance to Amnesty of the "prisoner of conscience." This also explains why Amnesty makes a special effort to monitor human rights abuses in the West (e.g., prisoners' rights in the United States).[45] In turn, Amnesty uses a variety of methods in its official campaigns. The strategies deployed seek mainly to "name and shame" governments via public forms of pressure (e.g., letter-writing), to provide a monitoring and informational function, and to extend and monitor international human rights law (e.g., via its support for treaty-making and revision).[46] And while Amnesty sometimes urges third-party governments to take (or continue) some form of international action[47]—e.g., the imposition of sanctions or trade embargoes, the establishment of post-conflict tribunals, or the maintenance and expansion of peace-keeping operations—it never urges outright military intervention.[48]

With this mediating concept in hand—the kind of universal moral, legal, and political concern relevant from the point of view of a human rights activist within a nongovernmental organization like Amnesty—the CSBV theorist can now turn to the defense of a specific *conception* of human rights under the mediating concept. What moral rights and correlated duties warrant the specific types of universal moral, legal, and political concern called for by an actor within Amnesty? To answer this further question, we say that the CSBV theorist ought to deploy the best and most comprehensive theory of the moral rights and correlated duties we have. What they should not do is to search for a single, master list of human rights and correlated duties that we can then use as a template or standard for the evaluation of all human rights practices and claims whatever their specific scope, origin, or aims. This is because, I have argued, there is none that can be faithful to the multiplicity of human rights practices.

Had we been the framers of the ECHR (or, indeed, the International Covenant on Civil and Political Rights [ICCPR]), we would have begun in a very different way. The ECHR governs a set of regional signatories and is a legal instrument created by treaty. The moral rights and correlated duties that ought to (partially) guide the formation of a list for the ECHR, as well as how they should be interpreted, will invoke a type of universal moral, legal, and political concern and a set of moral considerations of a different nature than the ones that went into the development of a human rights conception for Amnesty.[49] Therefore, we would have ended up with a different mediating concept and hence a different conception of human rights and their correlated duties. And it will be different again if we are statesmen and -women evaluating whether intervention would be justified (in part) in Syria or Libya or Egypt on the basis (partially) of moral human rights violations, determining how wide the scope of the right to self-determination in the ICCPR ought, as a moral matter, to be, or—to name a last example—deciding which legal human rights, if any, merit some recognition as *jus cogens* (or, alternatively, *erga omnes*).[50] In none of these cases would grasping for a master list of human rights be helpful.

Avoiding Merely Verbal Disagreement

One of the main merits of the CSBV is that it helps us avoid verbal disagreement. In this section, I explain how. This will also help us to further motivate our rejection of the Single Practice Assumption.

Recall the apparent disagreement between our Political and Orthodox discussants regarding whether the moral right to education should be considered a human right. Above I argued that the disagreement was only apparent since elimination of the term "human rights" from the dispute would make no substantive difference to their normative conclusions regarding violations of the underlying moral rights. I suggested that, if this was the case, then they should simply agree that they were talking at cross-purposes. I now want to argue that there are two ways that we can reframe their disagreement such as to restore its meaningfulness. Doing so, however, requires us at the same time to recast their disagreement in terms of the CSBV.

The first way the two participants could restore real disagreement would be to accept the Broad View and then simply adopt, for the sake of argument, either a Political reading of the parameter "universal moral, legal, and political concern," or a more Orthodox one. For example, they might continue in the following way: "Assuming, for the sake of argument, that human rights are those moral rights whose systematic violation would merit some kind of sovereignty-overriding interference, ought we to consider the moral right to education a human right?" Or: "Assuming that human rights are those moral rights whose systematic violation would be sufficiently urgent to justify an international advocacy campaign to stop them from occurring, ought we to consider the moral right to education a human right?" If they were to proceed in this way, they would be, in effect, converging on a single mediating concept and then exploring what follows regarding which moral rights we ought to count as human rights. Converging in this way on a mediating concept would mean that any disagreements about which moral rights can play the assigned roles would become *substantive, normative* disagreements rather than merely verbal ones. To continue our analogy, this would be equivalent to two interlocutors discussing Michael Jordan's height and agreeing to stipulate whether they are talking about Michael Jordan *as a basketball player* or *as a man* simpliciter, and then seeing what follows once they do so.

There is, however, a problem with this approach to restoring the possibility of disagreement. The problem is that the decision to use one or the other concept looks *ad hoc*. In particular, it is not clear what is normatively at stake in adopting one or the other (or some further concept under the Broad View). We can diagnose why the choice looks *ad hoc* using the CSBV. The choice looks *ad hoc* because neither party to the dispute has specified the particular context for which they are proposing their mediating concept of human rights. Are they wondering which human rights ought to govern the expansion of the legal rights protected by the ECHR? Are they trying to determine whether Amnesty should be more active in advocacy designed to prevent mass illiteracy in countries whose governments have the capacity to extend it to all? Are they trying to evaluate whether the moral right to education should have ever been part of the UDHR in the first place? Are they assessing to what degree the failure to educate children in US inner cities should be considered a human rights violation from the point of view of the American Convention on Human Rights (i.e., despite the fact that the United States has not signed or ratified the Additional Protocol protecting that right)? Are they doing the same as Black Lives Matter activists? And so on.

The CSBV claims that the most appropriate concept of human rights to deploy in each of these contexts should be allowed to vary depending on the interpretive specification of the role human rights claims are meant to play in that context. For example, if the context was the ECHR, then the relevant concept of "human rights" to use might be the Political one, given that the rights protected by the ECHR *do* license sovereignty-interfering judgments by the Court.[51] In the context of the ECHR, it would be very unclear what role the more Orthodox reading would have to play. But now let us say we are activists in the Black Lives Matter movement, who are considering whether it is appropriate to speak of the inadequate provision of education in US inner cities as a human rights violation. In *this* context, the Political view might seem an odd one to adopt: our primary concern is not (let us suppose) to get the international community or other states to interfere directly in the US government's policies in a sovereignty-overriding way. The Orthodox view, on the other hand, would be much more consonant with our aims. As activists, our use of the term "human rights" is intended to signal the gravity of the violations in light of the very point and purpose of any liberal democracy, and, in light of that fact, to seek a higher, constitutional status to the right to education within the United States. Finally, imagine we are wondering whether the right to education should have ever been included in the UDHR. Here we might be much less clear about what to think, given that the UDHR doesn't sanction any sovereignty-interfering action, and given the much broader role it has played in all kinds of political advocacy across the globe. Whatever concept we adopt in each of these cases, it should be clear by now that it would be a mistake to think that any single concept could pick out a single master list of human rights and correlated duties that meaningfully applies across all these different contexts.

Once we reject the Single Practice Assumption and adopt the CSBV, a new possibility for meaningful disagreement opens up: two interlocutors could be disagreeing about which mediating concept to use in light of either (a) a disagreement about the particular uses to which human rights claims ought to be put within a particular context or (b) a disagreement about which concept we ought to use given an underlying agreement about the role human rights claims are meant to play in that context. To return to our examples, two interlocutors might (a) disagree about the particular role that the UDHR ought to play in the international system, and so about which mediating concept of human rights is best suited to determining what counts as human rights for the purposes of the UDHR, or (b) two interlocutors might disagree about which mediating concept is best suited to play a role on which they already agree. Accepting this way of proceeding—and hence the CSBV—allows the interlocutors' conceptual disagreement to make sense in a way that it otherwise wouldn't have.[52]

It is useful to refer again to our example about height. The type of meaningful conceptual disagreement I have identified between an advocate of a Political view and an advocate of an Orthodox view is like the conceptual disagreement between two interlocutors advocating different thresholds for evaluating tallness. The disagreement makes little sense if it is construed as an attempt to derive a single threshold for tallness that will be valid in *any* context, but does make sense once we assume, for example, that they are basketball coaches selecting players to purchase in the draft. We now know *why* they are interested in tallness as a property of players, and so we have a background against which it makes sense to evaluate and disagree over the use of particular thresholds. In the same way, the conceptual disagreement between the Political and Orthodox theorists makes little sense if it is construed as an attempt to fix criteria for universal concern across all contexts, but does make sense if we assume they are, for example, activists in the Black Lives Matter movement (as opposed to, say, drafters of an international treaty).

How Does the CSBV Help to Satisfy the Four Desiderata?

In this section, we review how the Broad View satisfies the four desiderata with which we began.

The Subclass Desideratum

The Broad View meets the Subclass Desideratum at both the conceptual and substantive levels. At the conceptual level, the desideratum is satisfied by the qualifier that the systematic violation of the moral right must merit some specific kind of universal moral, legal, and political concern. But, more importantly, the Subclass Desideratum is also met at the substantive level. In moving from the general construal to a mediating concept, the Broad View *qua* CSBV isolates a particular *kind* of universal moral, legal, and political concern as relevant to a particular context. This further delimits the scope of "universal moral, legal, and political concern" and thus further precisifies and bounds the subclass.

The Fidelity Desideratum

As I have argued, the CSBV strikes me as faithful to the *diversity* of practices under the banner of human rights—indeed much more faithful than either the Political or Orthodox view, precisely because of the latitude it allows in identifying appropriate usage of the concept, and precisely because it allows us to explain the sense in which all the different practices in which human rights are invoked are referring to the *same* general concept (though with very different content). Again, the analogy to "tall" is instructive. The concept of tallness picks out a distinctive property of objects with a vertical dimension, namely that they are above some threshold in height, just as the concept of a human right picks out a distinctive kind of moral right, namely a moral right whose systematic violation merits universal concern. And, just as thresholds for tallness will vary with the contexts to which speakers intend to refer, what counts as the relevant kind of universal concern will vary with the contexts to which practitioners, advocates, and so on intend to refer.

But, at this point, someone might worry: "The Broad View doesn't strike me as very faithful to practitioners—whether lawyers, politicians, activists, professors—who overwhelmingly believe they are engaged in a *single* project."[53] Given the diversity of practitioners' motivations, aims, and cultural, institutional, political, and social backgrounds, there may be reason to doubt that practitioners in all these contexts really do conceive of themselves as engaged in a single project.[54] But let us assume, for the sake of responding to the objection, that human rights practitioners around the world really do conceive of themselves as engaged in a single overarching project. Even if we grant this assumption, it strikes me that abandoning the Single Practice Assumption does not require us to abandon the idea of a single project. An analogy: it seems clear that we can all be engaged in the project of building a vibrant city together, even though we have different ideas about what makes for a vibrant city, and even though we are each engaged in very different aspects of city-building (some of us are artists, others engineers, planners, restaurateurs). As long as we conceive of our activity as coordinated in the right kind of way, there is no need for us to conceive of ourselves as engaged in a single practice of "vibrant city-building" or to share much in the way of agreement on the truth-conditions for "vibrant city." It is enough if there is some very broad understanding of "vibrant city" that we can all be understood to be promoting, each in our own way, each in our own context. It is the same with the human rights project: we can each participate in a project that can loosely be described as securing the realization of moral rights that merit universal moral, legal, and political concern, but at the same time have very different, noncompeting ways of understanding what kind of universal concern we are interested in securing and how we conceive of ourselves as helping to secure it. On this reading, both the Justice of the European Court of Human Rights and the Amnesty activist can rightly conceive of themselves as participating in a single project but with different, noncompeting ideas of what that requires in the more specific, circumscribed contexts in which each of them work. Indeed, one might argue that the term's protean, yet still unifying, character is in fact part of what makes it such a powerful political ideal.

The Normativity and Determinacy Desiderata

The Normativity and Determinacy Desiderata can be discussed together. If one looked only at the conceptual component of the Broad View, then one might worry that it would have difficulty meeting the Normativity and Determinacy Desiderata. As we have seen, the Broad construal of the concept is so broad as to be *very* indeterminate. So indeterminate is it that one might wonder how one could have a normative reason to adopt it (other than that it permits us to encompass most contemporary usage). On the Broad View *qua* CSBV, however, the satisfaction of the Normativity and Determinacy Desiderata is relocated to the contextual and *substantive* level. Determinacy is gained by specifying a mediating concept that fixes a particular context of action and makes it clear what kind of universal concern is mandated by that context. And normativity is achieved by specifying the substantive moral rights that would justify the specific kind of universal concern envisaged. The Normativity Desideratum is satisfied, that is, by pointing to the normative force of the set of moral rights that can play the required roles.

CONCLUSION

In this chapter, I have argued that we should reinterpret both of the dominant philosophical accounts of the concept of human rights, namely Political and Orthodox views, as special cases of the Broad concept. According to the Broad construal of a human right, something counts as a (putative) human right when it is a moral right whose systematic violation ought to garner universal moral, legal, and political concern. I then argued that the evaluation of the truth of a human rights claim (understood in these terms) requires us first to specify a context, then a role that human rights are meant to play in that context, and finally the type of universal moral, legal, and political concern that is envisaged given that role. There is therefore no master list that can serve as a unitary system for the evaluation of all human rights practices. If I am right, then we should abandon the search for an overarching, general-purpose philosophical conception of human rights and turn rather to the piecemeal evaluation of particular human rights practices.

In Chapters 5 and 6, I will focus on a specific practice, namely the international legal human rights system. Rather than identify a general moral foundation for all human rights whatever the context, I will only identify a foundation for a specific context, namely the system of states, and will argue that the nature of the state system mandates a specific form of moral, legal, and political concern, namely the special protection of equal moral status by international law. In the rest of this book, I will therefore not claim to offer a general justification for all human rights whatever the context or an account of human rights practice as a whole—which, as I have argued in this chapter, would be misguided.

5

INTERNATIONAL LEGAL HUMAN RIGHTS AND EQUAL MORAL STATUS

IN THIS CHAPTER and the next, I seek to provide an account of a subgroup of moral rights that ought to garner a special kind of universal moral, legal, and political concern, namely protection by international law. More specifically, I will argue that we, as participants in the state system, have a special responsibility to protect, through international law, individuals against systematic violations, especially but not exclusively by states, of the moral rights that are constitutive of our status as moral equals. In Chapter 6, I will then contend that the international legal human rights that protect this status are themselves *fundamental,* and hence deserve a higher status in international law. To set the stage for the discussion, I will begin by provisionally leaving aside the distinction between "fundamental" and "nonfundamental" rights. This will be picked up again later in Chapter 6. I start therefore with the system of international legal human rights (ILHRs) as an undifferentiated whole.

It is uncontroversial that one of the highest-order aims of the ILHR system as it currently operates is to make the protection of a set of individual moral rights a matter of common concern for the international community.[1] By "international community," I mean the network of political and legal institutions that operates at the international level and that includes states, nongovernmental organizations (NGOs), and inter-national organizations. The most important of these institutions is the UN system, which is composed of myriad agencies, committees, com-missions, and associated treaty-based organizations (including the International Monetary Fund, the World Bank, the World Health Organization, and the International Labour Organization). Included are also various judicial and quasi-judicial bodies associated with the UN system, such as the International Court of Justice and the special crim-inal and arbitral tribunals, and UN-based human rights organizations (such as the Human Rights Council and the Convention on the Elimi-nation of All Forms of Discrimination against Women [CEDAW]), as well as NGOs such as Amnesty International, Human Rights Watch, and the International Committee of the Red Cross. Finally, flanking these UN-based institutions are also the regional human rights treaties and courts, such as the European Convention on Human Rights (ECHR) and the Inter-American Commission on Human Rights [IACHR], which also play an important role in the ILHR system.

ILHRs became a common concern of this community via compara-tive legal adjudication, officially mandated monitoring and information-gathering efforts, domestic implementation, and political and social mobilization. ILHRs provide, *inter alia,* a platform for domestic groups to pressure their governments; a touchstone for international pressure (diplomatic and otherwise); a set of standards for global governance; a basis for the use of comparative materials from foreign and interna-tional courts; a justification for organizing and channeling resources into NGOs; a basis and rationale for foreign aid and for the use of force; a set of duties to be implemented by domestic legislatures and courts; and, at least in the case of the ECHR, a ground for legal remedies ordered by an international court. It is in this way that ILHRs have become a *lingua franca* of inter-, trans-, and supranational politics.

There are a number of questions we might ask of the ILHR system and the institutions through which ILHRs are animated. We might ask whether, for example, the system is legitimate. Even if we do not believe it is the best system imaginable, we might wonder whether it deserves our compliance or support. And even if we did believe it deserves our compliance or support, and therefore has legitimacy *given the world as it is,* we might ask what an ideal system would look like if we could re-design the world from scratch. In such an imaginary reconstruction, there may not be states, and, indeed, there may therefore be no need for a system of ILHRs. Neither of these questions will be my concern here. This is not because I think they are not interesting or significant, but because I believe many compelling arguments have already been made on behalf of both.[2]

My concern will be another one. To set up the question, I proceed hypothetically. This will allow us to avoid begging any questions. The question is framed in the following way: *If* we assume the existence of states, is the creation and maintenance of an international legal human rights system morally mandatory? In what sense, for example, would it be wrong for states or their citizens to abandon engagement with human rights institutions (think, for example, of the British government's pro-posals to abandon the ECHR)? This is not a question about the legitimacy of the ILHR system. Inquiring about the legitimacy of an institution leads us to wonder whether we have duties to comply with and respect the institution *once it is already up and running.* It neither tells us whether we would do wrong to abandon the institution nor whether its creation is morally mandatory. An analogy: our local chess club might rightly deserve our compliance and respect, but, from this fact, it does not follow that we would have duties to create one if it didn't exist, or duties not to disband it once it does.

Having set the stage for the discussion to follow, I now want to focus the question still further by isolating one central aspect of the ILHR system and ask whether it deserves the universal moral, legal, and po-litical concern we have just specified, and so whether it might be suffi-cient *on its own*—and hence independently of whatever other aims the system might legitimately serve—to justify the creation and mainte-nance of the ILHR system. The aspect of the system I have in mind is the protection of our status as moral equals.

At the core of the current international system is a commitment to the moral equality of all human beings in the sense we identified in Chapters 1 and 2. This is most evident in its embrace of the "inherent and equal dignity" of the person as a central organizing value, which, as we have seen, is a placeholder for a commitment to moral equality.

But it is also evident in the pervasive concern with discrimination, persecution, and degrading treatment that extends across all the major human rights treaties as well as the major instruments of international humanitarian law (such as the Geneva Conventions, especially Common Article 3). A brief survey of each of these documents is sufficient to make this point. In addition to prominent roles in the UN Charter (where the clause "without distinction as to race, sex, language, or religion" is used four times), the ICCPR, and the ICESCR, anti-discrimination norms have a central place in three independent instruments covering discrimination on the basis of race, sex, and disability (the International Convention on the Elimination of All Forms of Racial Discrimination [CERD] [1969], the CEDAW [1981], and the Convention on the Rights of Persons with Disabilities [2008]). Finally, norms against cruel and degrading treatment and genocide are enshrined in the Torture Convention (Convention against Torture and Other Cruel, Inhuman or Degrading Treatment or Punishment [1987]) and the Genocide Convention (Convention on the Prevention and Punishment of the Crime of Genocide [1946]).

It is therefore surprising that philosophical approaches to human rights have spent so little time discussing the specifically *status egalitarian* aspect of human rights, let alone the place of anti-discrimination norms within that system. Allen Buchanan convincingly argues that this is because of the almost explicit focus in the philosophical literature on "minimal" conditions for human flourishing and the concomitant emphasis on rights to the basic exercise of our rational faculties, physical security, and subsistence (as in Shue's argument regarding basic rights, to which we turn in Chapter 6, or Griffin's argument regarding normative agency, discussed in Chapter 4).[3] While an emphasis on physical security, for example, might be enough to provide a very partial moral justification for the Torture and Genocide Conventions, it would entirely overlook the *distinctive* moral wrongness of torture, genocide, and cruel and inhuman treatment, and, indeed, what makes them similar to discrimination. As I argued in Chapter 2, what makes torture and cruel and inhuman treatment wrong is not simply the infliction of pain, let alone the mere fact that those practices severely limit the exercise of our rational faculties. Similarly, what makes genocide wrong is not simply that it is an instance of mass murder. To characterize the wrongness of each of these practices, I argued that we also need to train our attention on their relational, social aspect; we need to understand how they are ways of treating as inferior. In torture, the infliction of pain is wrong not just because pain hurts but because of the way the pain is mobilized to attack or obliterate another's capacity to develop and maintain an integral sense of self. In genocide, the murder—and, very importantly, the way the murders are prosecuted and carried out—are wrong not just because death is bad (for both the persons themselves and for those around them) but because of the way the fear of death, of *extermination,* is mobilized to humiliate and demean those who are the targets. As we have seen, those so targeted are treated as animals because they have lost the right to control the terms of their engagement with others; they have lost the right to be treated as bearing a subjective point of view and an interiority that deserves recognition. These relational aspects are not separable from the physical; the physical and the relational are both necessary for a full understanding of the social and political meaning of both practices.

Once we see genocide and torture as violations of our equal moral status, and once we see that there is no way to understand equal moral status without a deeper analysis of its essentially relational aspect, then it should be evident why anti-discrimination rights should also be so prominent in the ILHR system. As I argued in Chapter 3, practices of discrimination are wrong when and because they express, instantiate, or enable inferiorizing social cruelty. They therefore share the crucial relational feature that makes them instances of violating another's status as a moral equal. It is for this reason that they deserve to be considered *in the same class as* more severe violations of human rights, such as genocide and torture. Once again, it is revealing that very few philosophers writing on human rights have provided an explanation for why anti-discrimination rights should deserve such a special place in the ILHR system. The lacuna, once again, can be easily explained: if one is primarily concerned with minimal conditions for human flourishing, and the paradigmatic instances of falling below such a threshold are violations of physical security or subsistence rights, or limitations on the basic exercise of our rational faculties, then discrimination doesn't—in all but the most extreme cases—look as if it fits the bill.

So far I have raised a question about whether states and citizens have duties to establish and maintain the ILHR system and suggested that the moral rights constitutive of our equal moral status underlie that system. In the rest of this chapter, I will argue that our duties to establish and maintain such a system in fact flow from our commitment to moral equality. If the argument succeeds, it should serve as a vindication not only of the central place of status egalitarianism—including anti-discrimination norms—in the ILHR system, but also an explanation for why all states and citizens have duties to protect the equal moral status of both their own citizens and those in other states. In the first part of this chapter, I establish that all ILHRs must ultimately be justified, if they are justified at all, in terms of underlying individual moral rights. This clears the ground for the second part, which argues that we have obligations to create an ILHR system that protects the individual moral rights constitutive of our status as moral equals. I emphasize that I am not arguing that the ILHR system should be *limited* to the protection of equal moral status; I am only arguing that the protection of equal moral status provides a sufficient basis for our obligation to create and maintain the system. In Chapter 6, I then argue that these rights are in fact fundamental, and deserve priority in our moral reflection and legal practice.

A DEFENSE OF THE GROUNDING VIEW

My aim is to give an account of the moral rights underpinning the status egalitarianism of the ILHR system. But the aim, as stated, may seem to rest on a mistake. Recently, Buchanan has argued against what he calls the Mirroring View, or the view that the identification of an underlying moral right is both a necessary and sufficient condition for the justification of any legal human right. He claims that legal human rights can be justified solely on other, non-rights-based, grounds, including more general, nondirected moral duties (such as duties of beneficence) or broader social goals (such as the general welfare). In the discussion to follow, I will grant his rejection of the sufficiency claim, which strikes me as uncontroversial; merely demonstrating that some claim is in fact a genuine moral right is not sufficient to justify its protection as a legal human right within the ILHR system. It is one thing to justify the existence of a moral right but quite another to hold that it ought to be legally institutionalized.

Buchanan's argument against the necessity claim is, I believe, more interesting. I will argue that Buchanan is wrong to reject it. Indeed, I will go on to show that Buchanan himself must be committed to it.[4] If my argument is correct, then at the heart of any plausible justification of a legal human right (or set of such rights) will be a universal-concern-meriting moral right, by which I mean a moral right that merits *(pro tanto)* protection in international law. The object of this moral right need not "correspond" directly with the object of the particular legal human right (or rights) that it justifies, but the moral right must provide a necessary part of the overall justification for the legal rights. Other non-rights-based moral considerations might thus provide further reasons for implementing (or not implementing) the legal rights, but none of these further purposes can be either individually or jointly sufficient for its successful justification. To distinguish this view from the Mirroring View, I will call it the Grounding View.

To support his rejection of the necessity claim, Buchanan provides a series of examples, including rights to democratic participation, free expression, and to physical security. Here's one to which he often returns:

> [The legal right to health] admits of a powerful pluralistic justification that does not include an appeal to an antecedently existing moral right to healthcare. A legal entitlement to goods, services, and conditions that are conducive to health, which include but are not limited to healthcare, can promote social utility, contribute to social solidarity, help to realize the ideal of a decent or a humane society, increase productivity and to that extent contribute to the general welfare, and provide an efficient and coordinated way for individuals to fulfill their obligations of beneficence.[5]

To test this claim, imagine, as Buchanan suggests here, that the right to health is not in fact justified by any underlying moral right (and so, *a fortiori,* any universal-concern-meriting right). I will argue that, if the legal right was not ultimately grounded in such a moral right, it would lack the characteristic moral force and urgency attributed to human rights claims, and that is central to the point and purpose of the ILHR system as Buchanan himself characterizes it.

According to Human Rights Watch, there are an estimated 10 to 15 million artisanal gold miners working worldwide. In some regions, 20 percent are children. Most miners—including children—use mercury to extract gold from the ore. Prolonged exposure to mercury can cause severe cognitive impairments in children; in adults, symptoms of exposure include tremors, twitching, vision trouble, headaches, and memory and concentration problems; mercury can also adversely affect the cardiovascular system, the kidneys, the gastrointestinal tract, the immune system, and the lungs. Human Rights Watch mentions in particular Mali and Papua New Guinea, where there has been very little enforcement of health and safety regulations to protect workers, and where workers are not informed by employers or by the government regarding the effects of mercury.[6] This is a paradigmatic instance of a violation of the right to health.

Have any individual moral rights been violated? If we accept Buchanan's position, then we must conclude that there need not be. We must conclude that to explain the moral urgency and force of the workers' claims, it would be sufficient to advert to any of the broader social and moral goals listed in the passage cited above, such as solidarity, social utility, efficiency, beneficence, and so on. This doesn't strike me as plausible. The workers' claims are compelling not simply as aspects of broader and valuable goals or nondirected moral duties. Rather, they are compelling because they have morally weighty individual interests in living a life free of debilitating illness and cognitive impairment—interests that are sufficiently weighty to put employers and the governments under moral duties to inform and protect them (especially if they are children) from the harmful effects of mercury poisoning. These duties of notification and warning are thus grounded directly in the individual interests of the rightsholders, which makes it the case that when they are violated, we wrong the individuals concerned, rather than merely do wrong in general. The duties are thus *directed* to the rightsholders.* And where there are directed moral duties, there are moral rights. The legal human right to health is therefore justified, on this understanding, (in part) as a mechanism for protecting individual moral rights to notification and warning.

Buchanan could grant that the case *just mentioned* might best be accounted for by pointing to an underlying moral right but insist that this doesn't show that the legal right to health *in general* must be justified in the same way. In response, I want to claim that, if we miss this connection to moral rights, we miss a distinctive feature of the violation of *any* legal human right, and hence even legal human rights stated in their most general form. Violations of legal human rights trigger universal concern not simply because they serve moral duties or social goals owed to no one in particular but because they single out standards whose violation morally wrongs us *as individuals*. That is, in part, their very point.

And Buchanan himself, I now want to argue, is himself committed to this claim. Buchanan is surely right that many legal rights can be justified in terms of moral and nonmoral goals and nondirected duties that make no essential reference to individual moral rights. Many international legal rights are of this kind. For example, each party to the World Trade Organization (WTO)/General Agreement on Tariffs and Trade (GATT) treaties has a legal right to bring suit under its dispute resolution procedures. It is unlikely that the normative force of these legal rights must ultimately be explained in terms of moral rights possessed by the individual public officials who were responsible for signing, implementing, or negotiating the treaty. Similarly, diplomats enjoy international legal rights to immunity from prosecution under host state laws. These rights are protected by international law and possessed by individuals *qua* diplomats. Yet if a state fines a diplomat for a traffic violation, this does not morally wrong him. The reason is that there is no independent individual moral right that ultimately plays a central

---

*A directed duty is a duty owed *to* someone such that, in violating it, one wrongs that person. For example, by wrongfully breaking my promise to you, I violate a duty I have to you (but to no one else). A nondirected duty is owed to no one in particular. For example, I might have a duty not to swear in public, where this duty is not owed to anyone in particular. If this is the case, then in swearing, I do wrong, but I wrong no one in particular.

role in grounding the legal protection. Diplomatic protections are morally justified on purely instrumental grounds (namely as aspects of sovereign state immunity).

So why aren't diplomatic protections of this kind legal human rights? What distinguishes legal *human* rights from other legal rights protected at the international level, Buchanan argues, is their individualist focus. Buchanan writes:

> The basic idea of the system of international legal human rights is *to develop a regime of international law whose primary function is to provide universal standards for regulating the behavior of states towards those under their jurisdiction, **for the sake of those individuals themselves.***[7]

Diplomatic rights to immunity, although possessed by individuals, are not justified *for the sake* of those individuals themselves (i.e., diplomats), but for the sake of the states that are parties to the Vienna Convention on Diplomatic Relations. While the justification of diplomatic immunity rights might therefore ultimately refer to the way they contribute to individual interests *in general* (say, individual interests in peace served by protecting state interests), they are not justified in virtue of how they serve diplomats' interests for their own sake.

I agree with Buchanan. But this account of the point of legal human rights has an implication, I now want to argue, that Buchanan has missed: it is incompatible with the view that legal human rights might be justified by only nondirected moral duties and broader social goals. If there are legal human rights that can be justified only by appeal to nondirected moral duties and social goals, then those human rights will lack the essentially individualist concern of the human rights system *in Buchanan's view about what that concern entails.* In the example of the gold miners, if we focused only on the broader nondirected moral duties and social goals that the protection of the legal right serves, then we would miss the sense in which the legal right is justified *for the sake of the miners themselves.* What gives the claims moral urgency and triggers universal concern is the violation of stringent moral duties owed *to* the miners, and grounded ultimately in their individual interests in a life without significant impairment and without deceit. While the legal right might *also* be justified by the way it promotes broader social goals and nondirected moral duties (and so the interests of others, say, in a healthy, resilient workforce), none of those further goals and duties would be sufficient to explain the normative force of the right as a *human* right. This is not a peculiarity of the gold miner case but is an important normative aspect of all legal human rights (as Buchanan himself reminds us in the passage quoted above); if it wasn't, then we couldn't distinguish international legal *human* rights from international legal rights *simpliciter*.

We can expand this point by considering Buchanan's account of the two chief functions of the ILHR system. According to Buchanan, the ILHR system serves to protect and promote the equal moral status of all human beings and to help ensure that all have the opportunity to lead a minimally decent life.[8] As I explained in the introduction to this chapter, I couldn't agree more. But these two functions seem to lend themselves quite readily to statement in terms of moral rights. On this reading, the ILHR system is justified only if it protects and promotes the moral *rights* constitutive of our status as moral equals and constitutive of a minimally decent life. Putting Buchanan's own point another way, we could say that the protection of these rights must underlie the force and point of all legal human rights claims; that is what gives them their status as legal human rights claims rather than some other kind of legal right (such as a state's legal right to bring suit under the WTO / GATT or a right to diplomatic protection). This would confirm our reading of the gold miners' case as paradigmatic rather than peculiar. The gold miners' moral rights to live a life without significant impairment and without deceit by the powerful is, we might say, derived from the universal-concern-meriting moral right to live a minimally decent life on an equal footing with others. When we fight the injustice of the gold miners' situation, or when we bring attention to their plight in a Human Rights Watch report, we fight for *them* rather than for some broader nondirected moral duty or social goal owed to no one in particular.[9]

At one point, Buchanan recognizes that "one might formulate the commitment to equal basic status in rights-terms." But he goes on to argue that "it is not clear that the notion of a right is doing any work here. One could just as well say that the affirmation and protection of equal basic status for all is a fundamental moral value, one that grounds a very high-priority (mere) moral duty."[10] Buchanan here entertains the possibility that our commitment to equal moral status could be explained as the result of a general nondirected moral duty that makes no essential reference to the way in which the individual interests of those who have been treated as inferiors in the relevant sense have been set back. For all the reasons discussed in Chapters 2 and 3, this strikes me as implausible. We cannot explain our commitment to equal moral status without taking into account the effect of violations of that status on the particular individual interests of those who have been treated as inferior, taken one by one. If it were true that equal moral status is grounded in nondirected moral duties, then the individual who has been tortured would not be able to claim that he has been wronged in any sense; rather he would need to claim that the perpetrators have violated some general moral duty that benefits him only incidentally. But even if we reject the account in Chapters 2 and 3, it cannot be true, even in Buchanan's own argument, that duties to protect equal moral status are nondirected. This is because, as we have seen, it is not sufficient for ILHRs merely to *benefit* individuals—recall diplomatic rights. Once again, all international legal human rights must protect individuals, as Buchanan writes, "*for the sake of those individuals themselves.*" If protections of moral status merely served to realize nondirected moral duties, then they would only incidentally serve to protect the individuals whose equal moral status has been thwarted. The protections of equal moral status would be justified not for the sake of those who have been treated as inferior but for the sake of whatever more general interests the nondirected moral duty is meant to serve.

With these pieces in place, we are now in a position to deflate Buchanan's (and Sreenivasan's) other main argument. The argument is that the existence of an underlying moral right cannot be a necessary part of the justification of many important legal human rights—such as the legal human right to freedom of the press, democratic participation, and health—because the legal duties associated with each of these legal human rights far outstrip what could possibly be justified by appeal to the interests of the individual rightsholder alone.[11] To construe: The individual interests of any one person cannot plausibly ground stringent, third-party moral duties to set up, say, the wide-scale investment in public and social infrastructure required to realize a right to health, or the mechanisms for securing free and fair elections necessary to realize a right to democratic participation. Buchanan and Sreenivasan conclude that there cannot therefore be a moral right to health or democratic participation that justifies the corresponding legal right.

This would be a problem for the Grounding View only if it asserted that the existence of a universal-concern-meriting moral right must be *sufficient* to justify all the legal duties associated with a legal human right. And this is something I have been happy to deny. All I have said is that a universal-concern-meriting moral right must be a *necessary* part of the justification for the legal right. Indeed, the Grounding View doesn't even assert that the moral right in question must have the same content as the legal human right in question. For example, the Grounding View can deny that the justification of a legal right to democratic participation must make reference to a moral right with the same content (and hence with exactly corresponding moral duties). All it needs to say is that any successful argument in favor of the legal human right to democratic participation must make reference to the way the legal human right is designed, in part, to serve or protect some universal-concern-meriting moral right, such that paradigmatic violations of the legal human right would also count as wronging the individuals who have been so denied.

Which moral rights underlie any plausible justification for an international legal human right to democratic participation? Among these moral rights are surely the rights constitutive of our status as moral equals. This is not only because denials of democratic participation almost always carry a demeaning, inferiorizing message to those denied— imagine, for example, being a Swiss woman in the late 1960s (the federal franchise was extended to women only in 1971)—but also because democratic rights serve to protect citizens against the myriad forms of inferiorizing cruelty that typically come with authoritarian regimes. When we fight on behalf of international legal human rights like this one, we fight on behalf of those individuals who would be individually wronged by their denial. Without that essential tie to the morally urgent, universal-concern-meriting, rights-generating interests of individuals, international legal human rights would be no different than any other international legal right that serves good ends (such as diplomatic rights or WTO rights).[12]

So far I have argued in favor of the Grounding View, namely the view that all international legal human rights must be justified (in part) in terms of an underlying universal-concern-meriting moral right. I have, at the same time, conceded that the existence of such underlying moral rights will not always be sufficient for the justification of an international legal human right. I leave open, that is, what kinds of further moral and nonmoral considerations must be at play to justify the institutionalization of the legal right. This result is useful for our purposes, first, because it justifies our search for the key universal-concern-meriting moral rights that undergird the ILHR system. And, second, it sets a task description: Explain why the moral rights constitutive of our equal moral status should, in fact, be protected in a system of international law; explain, that is, why they merit universal concern in that specific sense. It is to those arguments that we now turn.

THE OBLIGATION TO ESTABLISH AND MAINTAIN
AN INTERNATIONAL LEGAL HUMAN RIGHTS SYSTEM

Recall that we began this chapter by making an assumption that would help us to narrow our focus: we assumed the existence of states. Our task here is not to argue that states are the most desirable political system for organizing our political life. Even if they are not, however, it still makes sense to ask whether, *given* the existence of states, we have any moral obligation to establish and maintain a system of ILHRs that protects our basic status as moral equals. I will argue that we do.

The most obvious source of obligation lies in the relation between a government and its citizens. If creating or maintaining a system of ILHRs improves the chances that a government will protect the equal moral status of its citizens or makes it less liable to backsliding, then it is clear that the government has a duty to its own citizens to create or maintain that system. But what about states for which this is not true (or at any rate where the danger of backsliding is less pressing)? What about, say,

Britain (to which we will return at the end of the chapter)?[13] In this case, it is less plausible to say that Britain has a moral obligation to join or create a system of ILHRs in order to provide assurance to its own citizens. Indeed, its own citizens might prefer to be free of any such international encumbrances. In cases like this, do the state and its citizens still have moral obligations to create and maintain a system of ILHRs?

There are, broadly speaking, three ways in which we might argue for the conclusion that they do. First, we might argue that we have positive moral obligations to protect anyone in the world against violations of their equal moral status and that the ILHR system is a good (though imperfect) way of doing so. Second, we might argue that our participation in the state system makes individuals more vulnerable to violations of their equal moral status than they otherwise would have been. We therefore have a duty to ameliorate the threats to people's equal moral status by establishing and maintaining an ILHR system. Third, we might argue that we have a positive duty to establish and maintain an ILHR system that protects equal moral status as a fair return for others' participation in a state system from which we benefit, but which makes individuals foreseeably and avoidably subject to a diverse array of threats to their equal moral status. While I will not reject the first two proposals, I will demonstrate how they face a number of problems. I will then argue in favor of the third, which strikes me as an appealing way of remedying the defects of the first two but is less often discussed.

The first argument ultimately rests on a Duty of Rescue. Imagine a state of nature in which we, in one village, hear about pervasive violations of equal moral status in a village some distance away, but with whom we have never had any contact. The Duty of Rescue tells us to attempt a rescue of the victims in the other village. But how stringent is this duty? Most concur that the duty is not very stringent: if the rescue would come at some, even small, cost to ourselves, we have no duty to do so. We might think that the duty to create an ILHR system that protects equal moral status is analogous. The ILHR system serves to protect those vulnerable to violations of equal moral status that are a result of state action (or inaction).[14] The problem is that participation in the ILHR system is costly. To make the system truly effective, it must be backed by the active participation of all states, who must not only make themselves liable to the monitoring and enforcement efforts of the system but must also contribute resources (and in some cases also troops) to the defense of individuals abroad. These costs, one might worry, extend beyond what the mere Duty of Rescue alone mandates, which gives us sufficient reason to look elsewhere to see whether there are any stronger arguments for ILHRs.

We turn now to the second argument. States do not exist in an institutional vacuum, like the villages discussed above. Both the juridical recognition of a state *as* a state and the ability of any one state to ensure the protection and well-being of its citizens depends, in our world, on its place in the wider *system* of states secured by the international order. In participating in the reproduction of our own states, we are therefore always also engaged in the reproduction of an international system of states.

For our purposes, there are three salient features of this system. First, the system is constituted by the recognition of a principle of international legal sovereignty, whereby it only recognizes groups that meet a certain number of (empirical) criteria, namely the possession of a defined territory, a government, a population, and the ability to enter relations with other states.[15] Second, the system is founded on the principle of noninterference, which allows states wide latitude in deciding for themselves their relations to foreign actors.[16] The only way norms against interference can be suspended is if states delegate powers, explicitly permit oversight and intervention (e.g., via treaties establishing monitoring schemes, or conditionality), or, in some cases, breach international law. Third, the system provides a background for extensive interdependence, mainly, though not exclusively, via treaty law (which enables, for example, the possibility of regulated trade and financial flows).

The system of states therefore seeks to provide a background for three essential goods: internal control, noninterference, and interdependence. But the existence of a system of states also exposes states and their citizens to three bads. First, sovereignty limits accountability (since states can always claim, behind the veil of sovereignty, "this is none of your business"). Second, interdependence creates vulnerability (especially in view of the extreme inequality in power among different states). And, third, the system envisages the possibility of (legitimate) wars between its constituent states.

These aspects of the international system conspire to make individuals vulnerable to foreseeable violations of their status as moral equals. We know, for example, that norms of noninterference make it possible for tyrants to promote cruelty with impunity and make it difficult for citizens to resist it. This possibility is further heightened by international norms such as the borrowing and resource privileges, which create incentives for smaller, organized groups to stage coups and then seek to maintain power through force and repression. We also know that wars, even legitimate wars, make innocents vulnerable to cruelty at the hands of occupying powers and warring parties (e.g., through rape, torture, and collective reprisals).[17] Border controls, furthermore, put those who struggle to flee from persecution, severe poverty, internal displacement, and war at severe disadvantages as they try to enter safe third countries. These disadvantages expose such migrants and refugees to violations of their status as moral equals, including severe exploitation, death, and starvation, whether at the hands of smugglers and traffickers or the states that try to turn them away.[18] And, finally, we know that the system of bargaining that supports, for example, trade deals serves to entrench patterns of poverty and underdevelopment that make it harder to meet individuals' subsistence needs.[19]

The second argument takes advantage of these facts to argue that, through our participation in the system, millions are made foreseeably and avoidably worse off than they otherwise would have been. The system of states therefore objectionably *harms*. We thus have *negative* duties to ameliorate the threats rather than merely positive duties to rescue.[20] All else equal, these duties are much more stringent than their positive counterparts: it is one thing, for example, not to save someone whom you could save at some cost to yourself, and quite another if you have deliberately, recklessly, or negligently put them in that position yourself. On this view, we therefore have stringent duties to mitigate the worst features of the international system, and, in our more specific case, to mitigate the threats to individuals' equal moral status issuing from war, economic and political interdependence, border controls, external unaccountability, and the borrowing and resource privileges.

The challenge this type of argument faces is to identify the baseline against which to make judgments of harm. When we say that millions are foreseeably worse off than *they would have otherwise been,* do we mean to compare their situation to how well off they would have been in the *absence of the state system?* But how do we identify how well off anyone would have been had the state system never developed? Would we imagine the counterfactual situation in which feudal suzerainty had continued? Or the system of Renaissance city-states? These seem like impossible counterfactuals to assess in any kind of determinate way. To assess them, we would have to turn the clock back to, say, the sixteenth century and then imagine how well off everyone would be now had the state system not emerged at all. There are obvious nonidentity problems: would we even exist? But even more seriously, it seems impossible to know what other causal circumstances to hold constant once we remove the state system from the horizon of history.

A state-of-nature baseline is a more plausible one to choose for two reasons. First, we have some sense of how bad a state of nature would be by looking at various situations across time and in various places that have approximated the condition (we might think of life in failed states, for example). Second, the state-of-nature baseline has a more intuitive match to our guiding question. When we ask how well off we would have been in the *absence* of the state system, we are not asking how well off we would have been *under some alternative system.* The latter question has most plausibility when we are considering forward-looking choices among feasible institutional schemes, which is not what we are doing here.

The trouble with a state-of-nature baseline is another one. Given how bad every state-of-nature-like situation we have known is, it looks difficult to argue that those most adversely affected by the state system would be any better off in its absence. This might be true of the most *extreme* violations of our status as moral equals, but not every violation will make people worse off than they would have been in the state of nature.[21] Indeed, it seems most plausible to argue that, on average, the state system provides massive benefits with respect to any state of nature with which we have ever been acquainted.

By far the most plausible baseline to use is, therefore, a *moralized* baseline.[22] According to this baseline, we ask to what degree the international order causally contributes to foreseeable and avoidable violations of equal moral status. If it does, then we can conclude that the international order harms those whose rights have been violated since it causes them to be worse off than they *should* be from a moral point of view, i.e., worse off than they would have been in a world in which their rights weren't violated. According to this argument, everyone who participates in the system therefore has a stringent duty to compensate victims of human rights violations that are a direct result of its operation. The greater one's participation, the greater the stringency and demandingness of this duty.

If, in turn, ILHRs provide an effective way of ameliorating each of the threats mentioned above at the international level, then we can argue that such a system provides one among many ways of providing the needed compensation. This looks plausible. When well-functioning ILHRs serve to make states accountable to their publics (e.g., by providing a global platform for social and political protests and by communicating information regarding the extent and nature of violations), to generate incentives for compliance (e.g., by naming and shaming, and the consequent impact on diplomatic, political, economic cooperation), to limit the capacity of states to expose migrants to death and starvation (e.g., through non-*refoulement* provisions and the power of global public opinion), to open a space for publics in weaker states to contest the exercise of coercive force by stronger ones in international negotiations, to secure the rights of noncombatants,[23] and so on. Of course, at the moment the ILHR system is quite weak and its capacity to do all of these things is limited. But, though the claim is controversial, the empirical evidence supports the view that ILHRs serve to promote each of these purposes rather than set them back, and that there is plenty of scope for improvement without jettisoning the entire project.[24]

At first glance, this looks like a powerful argument. There is, however, a problem with the view that should push us to look for alternatives. In the view just outlined, we ask to what extent the state system (and each of its participants) *causally contributes* to violations of equal moral status.[25] But what counts as a causal contribution? To answer this further question, we must ascertain the degree to which the state system (and each participant within it) *increases* the number of violations. But "increases" relative to what baseline? Note that, unlike the concept of harm, it would be implausible to use a moralized baseline to answer this further question. If we used a moralized baseline, an agent would count as causally responsible for a violation just in case there were feasible alternatives available in which such violations would not occur. This view of causation, however, would collapse the distinction between positive and negative duties on which the argument relies. To illustrate: If the availability of a feasible alternative scheme in which there are fewer violations is sufficient to make one causally responsible for all the violations one would fail to prevent by not selecting it, then there would be no causal (and hence, on this view, ultimately moral) difference between our pushing a baby into a pond and our failing to save it. In both cases, I would have foreseeably and avoidably caused the death of the infant and therefore been morally responsible for harming it. If we adopted this view of causation, then there would be no real difference between the second argument and the first.

To be successful, the argument must therefore use a *nonmoralized* baseline to determine by how much the state system—and *a fortiori* each of its participants—increases the number of violations and, indeed, whether it increases the number of violations at all. But which one to use? The subjunctive historical baseline in which the state system never emerged? A state-of-nature baseline? Either of these alternatives would generate exactly the same problems we noted above, but now with respect to determining the causal effects rather than the degree of harm. I conclude that we do better to look for alternatives.

Are there any alternatives that can preserve the force of the second argument as an alternative to the first? What we need is an argument that generates duties that are as stringent and demanding as (if not more stringent and demanding than) the second argument, but that can avoid making causal assessments of exactly how much each agent within the international order has contributed to violations of equal moral status. To bring out this argument, I begin by distinguishing three scenarios:

Scenario 1. You are on a climbing expedition on Everest. On your way up the mountain, you notice that a climber (whom you've never seen before) has been submerged by a rock slide. You can help, but it will be somewhat dangerous.

Scenario 2. You are on a climbing expedition on Everest. On your way up, you are not careful and you provoke a rock slide. You notice that you have submerged a climber (whom you've never seen before) who is climbing below you. You can help, but it will be somewhat dangerous.

Scenario 3. You are part of a climbing expedition on Everest composed of you and another climber. The two of you are on your way up Everest together, dividing tasks, sharing labor and provisions. There is a rock slide that buries the other climber. You can help, but it will be somewhat dangerous.

Your duty to help in Scenario 1 strikes me as the weakest of the three (and equivalent to our first argument). Scenario 2 is just like our second argument. Notice that because the causal relations are clearer, it is plausible to argue that you are in fact harming the other climber should you walk away. You therefore have a duty to rectify the injury that you have negligently caused by helping the other climber. Scenario 3 is the interesting one. Here I believe your duty is as stringent and as demanding as it was in Scenario 2. But why? Notice, for example, that there is no sense in which you have *caused* the rock slide. The scenario is thus structurally very different from Scenario 2. There is thus no question of rectification or compensation, and so no question of determining one's degree of causal or moral responsibility for the rock slide. And yet we feel that one's duty is much more stringent and demanding than in Scenario 1. The situation, we might say, *strengthens* the preexisting duty to aid that we had in Scenario 1.

I want to suggest that your duty to aid the other climber is a duty to provide a fair return; it is a duty of *reciprocity.* If you were to walk away, the other climber could rightly complain: "I've made it possible for you to get this far and now you abandon me." And, if you walk away because you stand to benefit in some way—suppose that if you help you won't be able to receive the large pay-out that comes with making the summit—then it will become true that you have also exploited him. You have taken unfair advantage of him as a climbing companion in order to get the money. I will refer to the duty that explains our commitment to the other climber as the Duty of Reciprocal Protection.[26] Absent countervailing conditions, we owe others in a joint endeavor a fair return for their participation captured (in part) by indemnifying them against foreseeable losses that are a result of participation in the joint scheme. The basis for this demand is a cost-sharing principle: we have an obligation not only to share the benefits but also to share the costs involved in producing those benefits, especially in cases where the costs are very high and the benefits important (or morally mandatory).

The duty, even in this rough form, is robust to a number of variations that will become relevant as we try to extend it to the international sphere. First, the duty binds those whose participation is nonvoluntary.[27] Suppose someone has no choice but to climb the mountain with you—this is his only chance to get food. In that case, it strikes me that he would still owe you a Duty of Reciprocal Protection when the rock slide submerges you. The duty even holds in conditions of legitimate coercion. There are several people who are stranded higher up, and you need his help over several days to save them. But, though he sees that there is no real danger in helping them, and though he sees he could do much good, he is tired and weary and refuses. So you coerce him by, say, threatening to burn his tent should he not join the rescue party. Now imagine that, on the way back down (after you have together saved the stranded climbers), there is a rock slide under which you have been trapped. It strikes me as uncontroversial that he has just as much a duty, all else equal, to help you as you did to help the other climber in Scenario 2. You have helped him to accomplish a morally mandatory task for which coercing him was (we assume) justified, all things considered.[28]

Second, the duty is robust to variations in contribution. Suppose the other climber has very limited abilities to climb and is not very strong, and you are both very strong and able. As a result, your and the other climber's contributions to the joint effort will be very unequal. Your contributions far outweigh the meager contribution of the other climber. It seems clear that the duties to aid in the case of the rock slide are just as stringent and demanding in both directions. But why? In situations like this, we do not compare the *absolute* contribution of each party; rather, we ask if each side has done enough judged in terms of their *fair share*. And we scale what counts as a fair share in terms of the *ability to contribute* of the parties involved. If the other climber has participated in the joint effort to the degree that they could, given the restrictions on their ability and strength, then we say they are entitled to equality of concern under the Duty of Reciprocal Protection. For you to insist on more, we say, would be unreasonably grasping. The only case in which we would say that it is reasonable to scale back what you offer in return is if the other climber is shirking (and hence exploiting your goodwill). And even there, we may give the benefit of the doubt. We may wonder whether they have done *enough,* especially if the risks that have materialized are very grave (as in the rock slide).

Of course, what will be appropriate under norms of reciprocity will vary according to the types of joint effort at stake and the relations among the participants. It will also vary by conventional background assumptions that govern the particular context of mutual cooperation. For example, some contexts will be more explicitly competitive, as in games, or governed by prior contracts, as in markets.[29] These background features will vary what counts as a fair share and a fair return (including how much indemnity other parties are owed in circumstances of loss). But where the joint endeavor is undertaken to overcome some significant adversity that all face (e.g., climbing a mountain), or where the joint endeavor is morally mandatory (e.g., the rescue), the governing norms of reciprocity will be of the kind just mentioned, where we scale what counts as a fair share according to one's ability to contribute. In other work, I have tried to establish further grounds for the principle of reciprocity on which the Principle of Reciprocal Protection rests, to explain what counts as a fair return given different background circumstances, and to suggest the special sense in which norms of reciprocity governing the joint overcoming of significant adversity are norms of solidarity.[30] But for now, I hope I have said enough to establish that in situations of this kind, we have more stringent and demanding duties to protect when compared to situations in which we are not joint participants in a cooperative project.

THE DUTY OF RECIPROCAL PROTECTION AND
INTERNATIONAL LEGAL HUMAN RIGHTS

We have now said enough to motivate the extension of the Duty of Reciprocal Protection to the international sphere, and, in particular, to explain why even relatively rights-respecting states, such as Britain, have a duty to establish and maintain a system of ILHRs.

The principle of extension departs from a conception of the state system, and the overarching framework of international law which regulates it, as a cooperative system. By cooperative, I mean that it is a joint endeavor sustained by the mutual support of its main constituents, namely states. In mutually recognizing one another and in governing their interaction under mutually accepted norms and rules, states create the international order. As we have seen, the point and purpose of the order is, at its most basic, to provide three goods: noninterference, the possibility of mutually advantageous cooperation, and internal control. All states participate in this order and therefore aid in its reproduction, and so aid in realizing each of these goods.

Participation in the international system is, furthermore, morally mandatory. Given the existence of states and the danger that their very existence poses to other states, states have a morally mandatory duty to seek an institutional framework to regulate their interaction. Without such a framework, each state cannot provide other states with assurance; without such assurance, it becomes morally permissible for states to protect themselves by engaging in preemptive and preventive strikes against other states that are seen as potential aggressors. And if one of the primary moral duties of a government to its own citizens is to procure their safety, then, in view of the likelihood of widespread wars and the difficulties states would face in ending them, states must create an international order guaranteeing their mutual existence and the possibility of mutual cooperation. Were a government to refuse to enter into some system of international law to regulate the interaction of its people with other states, it would be violating a duty to protect its own citizens from the ensuing chaos. States, in short, have a moral duty to exit the international state of nature.[31]

The state system, however, also produces a number of central bads as by-products.[32] As we have seen, the international system decreases the accountability of governments, thus making it more likely for them to violate the rights of their citizens with impunity; it gives governments borrowing and resource privileges, which increase the likelihood of violent coups and subsequent repression; it allows governments to secure their borders by force, which exposes refugees, asylum seekers, and economic migrants to exploitation and cruelty at the hands of smug-glers, traffickers, and border guards; it permits wide inequalities of power to operate at the international level, which can often lead to the entrench-ment of severe poverty and underdevelopment in weaker states; and it envisages the possibility of war, and therefore the near certainty that in-nocents will be subject to widespread violations of fundamental rights to equal moral status.

These bads are the known risks that go along with joint cooperation within the system of states. Under the Duty of Reciprocal Protection, we thus owe other states who participate in the system a fair return captured (in part) by indemnifying them against losses that are a foreseeable result of their cooperation. In the international case, there-fore, each state must be prepared to aid every other state against the foreseeable losses that go along with joint cooperation in the state system. Each state, that is, must be prepared to indemnify every other state against (at least) each of the losses associated with the risks just mentioned. Notice that, on this model, we don't need to know to what extent the state system as whole or particular governments or other actors are ultimately causally (or morally) responsible for the losses, and hence whether they count as having caused harm. All we need to know is that these losses (like rock slides on climbing trips) are a foreseeable consequence of international cooperation within a system of states from which all participants benefit and to which they contribute.

So far, I have been speaking about states and governments without distinguishing them. But it should be obvious that we need to. I have said that each *state* has a duty to indemnify every other *state* against the foreseeable bads identified above. But the bads include violations of equal moral status that are perpetrated by governments against their people. So if the government and the state were the same thing, the Duty of Reciprocal Protection would generate a duty to aid governments against themselves, and so lead us into a kind of practical contradiction (heightened by the fact that these are the very governments that will be insisting on a respect for their exercise of sovereignty). The solution to this apparent paradox is to distinguish the state from the government. The government both claims to represent and bring into being the "person" of the state as a collective actor, as Hobbes would say.[33] The state, therefore, is what we would today call the "people," not understood as a prepolitical body like the "nation," but as a politically generated collective that the government claims to represent and hence to act "on behalf of" or "in the name of." The government is then the agent of the people, its outward face. Once we draw this distinction, we can see that it is possible for the government to fail in representing the people (here we depart from Hobbes). Rather than to act on its behalf, it can begin to act against it. In those cases, there is a division between a government and the people. If we further assume that any legitimate government must act to protect (at the very least) the rights to equal moral status of its people, then we can say that a government that systematically violates those rights fails to act in the name of the state *qua* people. In those cases, it has lost legitimacy and hence the right to say to outsiders "this is none of your business."[34]

Seeing things in this way affects the sense in which the state system is rightly perceived to be cooperative. Consider: To *whom* do we owe a fair return for the protections afforded by an international order that recognizes our internal autonomy and right to noninterference, and that provides a background framework for economic, social, cultural, and political exchange and cooperation? My suggestion is that we owe the fair return to peoples, and to governments only derivatively, namely only as and when they successfully represent them. The reason is straightforward. If the constitutive aim of a government is to rule on behalf of and in the name of the people, and it is the people who ultimately provide the government with the resources to govern in their name (via taxation, labor, compliance, and so on), then it becomes clear that it is to the people, and not the government (or at any rate the government only derivatively), that we owe a fair return.

With this picture in place, we can return to the ILHR system. In the context of the goods and foreseeable risks just canvassed, the Duty of Reciprocal Protection mandates some mechanism for protecting peoples against their governments, should those governments attack their rights to equal moral status, and hence subject them to cruelty. (Recall that I here leave aside whether the duty also mandates more extensive protections; our focus is on equal moral status.) If the empirical evidence on behalf of the effectiveness of the ILHR system to which I adverted above is correct, and if there are no alternative feasible institutional schemes in the foreseeable future that could do better, then the Duty of Reciprocal Protection mandates our participation and support for ILHRs. There are, of course, a number of corollary duties, among which is a duty to improve the effectiveness of the system; to ensure that international negotiations do not entrench severe poverty and underdevelopment; to protect asylum seekers, refugees, and economic migrants from social cruelty; and so on. But it is enough for now if we have established a case for why the creation and preservation of an ILHR system is not just an act of beneficence but a morally mandatory duty. When, say, the British or the Americans want to diminish their exposure to the ILHR system (e.g., by withdrawing from the ECHR), we can say that they owe it to the Ukrainians, Russians, Romanians, Liberians, and so on, to stay in. It is only because of the support and contributions of all these other peoples to the international order that the British and the Americans are so well off. To undermine the system by withdrawing or by hollowing out their commitment via reservations is to leave those others stranded.

LOOKING AHEAD

In this chapter, I have sought to do three things. First, I began by suggesting that an accurate understanding of our commitment to equal moral status is necessary to make sense of some of the most central moral rights underlying the ILHR system (such as rights against discrimination). Second, I have argued that at the heart of every ILHR lies a moral right; even though there need not be a correspondence between the object of the moral and the legal right, the legal right must ultimately be justified in terms of an underlying moral right. The moral right serves as what we might call the "moral compass" of the corresponding ILHR. While the Mirroring View is rightly rejected by Buchanan, the Grounding View cannot be. Third, I have sought to explain why the creation and preservation of an ILHR system is morally mandatory for states, given the nature of their cooperation at an international level. Chapter 6 will show how the moral rights constitutive of equal moral status that we have discussed in Chapters 2, 3, and 5 are in fact *fundamental* rights that deserve, as a result, both priority in our moral reflection and special protection within the ILHR system.

6

FUNDAMENTAL RIGHTS, INDIVISIBILITY, AND HIERARCHY AMONG HUMAN RIGHTS

WHAT MAKES A MORAL right *fundamental?* Henry Shue has done the most to identify a strategy for distinguishing fundamental from non-fundamental moral rights.[1] In this chapter, I remind the reader of his definition of a basic right, argue for several key revisions, and then use the revised criterion to demonstrate that the rights constitutive of our equal moral status are, in fact, fundamental in the specified sense. I will then argue that fundamental rights—and so the rights constitutive of our equal moral status—are the moral heart of the super-norms of international law, namely *jus cogens, erga omnes,* and rights nonderogable in states of emergency.

BASIC RIGHTS

For Shue, a moral right is *basic* just in case its enjoyment is necessary for the enjoyment of any other right.[2] But what does it mean to *enjoy* a right? For Shue, one enjoys a right when the right is *socially guaranteed.* Socially guaranteeing a right requires others not only to respect the right, but also to aid and protect individuals against standard threats to the enjoyment of the object of the right. But what does it mean for the enjoyment of one right to be *necessary* for the enjoyment of another? There are two different types of necessity that Shue invokes but that are not clearly distinguished. The two different types I have in mind are *conceptual* and *empirical.*

Sometimes Shue seems to have in mind a kind of *conceptual* necessity. Referring to the connection between the socially guaranteed enjoyment of a right to physical security and the socially guaranteed enjoyment of a right to free assembly, he writes that physical security is an "inherent necessity" or "essential element" of the right to free assembly: "Being secure is an essential component of enjoying a right of assembly, so that *there is no such thing* as a situation in which people do have social guarantees for assembly and do not have social guarantees for security."[3] If one doesn't enjoy physical security, then one cannot be said to be *really* free to assemble. The necessity is conceptual because, on this reading, enjoying what we might call *genuine* or *fully effective* freedom of assembly conceptually entails that one also enjoy physical security. Enjoying physical security is just part of what it *means* to enjoy genuine freedom of assembly.

But this seems false as a conceptual claim. Suppose, for example, that women in some society are subject to domestic violence, but the domestic violence is never directed at preventing women from assembling in public. Suppose furthermore that the society does nothing to criminalize domestic violence (either because they don't enforce laws on the books against it or because there are no such laws), and that women quite frequently assemble in public for all kinds of purposes (indeed, this is often a way of getting away from abuse in the home). In this case, it looks as if women do not enjoy a socially guaranteed right to physical security but they do enjoy a socially guaranteed right to assemble in public. In response, a defender of the conceptual reading might say that this just shows that there is no basic right against domestic violence, or that a right against domestic violence is not in fact part of the basic right to physical security. But this strikes me as implausible: if physical security is a basic right, then surely the right against physical abuse in the home is.

We can generalize the result. Because the claim is a conceptual one, all that is needed to falsify it is to imagine cases in which one does not enjoy socially guaranteed physical security or subsistence, but where it is *conceivable* to enjoy any other socially guaranteed nonbasic right or combination of such rights (rights to assembly, fair trial, free expression, and so on). Consider subsistence rights. We can *imagine* societies that do not socially guarantee basic sanitation, shelter, or food, and where most people do not enjoy access to any of those things, but where people still enjoy socially guaranteed freedoms to assemble, participate publicly, express themselves freely, and so on, and still assemble, express themselves, and so on, to the same extent they would have done had subsistence been socially guaranteed. Such people might just be very resilient, or not care about or need food, shelter, and sanitation, and so the lack of each of these things would have no effect on their ability (or desire) to do each of those things. This is *empirically* unlikely, but that is not germane to the point here, which is that there is nothing *conceptually entailed* in the concept of enjoying a socially guaranteed right to free assembly, free expression, and so on, regarding whether one has a roof over one's head, enough food to eat, or access to basic sanitation, or whether the society in which one lives socially guarantees each of those things.

The claim, to be plausible, must be another one. I propose that the best way of construing Shue's position is in terms of an *empirical* relation between one right (or set of rights) and another. On this view, Shue means that the socially guaranteed enjoyment of subsistence and physical security rights is *empirically necessary* for the socially guaranteed enjoyment of other rights. What does it mean for something to be *empirically* (rather than conceptually) necessary? I will assume for the sake of argument that the most plausible understanding of empirical necessity in this context is the following: if it is highly unlikely, given the world as we know it, that one set of rights will be either socially guaranteed or enjoyed without socially guaranteeing the enjoyment of the other set, then the latter set is empirically necessary for the former, and hence basic. To illustrate: On this view, Shue would be asserting that if people do not enjoy socially guaranteed rights to physical security, then it will be highly unlikely for people to enjoy socially guaranteed rights to free assembly. The idea of necessity in this sense is loose and contextually sensitive, but adequate.

Even in this more plausible form, however, the claim needs further elaboration. Are we principally concerned with the enjoyment of the *object* of these rights (physical security, free assembly)? Or are we principally concerned with whether the objects are *socially guaranteed* (by law, for example)? We might think that, given the political context of the discussion, the claim must principally concern social guarantees. This would be under the plausible assumption that one's *robust* and *resilient* enjoyment of the object of a right will depend on whether or not the right (and so its object) is, for example, legally or socially enforced or implemented.[4]

But, even if we grant this assumption—even if we grant, that is, that socially guaranteeing the object of a right is necessary for the full enjoyment of the right—there is an important equivocation that must be resolved before we can proceed. It is one thing to affirm that

a. if a regime fails to provide socially guaranteed rights to physical security (or subsistence), then it will be highly unlikely that the regime will seek to provide a socially guaranteed right to freedom of assembly,

and another to affirm that

b. if a regime fails to provide socially guaranteed rights to physical security (or subsistence), then it will be highly unlikely for individuals to possess effective opportunities to assemble freely (whether or not the regime seeks to socially guarantee their right to assemble).

In the first case, we ask about the rights-violating character of various regimes. We wonder, for example, whether regimes that do not socially guarantee rights to physical security are also highly unlikely to socially guarantee rights to freedom of assembly. In the second, we ask whether a failure to socially guarantee the enjoyment of rights to physical security (or subsistence) makes it highly unlikely that individuals will have an effective opportunity to assemble freely (or to receive a fair trial, to participate politically, and so on). Which one ought we to be concerned with? It seems clear that Shue would answer *both*. Given our ultimate concern with the resilient and robust opportunity to enjoy the objects of our rights, we will want to know *both* the likelihood that regimes that fail to guarantee one set of rights will also fail to guarantee others *and* the likelihood that regimes that fail to guarantee one set of rights will likely undermine individuals' opportunity to enjoy the objects of other rights (whether or not the regime attempts to guarantee them). On this reading, physical security and subsistence rights are basic because (a) it is highly unlikely that any regime that fails to satisfy either will socially guarantee other rights, and (b) it is highly unlikely that individuals will have effective opportunities to enjoy the objects of those other rights (whether or not the regime attempts to socially guarantee them by legislation, for example).

This then provides a way of answering the objection directed at the conceptual reading. If women are systematically subject to domestic violence, and the regime officially and unofficially condones such violence, then it is highly unlikely that women's other rights will be guaranteed.[5] Women will very likely be subject to comprehensive restrictions on their freedom of movement, free expression, and religious liberty and have limited access to socially guaranteed welfare or fair trials. Similarly, if women are systematically subject to domestic violence and the society officially and unofficially condones such violence, then it will also be highly unlikely that women will have effective opportunities to assemble freely or express themselves publicly (whether or not the government attempts to socially guarantee those further rights). This is because women will be highly likely to be subject to intimidation and coercion upon attempting to exercise those freedoms, and, even in the absence of such specific threats, such violence will be highly likely to have a debilitating impact on women's sense of self, and so will be highly likely to impede their effective opportunity to enjoy those further rights. Similar things can be said with respect to subsistence. As Shue writes, "because the actual deprivation of [physical security or subsistence] can be so very serious—potentially incapacitating, crippling, or fatal—even the threatened deprivation of either can be a powerful weapon against anyone whose security or subsistence is not in fact socially guaranteed."[6]

So far, I have argued that Shue's account of the basic-ness of a right rests on (a) empirical judgments regarding the high likelihood that violations of physical security and subsistence rights will also be associated with violations of all other rights, and on (b) the high likelihood that violations of physical security and subsistence rights will have an impact on individuals' effective opportunity to enjoy *every* other right. But even this amendment looks implausible, since there will be at least *some* rights whose enjoyment may not be strongly correlated with the violation of rights to security and subsistence. One might, for example, fully enjoy a right not to be arbitrarily deprived of one's nationality in many regimes where one's physical security and subsistence rights are not socially guaranteed. To cope with this problem, I suggest a further amendment to Shue's account. Instead of requiring that basic rights are those rights whose enjoyment, when socially guaranteed, is empirically necessary for the enjoyment of *all* other social, political, cultural, and economic rights, we should substitute "most other rights." What this amendment loses in neatness or elegance, it gains in plausibility.

I now want to suggest that there is another, related concept of basic-ness that looks less at the empirical correlations among social guarantees and more at the structure of value underlying such judgments. With these two concepts of basic-ness in hand, I will then return to the anti-discrimination norms discussed in Chapter 3.

FUNDAMENTAL RIGHTS

Consider the causal mechanisms by which lack of physical security and subsistence have an impact on one's effective opportunities to enjoy other rights. One route is by making it physically impossible for one to do so. For example, if the government kills all who attempt to participate in a public protest, then it will be true to say that these people do not have the effective opportunity to carry out the protest. Similarly, if one is starving, then one will not have the strength (even if one has the will) to, say, assemble in public. But this is not the predominant way in which effective opportunities to enjoy other rights are diminished. The predominant way is via the chilling effect that *fear* has on individuals' exercise of their liberties.[7] If individuals fear being beaten, raped, starved, or killed, they will be very unlikely to engage in any of the activities that would expose them in these ways; it will then be correct to say that they lack, because of these fears, effective opportunities to fully enjoy most of their political, economic, cultural, and civil liberties.

But why does fear of deprivation matter morally? Of course, in part it matters because of its chilling effect on our effective opportunities to enjoy things such as assembling in public, expressing ourselves freely, participating politically, and so on. But why do each of those further things matter morally? What I want to suggest is that, ultimately, fear of deprivation matters because of the particular way it impacts our interests, and hence our capacity to flourish. Recall what I referred to, in Chapter 2, as the most important goods in a human life, things like love, pleasure, the raising of a family, friendship, knowledge, and accomplishment and skill. Fear of deprivation matters morally, then, not simply because it makes it less likely that we will be able to enjoy economic, civil, political, and cultural liberties. It matters, more fundamentally, because it impinges not just on any one of our important interests, but on most of them at once. A life lived in constant fear of deprivation is a life that lacks one of the structural conditions for living a flourishing life. Put most directly and plainly, constant fear of deprivation—whether deprivation of basic physical security or subsistence—makes it very difficult to focus on anything other than the fear.[8]

A right is *fundamental,* then, just in case it protects interests that are structural aspects of a flourishing life. An interest is a *structural* aspect of a flourishing life when setting it back (by, for example, violating the rights that are meant to protect it) pervasively undermines the pursuit of most of our other interests, and most significantly, our interests in the most important goods. (From now on, when I refer to Shue's concept, I will use the term "basic" right; when I refer to my own, I will use the term "fundamental.") On this account, for example, a failure to socially guarantee our physical security or subsistence sets back our structural interests not only in life itself but also in a life free from the constant fear of deprivation; as we have seen, those interests are structural because of their role in the pursuit of the most important goods. We can therefore determine whether a right is fundamental in my sense without measuring whether its abrogation will have an effect either on the likelihood that other rights will be socially guaranteed or on our opportunities to enjoy those other rights. The focus is directly on how the violation affects our structural interests in the most important goods, rather than, more narrowly, on how the violation affects the social protection or enjoyment of other social, political, cultural, or economic rights. This is one of the key differences from Shue's concept of basic-ness. At the same time, however, it is of course true that basic-ness and fundamentality will often go hand-in-hand: if the failure to socially guarantee a right diminishes one's opportunity to enjoy most other rights, or makes their protection less likely, then this failure will most likely also set back our structural interests (and vice versa).

Focusing on whether a right is fundamental rather than basic has two further advantages. First, it allows us to reflect more carefully on *how* violations of rights have an impact on other rights. We can see this by returning to physical security, subsistence, and the constant fear of deprivation. Consider, for example, *under what conditions* rights to physical security and subsistence are most often violated. It is very unusual for rights to physical security to be violated by widespread random violence, or rights to subsistence to be violated because of mere oversight.[9] Most often, rights to physical security and subsistence are violated in conditions where individuals are *targeted,* whether at the hands of other individuals or groups or at the hands of governments. Consider further the *social context* against which individuals are targeted. Most often, they are targeted because they are of the wrong race, ethnic group, political party, or religion, or because they are too poor to matter. (Think, for example, of ethnic conflict in, say, Darfur; or starvation as a political tactic in Ukraine under Stalin; or first-world agricultural subsidies and their effects on developing countries.) Or, if physical security is undermined by widespread criminality, this is often because governments fail to protect individuals in those neighborhoods. Once again, this often happens as a result of either discrimination, negligence, or indifference. (Think, for example, of townships in South Africa, or slums in Brazil, or Sen's "missing women."[10]) In each of these cases, then, individuals do not suffer fear of deprivation simply as a result of wrong-headed policies whose effects were not foreseen or foreseeable; they suffer it as a result of who they are, what they believe, or what their status is in that society. Deprivation thus has an ineliminable *social* dimension, setting back our interests not only in being free from the constant fear of material and physical deprivation but also our central interests in being recognized by the societies of which we are a part. Such deprivations therefore attack another structural aspect of a flourishing life, namely our capacity to maintain and develop an integral sense of self in a wider society of others. They are more often than not instances of inferiorizing social cruelty, and hence violations of our status as moral equals.

This predominantly social aspect of deprivation was overlooked by Shue; no doubt this is because he operated under the assumption that the basic-ness of a right turned on whether it made it *physically* or *conceptually* impossible for individuals to enjoy other rights. But if our critique of Shue is correct, then his emphasis was far too narrow. This allows us to return to rights against discrimination. It is revealing that Shue doesn't mention rights against discrimination at all in *Basic Rights*—despite the centrality of such rights in the international system of legal human rights. This was, I believe, a mistake: rights to discrimination can be both *fundamental* and *basic* in the senses just outlined. As we have seen in Chapter 3, they are essential to the protection of our structural interests in developing and maintaining an integral sense of self. As we have also seen, the effects of the social cruelty intrinsic to widespread and systematic discrimination ramify throughout a person's life, thereby significantly setting back one's interests in enjoyment of the most important goods. Furthermore, regimes that fail to socially guarantee rights against discrimination are highly likely to fail to guarantee most other rights (think of the American South in the 1940s and 1950s, for example). Affected individuals in societies that fail to socially guarantee rights against discrimination will also be highly unlikely to have effective opportunities to enjoy most other civil, political, social, and cultural rights (whether or not the government tries to socially guarantee them—again think of the American South in the late 1960s). Such rights are therefore also *basic*.

This brings us to the second advantage of the account offered here. To see it, we ask the following question: When we say that rights against discrimination (or rights to physical security or subsistence) are fundamental, does that imply that all *violations* of discrimination, security, or subsistence rights are also fundamental? No. Rights are violated when the duties correlated with them are violated. But both the correlated duties, and the ways of violating them, are diverse and shifting with background circumstances.[11] Let us suppose that a government has a duty to provide us with protection against fires, and that this duty flows from our rights to physical security. And let us imagine that this duty is violated when the state closes down a number of fire departments; there is now evident underprovision of fire protection. In this case, *ex hypothesi,* we have reasonable grounds to complain. But the government otherwise protects every other aspect of our right to physical security and hence every other correlated duty. In this case, it strikes me as implausible to argue that this violation is fundamental, or part of a pattern of violations that are fundamental, since the closing of the fire stations does not ramify across all our interests, either by killing us, causing constant fear, or by attacking the integrity of our sense of self. Other violations of the right to physical security, on the other hand, do ramify in those ways. When violations do ramify, then we can rightly say that the violation was fundamental. It is therefore misleading to speak (as we have been doing thus far) in terms of moral and legal human or constitutional rights (such as the right to free assembly), or sets of such rights, as fundamental or basic. It is particular rights *violations* and patterns of rights violations that are fundamental, not the rights themselves.

The same kind of analysis applies to the violation of all international legal human rights (ILHRs), moral human rights, and constitutional rights. Violations of such rights will only be fundamental when they significantly impinge on our structural interests. The cases we have discussed above, including the cases of sexual harassment and racism in the American South, are structurally significant.[12] Others will not be. This is not to say, of course, that nonfundamental rights violations are not important. It just means that such violations are not fundamental in the sense I described.

If this analysis is correct, it becomes clear that it is misleading to focus, as Shue's framework urges us to do, on groups of classical political, civil, economic, and cultural liberties, such as the right of free assembly or even rights to physical security. If we are interested in identifying fundamental rights, we should focus primarily on rights *violations* or patterns of rights violations, tracking those that significantly impinge on our deepest, structural interests, such as the three central interests we identified in Chapter 2, or our interests in a life free of the constant fear of deprivation.[13] We need not, however, entirely revise our usage, which would be cumbersome and awkward. Instead, we can just be clear that when we add *basic* or *fundamental* as a modifier for a more general right, as when we speak of fundamental rights to physical security, we are not saying that all violations of the more general right to physical security are fundamental, just that some are. The modifier then picks out those aspects of the right that are fundamental or basic in the required sense.

Once we put things in this way, it suggests a more radical revision of Shue's framework. Once we allow for the modifier *basic* or *fundamental* to pick out an aspect of a right rather than the whole right (and hence all of its correlated duties), then why try to parse classic ILHRs or constitutional rights into two categories, namely those that are basic or fundamental and those that are not? Why not simply allow for violations of *any* classical liberty or human right to be fundamental or basic depending on the character of the violation? We return to this question in the next section.

I have thus far spoken of fundamental and basic rights (or rights violations) as opposed to nonfundamental and nonbasic rights as if the distinction was binary. But this is obviously false. Once we begin focusing on how likely it is for one type of rights violation to have impacts on other rights and other interests, then it should be clear that the degree and character of these impacts varies along a continuum. So we really ought to speak of more and less fundamental or basic rights violations, with clearly fundamental instances on one side of the continuum and clearly nonfundamental instances on the other; in the middle, rights violations will vary in their degree of fundamentality according to how far they are from the clear cases. This does not, however, imply that it is never useful to revert to a binary distinction with a distinct threshold. But its usefulness must be evaluated by the role it plays in the particular discourse we are interested in. For example, as we will see in the next section, speaking of a rights violation as being *either* fundamental *or* nonfundamental can be very useful in the context of the law, where we need to fix certain definite categories of remedy to particular types of violations. The threshold chosen will, in many of those cases, be more or less arbitrary, given the fluidity of the underlying notion, but this vagueness in the borderline of the concept shouldn't bother us any more than, say, age limits for any number of rights and privileges does (voting, driving, drinking, etc.).

INDIVISIBILITY AND HIERARCHY AMONG HUMAN RIGHTS

So far I have argued for a novel conception of what makes a right (or aspect of a right) fundamental. A right (or aspect of a right) is more or less fundamental according to the degree to which its violation structurally undermines the pursuit of all or most of our interests, and most significantly, our interests in the most important goods. In the conclusion of this chapter, I want to use this account to reflect on a controversy within debates on human rights, namely whether there is a hierarchy among human rights norms, and, if there is, how to characterize it. There has been very little philosophically written on the topic, so it is worth seeing whether the categories and theses we have been developing can be brought to bear on it.[14] This will also allow us to come full circle in our attempt to show that one of the central and most important aims of the international law of human rights is to protect our status as moral equals.

It is official UN doctrine that human rights are "indivisible." Already in 1968, the UN's Proclamation of Teheran stated: "Since human rights and fundamental freedoms are indivisible, the full realization of civil and political rights without the enjoyment of economic, social and cultural rights is impossible."[15] In a 1977 resolution, the UN General

Assembly endorsed indivisibility but dropped the important qualification about full realization.[16] And, finally, indivisibility was reaffirmed in the 1993 Vienna Declaration (without the qualification): "All human rights are universal, indivisible and interdependent and interrelated. The international community must treat human rights globally in a fair and equal manner, on the same footing, and with the same emphasis."[17] References to indivisibility are legion in documents issuing from the various UN human rights bodies.[18] The rhetorical aim of invoking indivisibility was evident: at a time when many saw social, economic, and cultural rights as the bastard second cousins of civil and political rights, indivisibility was meant to reinforce the significance and importance of the former (much along the lines of Shue's main thesis in *Basic Rights*). But, above and beyond the rhetoric, is the idea of indivisibility helpful, and, given some charitable interpretation of that idea, is it true?

The first interpretation of indivisibility is the following: all human rights (i.e., all human rights listed in at least the International Covenant on Civil and Political Rights [ICCPR] and the International Covenant on Economic, Social and Cultural Rights [ICESCR]) are equally basic in the sense I discussed above. This is a generalization and expansion of Shue's claim that only a subset of human rights are basic. The full, socially guaranteed enjoyment ("full realization") of any one right—say the right to assembly—requires the full, socially guaranteed enjoyment of all the others—say the right to health. On this reading, no citizen could fully enjoy a socially guaranteed right to assembly if she didn't also fully enjoy a socially guaranteed right to health. But this seems false. While of course one will need to have enough health to make use of the right to assembly, this doesn't require one to have access to a healthcare system. In response, one could simply build into the concept of the "full enjoyment" of any one right that one must fully enjoy every other, but that would win the argument by a mere conceptual fiat: What reason do we have to believe that the "full enjoyment" of any one right must conceptually include the "full enjoyment" of every other right? What would that add to the idea that all legal human rights ought to be realized? The claim, for example, would not exclude, when "full enjoyment" is not possible, giving priority to some rights over others. It would also not help us in identifying which rights should deserve such priority.

It would be more plausible to claim that socially guaranteeing the enjoyment or realization of any one human right (to whatever extent) can *contribute* to the enjoyment or realization of other rights. But determining *how much* the realization or enjoyment of one right will contribute to the realization or enjoyment of another will vary tremendously not only by cultural, political, legal, or social circumstances but also by right. Indivisibility, on the other hand, seems to affirm a binary rather than scalar claim; either a group of rights is indivisible or it is not. There are no degrees of indivisibility. Furthermore, on this reading, there is no sense in which the enjoyment or realization of one right is "necessary" to the realization or enjoyment of any other right; this interpretation therefore seems to abandon what makes a claim of indivisibility distinctive. Finally, and closely related, the interpretation fails to distinguish indivisibility from the claim that human rights are, as the Vienna Declaration puts it, "interdependent" or "interrelated." I therefore leave this interpretation to the side.

On a second reading, "indivisibility" implies that the full enjoyment of each human right is as (morally?) important as the full enjoyment of any other. There is no hierarchy among single human rights or groups of human rights. The realization of economic, cultural, and social rights (to some specified degree that is comparable across rights) is just as important as the realization of civil and political rights. But important for what, or in what sense? Perhaps the claim is that the different rights are just as important for human flourishing. But, again, this seems evidently false. As we have seen, some rights violations are much more comprehensively damaging than others. Why must we assume that a violation of any one human right is as bad as a violation of any other human right?

Is there a more plausible reading? Building on the account above, I want to suggest a reading that is avowedly creative, but that captures some of the spirit of the Vienna Declaration, and is, at least, more plausible than the first two. Indivisibility refers to the idea that we ought to resist the temptation to rank the classical groupings of human rights (such as civil and political rights) as more basic or fundamental than others (such as social and economic rights). But this does not imply, on this reading, that all rights are somehow equally important. The commitment is negative and implies only that violations within any one group of rights, whether cultural, economic, social, civil, or political, can be as grievous and as consequential for human flourishing as violations of rights in any of the others. It is also compatible with the idea that there are some core rights (within each group) that deserve special protection in international law. What matters is the context within such rights are violated, and how they are violated. Emphasizing the indivisibility of human rights, furthermore, can serve to remind us that often violations of human rights go together, and that a full analysis of any specific rights violation requires attention to co-occurring violations.

This less ambitious formulation also has another key advantage: its compatibility with an assertion of hierarchy among human rights norms, to which we now turn. A central question in international law is whether there is (and ought to be) a hierarchy among international legal norms analogous to the hierarchy within domestic legal systems between, say, constitutional norms and ordinary legislation. Are there (and ought there to be) norms within international law that are binding on all states (and other international actors); cannot be abrogated by other sources of international law, such as treaty law; and for which states can be held liable even if they are "persistent objectors"?[19] For such "super-norms," international jurists most often look to human rights law to provide a basis for three different types of norms: *jus cogens, erga omnes,* and rights nonderogable in times of emergency. Regarding *jus cogens* norms, jurists commonly cite Article 53 of the Vienna Convention on the Law of Treaties, which defines *jus cogens* as a norm of "general international law accepted and recognized by the international community of States as a whole as a norm from which no derogation is permitted and which can be modified only by a subsequent norm of general international law having the same character."[20] But there is great disagreement among jurists regarding which norms, exactly, have or should have this character. Should all human rights norms be considered *jus cogens?* Or only some core? How do we identify this core?[21]

Theodor Meron, for example, famously noted the distinction between fundamental or core human rights and nonfundamental ones in international human rights law, and also remarked on the former as a source for *jus cogens,* but bemoaned the lack of consensus on what makes a right fundamental.[22] More recently, in one of his last essays, which were meant to sum up a long and illustrious career as both judge and jurist, Antonio Cassese called for a renewed emphasis on the "existence of peremptory rules of international law *(jus cogens)* on human rights, which are at the summit of the international legal order and may not be derogated from by any state. Such rules are gradually constituting the constitutional principles of the world society." He then goes on to outline three avenues for providing more formal recognition of such norms in international law. He does not, however, say much about which rights should deserve this higher status, leaving it to "future practice."[23]

Regarding *erga omnes* norms, which are related but distinct from *jus cogens* norms, jurists commonly cite the International Court of Justice's (ICJ) *Barcelona Traction* decision (1970). The decision declared the existence of obligations which are

> the concern of all States. In view of the importance of the rights involved, all States can be held to have a legal interest in their protection; they are obligations *erga omnes.*
>
> §34. Such obligations derive, for example, in contemporary international law, from the outlawing of acts of aggression, and of genocide, as also from the principles and rules concerning the *basic* rights of the human person, including protection from slavery and racial discrimination.[24]

Erga omnes obligations were, for example, invoked in *Belgium v. Senegal* (2012) to justify bringing suit under the ICJ.[25] In that case, Belgium instituted proceedings on the grounds that Senegal had failed to prosecute the former president of Chad, Hissène Habré, for crimes against humanity and torture, and for failing to extradite him to Belgium to stand trial for those crimes. Belgium claimed to have a legal interest in the case because the obligations violated (torture, crimes against humanity) were *erga omnes.* But, again, jurists divide on which norms (in addition to crimes against humanity and torture) should count as *erga omnes*. It is clear that international jurists agree that there is a category of "basic" or "fundamental" or "core" rights that forms a subset of all legal human rights, but which ones are fundamental? As the International Law Commission's statement on these paragraphs explained: "In the Court's opinion, there are in fact a number, albeit a small one, of international obligations which, by reason of the importance of their subject-matter for the international community as a whole, are—unlike the others—obligations in whose fulfillment all States have a legal interest."[26] Once again, how are we to decide what class of rights is so important as to be a "subject-matter for the international community as a whole"?

And, finally, international jurists look to human rights treaties, such as the European Convention, the ICCPR, or the American Convention on Human Rights, for those rights that are declared to be nonderogable in states of emergency (including war).[27] Although these norms are treaty-based, many jurists believe their status as nonderogable flows from their special character rather than from their basis in treaty.[28] And here again we find the same disagreement, which is evident since each of those human rights treaties protects different rights as nonderogable.

My aim here is not to provide a legal argument that purports to establish which norms are currently recognized as *jus cogens, erga omnes,* or nonderogable in times of emergency. My aim is also not to identify how jurists or judges ought to go about identifying such norms as a matter of law. For example, I will not seek to identify how wide state practice must be to assert some such norm as legally binding, or what kind of *opinio juris* is required to affirm it.[29] Rather, my interest in these questions is in the kind of *moral* reasoning that ought to underlie our judgments in this area. What human rights norms *should* we, as a matter of morality, recognize as meriting a hierarchically superior status (whether as *jus cogens, erga omnes,* or as nonderogable in times of emergency)? This is the kind of reasoning that Dworkinians believe is silent prologue to any decision at law, and positivists believe is *not* (unless you have some legally sanctioned discretion to employ such reasoning). Here I need take no stand on this dispute in the philosophy of law: my argument is unabashedly moral rather than legal. I also note that my aim is not to provide an *all-things-considered* argument for which norms ought to be recognized as hierarchically superior in each of those ways. Such a judgment would require much more attention to the specific remedies, procedures, and venues available for invoking each of those norms. And, in the special case of nonderogable rights in times of emergency, it would require much more attention to the special nature of public emergencies. Rather, my aim is the much more modest one of individuating the type of moral reasoning that must—as a necessary but not sufficient condition—go into any (moral) assessment of hierarchy among human rights norms in international law. As we noted in Chapter 5, our aim is to find the moral compass that underlies judgments regarding *jus cogens, erga omnes,* and nonderogable norms.

Such an inquiry will also allow us to tie together the strands of the arguments pursued in Chapters 1 through 6. I began by wondering about the grounds of our commitment to moral equality. I then suggested that the concept of dignity in its three most influential forms could not provide this basis and argued in favor of what I called the Negative Conception. According to this approach, we ought to pay closer attention to our social practices of treating each other as moral equals, including the role that attitudes like respect play within them. I also claimed that the best way of characterizing such practices was to consider what is at stake in *denials* of moral equality, what it is to treat people as *inferiors* in the relevant sense. The wrongness of all instances of such treatment, I contended, can be explained by noting, *inter alia,* how they involve a special kind of cruelty, namely social cruelty. What makes such cruelty wrong is that it seeks to attack a structural ingredient of any flourishing life, namely our capacity to develop and maintain an integral sense of self in a community of others. In Chapter 3, this account was then used to provide an account of the moral wrongfulness of discrimination, which is one of the paradigmatic instances of treating another as inferior in the relevant sense.

I then turned to human rights. After rejecting the Single Practice Assumption along with the two predominant theories of human rights that endorse it, I agreed with Allen Buchanan that we ought to spend more time thinking about the moral bases of the system of international legal human rights. I proposed that we could do so by reflecting carefully about one of the constitutive aims of the international legal human rights system, namely the protection of our equal moral status. But why do we have an obligation to pursue that protection at an international level and to embody it in a system of public norms at that level? And, just as importantly, what does that protection involve?

Deploying the account of moral equality defended in Chapter 2, I established that we have a special obligation to pursue the protection of individuals against standard threats to our equal moral status at the international level because of the way we participate in and benefit from the state system. I then argued that, if one of the constitutive aims of the international system of legal human rights is to protect our equal moral status, and if that moral status is composed of rights against inferiorizing social cruelty, then one of the constitutive aims of international human rights must be, in turn, the prevention of inferiorizing social cruelty. With this account in hand, it became evident why anti-discrimination rights—which protect individuals from the inferiorizing social cruelty of stigmatization, dehumanization, infantilization, objectification, and instrumentalization—are rightly considered to be so important in the ILHR system.

With this summary, it should be clear how the account I have offered can be brought to bear on the question of hierarchy and indivisibility among human rights norms in the international legal system. We have established, first, that one of the constitutive aims of international human rights law is the prevention of the systematic and public social cruelty associated with the existence of the state system. Second, I have also established that public and systematic social cruelty attacks a structural element in our pursuit of the most important goods, namely our capacity to develop and maintain an integral sense of self. If, in turn, all violations of legal human rights that structurally undermine our ability to pursue the most important goods are *fundamental* violations, then this entails two conclusions. First, the protection of equal moral status is not just *an* aim but a *fundamental* aim of the international system. Second, any violation of a legal human right that counts as a public and systematic instance of inferiorizing social cruelty is therefore a *fundamental* violation, and hence merits special and higher consideration in international law.[30] The Negative Conception, in other words, can provide a basis for reflecting on which norms (or aspects of norms) should be treated as underpinning the law governing fundamental or "core" human rights once we abandon the search for dignity. Of course, any particular application requires the exercise of moral and political judgment and must take into account a variety of more contingent factors, but my hope is that the account can provide an interpretive compass for such judgments. If I am right, then it will be obvious why international human rights law should take a particular and special interest in practices such as genocide, slavery, inhuman and degrading treatment, invidious discrimination, retroactive punishment, avoidable mass starvation, indefinite detention without due process of law, religious persecution, war crimes, and so on. As I have tried to show, these are all practices that involve tremendous cruelty and that are all a foreseeable and regrettable by-product of the state system in which we are all complicit, and from which we all benefit.

· · ·

Many questions remain to be answered. For example, what other functions ought the ILHR system to serve? In this book, I have only focused on one function, namely the protection of our status as moral equals, and hence on the prevention of the inferiorizing social cruelty associated with a system of states. I do not deny that there may be others.[31] At several points, for example, I have allowed that the realization of minimal human flourishing might also be among them. But I have not said anything about this function or about its relation to equal moral status.[32] All I have said is that focusing solely on this function leaves important things out. Similarly, I have not assessed to what extent the *current* ILHR system succeeds in protecting equal moral status (though I have granted that this protection is better than it would be in the absence of such a system). All I have done is to provide a set of moral criteria for evaluating its success.

I have also left aside several important questions regarding the foundations of my view. What, for example, is the connection between moral equality as I have construed it in this book and other kinds of equality, such as what is sometimes called *social* and *distributive* equality? I have said almost nothing about those connections in this book, yet the question is important.[33] I have also said little about the implications of the Negative Conception for the ethics of euthanasia, animal ethics, human enhancement, disability, and many other things besides.

My aim has been more modest. I first tried to shake our faith in the idea of dignity as a basis for our commitment to moral equality. Dignity, in its various modern manifestations, cannot provide a master value through which to defend our commitment. I then sought to outline a novel approach to moral equality to take the place of dignity, which urges us to look more closely at paradigmatic practices and modes of *treating as inferior*. All such practices and all such modes of inferiorizing treatment are wrong, I argued, when and because they are socially cruel. If I am right, our commitment to moral equality, and hence our affirmation of human rights, are best explained as a commitment to a way of treating others with humanity rather than as a recognition of a mysterious, transcendental property that is possessed to an equal extent by all of us.

NOTES

PREFACE

1. The *humanities*, in turn, are those studies that promote the virtue. For this usage, see, e.g., Kristeller 1978.
2. Kant 1999, p. 50, G4:394.
3. Rousseau 1997, p. 187.

BOOK EPIGRAPH

Dostoevsky 1991, p. 238.

INTRODUCTION

1. From now on, I will refer to "persons" as beings that are self-conscious, with some sense of themselves as existing through time and with some minimal capacity to respond to both practical and theoretical reasons.
2. Vlastos 1984, p. 55.
3. The argument therefore will bring moral equality much closer to what has been called "social equality" in the literature. There are still important differences, however, since social equality usually refers more narrowly to the requirements of egalitarianism among citizens and residents of states rather

than among human beings as such. I discuss the relation between moral, social, and distributive equality in more detail in Sangiovanni 2013, forthcoming-b. For the idea of social equality, see Fourie, Schuppert, and Wallimann-Helmer 2015.

4. I am appealing to a conception of "definition" and "grounding" here that is similar to G. Rosen 2010, 2015, respectively. Many thanks to Eliot Michaelson for discussion. I return to this in Chapter 2.

5. Cf. Scheffler 2015.

6. I leave it open, therefore, whether there might be ways of treating others as inferior that are wrongful, but *not* because they constitute violations of equal moral status.

7. See Shklar 1984, 1989. See also Margalit 1996 and Glover 2012, from which I have learned much.

8. Montaigne 1965, "Of Cruelty": "Of all vices, I cruelly hate cruelty, both by nature and by judgment, as the extreme of all vices" (p. 313).

9. Nussbaum 1996.

10. See, e.g., Schofield 1999; Vogt 2008; Cooper 2012, chap. 4.

11. On Stoic sociability, see, e.g., Engberg-Pedersen 1990.

12. See, e.g., Cicero 1991, I.11–16; Cicero 2001, III.

13. Cooper and Procopé 1995, *On Mercy*, 1.25.

14. On *humanitas* as a virtue, see Kristeller 1978; Veyne 1993.

15. Hume 1998, p. 272, section 9.6.

16. See, e.g., Lipton 2004.

17. See Daniels 1996 on the role of inference to the best explanation in reflective equilibrium. The notion of explanation here is obviously normative, not causal. We are not interested in (causally) explaining how we came to have certain principles (e.g., we read this or that book, or grew up in this or that place).

18. Rawls 1999b, p. 508.

19. The methodology I deploy is therefore a more regimented instance of reflective equilibrium—more regimented because it relies heavily on one kind of inference, namely inference to the best explanation, and one kind of social interpretation, namely an interpretation of our practices of treating one another as equals. On reflective equilibrium, see Rawls 1999b, pp. 42–45, 508–509. On interpretation, see Sangiovanni 2008, 2016. However, it is important to note that though the methodology I use in this book is consonant with the views regarding the role of practices in political philosophy defended in those papers, it does not require adherence to them.

1. AGAINST DIGNITY

1. Quoted in Beitz 2013, p. 265. Beitz's article, to which I am indebted, also expresses skepticism regarding whether human rights can be derived (in whole or in part) from the idea of dignity.

2. *Omega, Port Elizabeth, Grootboom, Pretty, Cruzan, Casey, FCC Abortion cases,* etc. For these cases and for excellent discussion, see McCrudden 2008.

3. See, e.g., Rao 2007; Pinker 2008.

4. As Allen Buchanan notes, "a theory that does not provide a justification for the prominent role of equal status in I[nternational] H[uman] R[ights] is either radically incomplete (if it retains the emphasis on equality) or deeply revisionist (if it recommends that this emphasis be jettisoned)" (Buchanan 2010, p. 591).

5. For the distinction between treating someone "with dignity" and treating them "in accordance with their dignity," see M. Rosen 2012.

6. In this usage, someone who is deserving of something (or "worthy" of it) is, in the Latin, *dignus,* or, in Italian, *degno.*

7. For Aristotle, only men were capable of *megalopsychia.*

8. Grosseteste 1972, Clavis 26.2.2 (M), p. 211.

9. *Dignitatis* is used to delineate an elevated social standing throughout *De Officiis,* and *dignus* is used to identify those virtues, attitudes, and bearing that makes one *worthy* of that standing.

10. Cicero 1991, pp. 37–59, §§91–151.

11. Cicero 1991, p. 41, §106.

12. For the Stoic sources of this doctrine, see, e.g., Cooper 2012.

13. The four categories subdivide into those involved with the perception of truth (including wisdom), the preservation of fellowship among men (including justice), the pursuit of greatness (including fortitude), and seemliness. See Cicero 1991, pp. 6–7, §§11–15.

14. On this point, the Stoics disagreed, since they believed that true virtue could be possessed even by a slave. Consider, for example, Epictetus. But even for the Stoics, esteem and worth come only from action in accordance with nature or virtue, not mere membership in the human species.

15. See, for example, the influence it had on etiquette books during and after the Renaissance, such as Giovanni della Casa's *Galateo.* And for the eighteenth century, see, e.g., Klein 2002.

16. See, e.g., Sensen 2011. As we have seen, *dignitatis* and *dignus* in Cicero's Latin both imply a reference to value or worth.

17. Castiglione 2002, p. 74, II.10.

18. For further examples, see also I.3, I.34, and II.11–13, 49. And for maintaining the dignity of the courtier in his relations with the prince, see IV.44–47.

19. On the *querelle,* see Kelly 1982.

20. Castiglione 2002, p. 143, II.98.

21. For the comparison between painting and sculpture, see also *Book of the Courtier*, I.50–52, and Leon Battista Alberti, *Della Pittura* (1435) and *De Statua* (1450). Other instances of this kind of metaphorical use of dignity as applying to a genre appear also in Cicero 1991, II.66. See also Montaigne on "letters." See also *Book of the Courtier*, I.45–47, for the *paragone* between letters and arms.

22. The notes were first copied and collected in the *Codex Urbinas Latinus* around 1542 and only published later by Raffaelo du Fresne in 1651.

23. Vinci 1804, §33; my translation.

24. Vinci 1804, §32; my translation.

25. Kolnai 1976, p. 254.

26. On whether nobility of birth is "essential," see also Castiglione 2002, p. 22, I.15, where Castiglione's interlocutors discuss both sides of the question.

27. Kolnai 1976, p. 260.

28. See, e.g., Miller 2012, p. 413: "Societal needs are the needs people have qua members of particular societies, and they can be defined as the conditions that must be fulfilled in order for a person to lead a minimally decent life in the society to which he or she belongs. Such needs depend on contingent social norms that define standards of decency."

29. Nussbaum 2011, pp. 29–33. See also the Universal Declaration of Human Rights, Art. 23.3.

30. See, e.g., Montaigne 1965, "Of Cruelty"; Lipsius 2006.

31. As in Pico Della Mirandola 2012.

32. Cf. Augustine, *On Christian Teaching*, 1.22.21: "Neither ought any one to have joy in himself, if you look at the matter clearly, because no one ought to love even himself for his own sake, but for the sake of Him who is the true object of enjoyment," as cited in *Rerum Novarum*.

33. For an account of the immediate background to the writing of *Rerum Novarum*, including the influence of neo-Thomists such as Matteo Liberatore and others that were part of the influential Jesuit publication *Civiltà Cattolica* on the encyclical, see Misner 1991.

34. See, e.g., the influential tract by Juan Donoso Cortés (1879). See also McGreevy 2009.

35. See, e.g., O'Malley 2010, chap. 2.

36. Cf. his *Diuturnum* (1881) on the foundations of civil power in ecclesiastical power.

37. Quoted in Moyn 2013, p. 58.

38. Moyn 2013.

39. Quoted in Moyn 2013, p. 59.

40. It is relevant here that the contemporary Catholic theology is mostly Thomist, especially the strand that is well represented by Maritain.

41. Lee and George 2008.

42. Finnis 1997.

43. Lee and George 2008, p. 190.

44. For an excellent overview of this Thomist conception of the soul as rational nature, see Stump 2008, on which I rely here.

45. Finnis 1997, pp. 49–50.

46. See also the rejection of the "simple reading" of the Kantian Regress argument, which I discuss below, which applies in equal measure to the Lee and George argument.

47. Cf. Korsgaard 1996a, pp. 110–111.

48. Respect for Kant demands not only obedience but also reverence. See, e.g., Kant 1999, pp. 209–210, CPrR5: 86–87. See also Feinberg 1973. The reverential aspect of Kant's account of respect is not relevant to our discussion, so I leave it aside.

49. Korsgaard 1996a, 2004. See also Wood 1999, though Wood gives a more realist reading of the conclusion than Korsgaard allows.

50. For Korsgaard's arguments against the (predominantly Moorean) realism of the sort adduced in (2), see Korsgaard 2003, 2004.

51. Korsgaard 2004, p. 123.

52. Note that I have stated the argument in its transcendental form, such that what it establishes is what we *must presuppose* about our value. It is a further question whether what we must presuppose about our value actually establishes that we do, in fact, have that value. For Korsgaard's attempt to bridge this gap, see Korsgaard 2004, p. 47. See also Stern 2011. I am happy to grant that there is no "external" perspective from which to put that presupposition into question: asking ourselves whether we must value humanity is the same, on this view, as asking ourselves whether humanity has value.

53. This argument is not present in Korsgaard, but I think it is a plausible extension of her view. Cf. also Hill 2000.

54. Korsgaard 2004, p. 91.

55. Korsgaard 2004, p. 44.

56. Korsgaard 2004, p. 47.

57. Korsgaard also believes that such practical states of mind can, however, be mistaken (and hence, she says, true or false) if they don't conform with the necessary presuppositions of rational willing or valuing. See Korsgaard 2004, p. 35.

58. Korsgaard 2004, p. 122.

59. I am indebted here to discussion in Gibbard 1999.

60. I also do not report my state of mind when I express my anger and my endorsement of a set of parental norms. Saying "I am angry!" or "I am reflectively endorsing parental norms!" is not the same as saying "You ought to have picked up the kids!" The distinction between expressing and reporting a state of mind is a staple of expressivism. See, e.g., Gibbard 1990, pp. 153–154.

61. As expressivists like Blackburn and Gibbard believe. See Blackburn 1998; Gibbard 2003.

62. For convincing answers to metaphysical and ontological skepticism regarding the existence of non-natural moral properties, see Parfit 2011, chap. 31, and Scanlon 2014, lecture 2.

63. For more on the possibility of intrinsic but only relational goodness, see, e.g., Kraut 2011, pp. 15–20.

64. The idea of a practical rather than conceptual requirement may be necessary to avoid what David Enoch calls the "Agency, Shmagency" objection. The issue isn't about what our concepts commit us to, but about what our practical action and freedom commit us to. See Enoch 2006.

65. Velleman 1999b.

66. Velleman 1999b, p. 613.

67. For that argument, see below on what I call *basic* moral status.

68. Cf. Nagel 1979b.

69. B. Williams 2005, p. 102. See also Pojman 1992; Arneson 1999.

70. Rawls 1999b, pp. 441–449.

71. Waldron 2002, p. 77.

72. See, e.g., Carter 2011; Arneson 2014; Christiano 2014.

73. Kant 1999, p. 202, 5:76–77.

74. Kant 1999, p. 269, 5:161.

75. Kant 1998, p. 546, CPuRA558/B586.

76. Kant 1998, pp. 533–534, CPuRA534/B562. See also Kant 1999, pp. 95–96, G448.

77. Kant 1999, pp. 209–211, 5:86–89.

78. See Fara 2008 on masked abilities, on which I rely here. Fara gives the following analysis of a masked ability: "An agent's ability to A in circumstances C is *masked* iff *(i)* The agent tries to A; *(ii)* circumstances C obtain; *(iii)* the agent retains the ability while trying to A; yet *(iv)* the agent does not succeed in Aing" (848).

79. See, e.g., McMahan 2002, pp. 252–253; B. Williams 2005.

80. Kant 1999, p. 84, G435.

81. Forst 2011, p. 49.

82. Forst 2011, p. 1; emphasis added.

83. See, e.g., Forst 2011, pp. 129–130.

84. Darwall 2006, pp. 114–115. See also the excellent discussion of these passages in Watson 2007, to which I am indebted for the points made here.

85. Cf. Thucydides's account of the Peloponnesian War, in which the Athenians enslave the Eionians, Chaeroneans, Ambraciots, Mityleneans, Toronaeans, Scionians, Melians, and Hyccarians.

86. Darwall 2006, p. 268.

87. R. Jay Wallace (2007) also objects to what he refers to as Darwall's voluntarism.

88. Darwall 2006, p. 266; emphasis added.

89. Forst 2011, p. 61.

90. This leaves open whether the Kantian view has the resources to explain in what sense beings that lack a competence to understand or evaluate reasons can have moral standing, such as nonhuman animals and severely disabled human beings. For Darwall's views on this, see Darwall 2006, pp. 43, 95, 302. I return to this issue below.

91. Another way to make the same point is by emphasizing that, even if a certain structure of reason-giving *qua* justification *did* presuppose the full moral equality that Forst wants, we can always ask: Why, in giving reasons and offering justifications, *must* we adopt that mode of reason-giving *qua* justification? Why not adopt a thinner mode that only presupposes the formal characteristics of reasons in the generic sense? I make this point at greater length in Sangiovanni 2014.

92. Forst 2011, p. 56.

93. Forst 2011, pp. 38–39.

94. Forst 2011, p. 59.

95. For example, Forst 2011, p. 41.

96. Because its conscious mental life has, *ex hypothesi,* no functional or causal role to play in its behavior, if the being acts to avoid or to pursue things, it would do so as a result of causal processes that are entirely independent of its conscious mental life.

97. Cf. Nagel 1979b.

98. I emphasize that we are here focusing on the utilitarian's view regarding what it is that gives a being *a* moral standing in the first place. It is a further question how this moral standing ought to figure in our best first-order account of morality, including whether there are any agent-relative constraints and whether we always have reason to act so as to maximize the sum total of welfare.

99. I thank Arnon Kernon for helpful discussion on this point. For more on this distinction, see Sangiovanni 2016.

100. Korsgaard 2004, pp. 38–40.

101. Cf. Scanlon 2014, pp. 9–11.

102. The argument I give therefore has a structural similarity to both Rawls's "congruence" argument, which shows how his principles of justice affirm each person's good (Rawls 1999b, pp. 496–505), and the "interpretive" approach that Dworkin defends (Dworkin 2011, pp. 184–188), which seeks to "identify conceptions of happiness and of the familiar virtues that fit well together, so that the best understanding of morality flows from and helps define the best understanding of ethics" (16).

103. Cf. Prichard 1912.

104. Cf. Rawls 1999b, pp. 497–498.

105. Hume 1998, p. 272, §9.6: "But when he bestows on any man the epithets of *vicious* or *odious* or *depraved,* he then speaks another language, and expresses sentiments, in which he expects all his audience are to concur with him. He must here, therefore, depart from his private and particular situation, and must choose a point of view, common to him with others; he must move some universal principle of the human frame, and touch a string to which all mankind have an accord and symphony. . . . He has chosen this common point of view, and has touched the principle of humanity, in which every man, in some degree, concurs."

106. I explore the tight connection between morality and empathy in more detail in Sangiovanni 2014, in which I also discuss psychopathy and autism as conditions in which our capacity for empathy is generally set back. In that paper, however, I was trying to demonstrate that the normative authority of practical reasons stems from what is (contingently) true about us as both rational and empathic beings. As should be clear in the text, I now believe that no such account can be successful, but that such an account can be used to further justify the role claimed for such reasons in our practical reflection. See also Forst 2014, to which I am indebted.

107. Cf. Scanlon 1998, pp. 162–167.

108. See, e.g., Hume 1998, p. 276, IX.1.225, and Frans de Waal: "empathy is the original pre-linguistic form of inter-individual linkage that only secondarily has come under the influence of language and culture" (Waal 2009, p. 24).

109. See, e.g., A. Smith 1982, p. 13, I.1.1.4.

110. Of course, empathy can be turned toward bad ends, but *insofar as* it is an essential and sustaining part of the infrastructure of the most important goods in a human life, it is itself good.

111. Christiano 2014, p. 59.

112. On the limited character of the idea of treating as "mere means," see Chapter 2 on consent and Chapter 3 on objectification and instrumentalization.

113. And so right to question Bernard Williams's inference (in B. Williams 2005) from the fact of having a point of view to a conclusion about moral equality.

2. MORAL EQUALITY, RESPECT, AND CRUELTY

1. Cf. the strategies pursued with respect to distributive equality in Wolff 1998; Anderson 1999; Scheffler 2003, 2015.

2. P. Strawson 2008. See also Wallace 1994; Bird 2013.

3. Goffman 1963.

4. See, e.g., Korsgaard 1996a; Wood 1999, pp. 111–155, for influential versions of this reading.

5. See, e.g., Wolterstorff 2010 and Pope John Paul II's encyclical *Evangelium Vitae* (1995) and, most recently, Waldron forthcoming-b.

6. Cruelty is wrong, on this view, *because* it is a type of unauthorized use of another's vulnerability to inflict harm or suffering. But note that cruelty is a thick concept, so to determine whether some action falls in the extension of the descriptive, wrong-making properties mentioned on the right side of the "because"—and thus counts as a relevant type—we need to do some evaluation.

7. See, e.g., Kekes 1996.

8. On the objective meaning of actions, see Scanlon 2008, p. 4: the meaning of an action is "the significance, for the agent and others, of the agent's willingness to perform that action for the reasons he or she does." See also pp. 53–55 on the sense in which there is an objective fact regarding the meaning of an action such that one could be mistaken in one's assessment of it. I return to the relevance of social meanings in much more detail in Chapter 3.

9. Sussman 2005.

10. Amelia Hill, "Winterbourne View Care Home Staff Jailed for Abusing Residents," *Guardian*, October 26, 2012.

11. See, e.g., Power 2002, p. 36.

12. Cf. Card 2003: "the special evil of genocide lies in its infliction of not just physical death (when it does that) but social death, producing a consequent meaninglessness of one's life and even of its termination" (73).

13. Cf. Patterson 1982: "This [natal alienation] is achieved in a unique way in the relation of slavery: the definition of the slave, however recruited, as a socially dead person. . . . The ritual of enslavement incorporated one or more of four basic features: first, the symbolic rejection by the slave of his past and his former kinsmen; second, a change of name; third, the imposition of some visible mark of servitude; and last, the assumption of a new status in the household or economic organization of the master" (5, 52).

14. The term—"Muslims"—was used because of the prostrate position of prayer, which invokes the prostration and submission of the "drowned" to their fate.

15. Levi 1996, p. 100.

16. Levi 1996, p. 181. See also the account of how slavery can fracture in Morrison 1987.

17. Cf. Nozick 1974, p. 29.

18. I am indebted to Velleman 2006, chap. 9, "The Self as Narrator," for this account of the interaction between these two aspects, or guises, of the self.

19. Joan Didion: "We might expect if the death is sudden to feel shock. We do not expect the shock to be obliterative, dislocating to both body and mind. We might expect that we will be prostrate, inconsolable, crazy with loss. We do not expect to be literally crazy, cool customers who believe that their husband is about to return and need his shoes" (Didion 2007, p. 188).

20. Cf. Frankfurt 1999, pp. 100–107.

21. Cf. Montaigne 1965, p. 857.

22. Lugones 1990, pp. 138–139. I am indebted to Calhoun 1995 both for the example and for discussion.

23. For discussion of cases like this, see Frankfurt 1988, pp. 180–190. For Huck Finn, see Arpaly and Schroeder 1999.

24. Cf. Raz 1986, pp. 281–283, 306; Raz 2001, p. 148.

25. Cf. Sartre 1983. And see Dante 2010, Canto V, lines 100–108, where Paolo and Francesca are condemned to be bound irrevocably together in the thrall of a desire they cannot, as mere souls, ever consummate. On the good of solitude, see Montaigne 1965, "On Solitude." I thank Marco Sangiovanni for discussion.

26. For more on the possibility of extrinsic values that are not instrumental in a causal sense, see Korsgaard 1996b and Raz 1986, pp. 200–202.

27. I am indebted to Goffman 1956 for the idea of self-presentation, and Velleman 2006, chap. 3, which develops a similar line of thought to explore the origin of shame.

28. Cf. A. Smith 1982, I.2.i.

29. Cf. A. Smith 1982, I.4.viii.

30. Cf. Nagel 2002, p. 6.

31. Cf. Freud's initial worries about his divulging information about the "Rat Man" in his famous case study: "the paradoxical truth that it is far easier to divulge the patient's most intimate secrets than the most innocent and trivial facts about him; for, whereas the former would not throw any light on his identity, the latter, by which he is generally recognized, would make it obvious to every one" (Freud 1960b, p. 156). See also Shklar 1984, pp. 75–78, on the moral ambiguities of hypocrisy and, especially, the desire to unmask it.

32. Only ever partially, of course, since we can always betray ourselves in all sorts of ways, conscious and unconscious.

33. Once again, only ever partially, since the terms that we set are often set for us. The point is that to maintain an integral sense of self, we need to have significant leeway in determining those terms and their meaning.

34. See, e.g., Luban 2007, p. 1431: "The world of the man or woman in great pain is a world without relationships or engagements, a world without an exterior. It is a world reduced to a point, a world that makes no sense and in which the human soul finds no home and no repose." For a similar point, see also Sussman 2005, p. 7. But see also Kramer 2014, esp. pp. 180–182, for critique of Sussman and the defense of a much more perpetrator-focused account of the wrongness of torture.

35. Goffman 1961, p. 47.

36. Goffman 1961, p. 40.

37. Levi 1996, p. 172.

38. Goffman 1961, p. 19.
39. See, e.g., the powerful account of the wrongness of racial inequality, and its roots in stigma, in Loury 2009, chap. 2. Of the racist vitriol he was recently subject to as a result of publishing a letter on the structural pervasiveness of racism, George Yancy says, "The comments were not about pointing out fallacies in my position, but were designed to violate, to leave me psychologically broken and physically distraught. . . . I felt violated, injured; a part of me felt broken," Brad Evans and George Yancy, "The Perils of Being a Black Philosopher," *The Stone,* April 18, 2016, http://opinionator.blogs.nytimes.com /2016/04/18/the-perils-of-being-a-black-philosopher/?_r=3.
40. Perhaps less obviously, dress is also an important part of our bodily self-presentation. It is significant that most of Goffman's total institutions impose the use of uniforms (or in some cases nakedness) and the shearing of one's hair to denote the inferior status, and deserved shame, of the inmates.
41. Card 2003.
42. As we will see below, I believe a specific kind of recognition respect, namely opacity respect, governs our commitment to moral equality. Cf. Darwall 1977, p. 38.
43. For the notion of opacity respect, I am indebted to Ian Carter's ground-breaking discussion in Carter 2011. On my account, the role and value of opacity respect is not explained via an account of "external dignity" (see Chapter 1 for a critique of Kolnai's view, on which Carter bases his conception) but via the idea of persons as self-presenting beings. Furthermore, opacity respect, on my view, isn't focused on a narrower concern with the harm (sometimes) involved in evaluating people's agential capacities or on the importance of evaluative abstinence, but on the way violations of opacity respect in general make people liable to social cruelty. Those two differences noted, the two accounts are, I believe, compatible, and, indeed, mutually reinforcing.
44. In determining the point of respect in our practices, I am using a methodology similar to the one recommended by Miranda Fricker in Fricker 2016: we attempt to determine what the core function of respect is in our practice of treating one another as equals, and then try to interpret other instances of more "everyday" respect as derivative.
45. Cf. Hume 1998, p. 261, §8.
46. Note that a violation of opacity respect is neither necessarily nor always, in our world, cruel: all I have asserted is that violations of opacity respect, when pervasive, can make us *liable* to cruelty, and part of their very point is to protect us from such liability.
47. Nagel 2002, p. 8.
48. Contrast, for example, denying the vote to children, or to noncitizens.
49. I return to invidious discrimination in Chapter 3.

50. Cf. Du Bois 2007, p. 8.
51. Cohen 2013, p. 195.
52. Cohen 2013, p. 195.
53. Cohen himself never takes a stand in the unfinished sketch cited above (which was only published posthumously).
54. For illuminating remarks on social stigma, see Goffman 1963, pp. 2–3.
55. It is worth recalling that violations of opacity respect are not always instances of treating as an inferior, and are therefore not always violations of equal moral status. Disrespect can just be rude or callous or insulting without being an instance of treating as inferior.
56. I return to the importance of social meanings in Chapter 3.
57. Woolf 1974, p. 245. See also Andrea Westlund's (2003) discussion of the Angel.
58. See also the discussion of infantilization *qua* objectification in Chapter 3.
59. Woolf 1974, p. 246.
60. I therefore agree with Nussbaum's (2001) insightful rejection of theories that try to explain the morally problematic character of preferences like those of the Angel in the House in terms of the irrationality of adaptive preferences, and I also agree that we need an assessment of the person's good from their own point of view, but an assessment that cannot be reduced either to the preferences they actually express or that they would express in the absence of false empirical beliefs.
61. Cf. Owens 2011. Note that I do not deny that a normative power to give and withhold consent may also have noninstrumental value. We may, for example, also have what Owens calls "normative interests" in such powers for their own sake. For the idea of a normative interest, see Owens 2012.
62. Richard Baldwin writes, "Love takes off the masks that we fear we cannot live without and know we cannot live within," quoted in George Yancy, "Dear White America," *The Stone,* December 24, 2015, http://opinionator.blogs .nytimes.com/2015/12/24/dear-white-america/.
63. For the "pure" rape case (in which the victim does not know that they have been raped), see Gardner and Shute 2000. Notice further that in both cases, someone's body is used as a mere means, and hence in ways to which they "could not possibly consent" because they have never been given the chance to consent. Cf. O'Neill 1989, chap. 6; Korsgaard 1996a, pp. 138–140; Gardner and Shute 2000. I develop this critique of the Kantian view further in Sangiovanni 2012, forthcoming-d. See also Barbara Herman's discussion of the difficulty the Kantian faces in explaining the wrongness of violence in Herman 1989.
64. Cf. Kant 1999, Ak6:434–435 and Anderson 2008: "Yet Kantian ethics cannot do without any notion of superior and inferior beings. . . . Kant's solution was to displace rankings of respect from the social hierarchy and project it instead on the order of nature" (139).

65. For this usage, see Waldron 2012; Beitz 2013, p. 273.
66. Hohfeld 1964.
67. Cf. Westen 1982; Raz 1986, pp. 220–229; Shin 2009; Nathan 2014.
68. This account can also serve as a response to Jo Wolff's puzzlement about the apparent priority of social inequality to equality in Wolff 2015.
69. Note that, for example, opacity respect could be highly damaging to beings that lack a capacity to develop and maintain an integral sense of self (imagine treating an infant or someone with advanced dementia with opacity respect, which would almost certainly lead to their hurting themselves).
70. P. Strawson 2008, p. 9.
71. Hurston 1990.
72. On the role of such counterfactuals in making sense of the wrongness of attempts that are bound to fail, see the helpful discussion in Westen 2008 and Duff 1996, pp. 219–263. According to Westen, "we use 'threats' and 'risks' of harm to refer in retrospect to how easily counterfactual events could have obtained that, had they obtained, would have produced harm that, thankfully, did not occur" (547).
73. See, e.g., Steinhoff 2014.
74. Or at least absolute without much further qualification.
75. Cf. Nagel 1979a.
76. See, e.g., Guenther 2013.
77. For Kant on punishment, see, e.g., Byrd and Hruschka 2010.

3. WHEN AND WHY IS DISCRIMINATION WRONG?

1. Eidelson 2015, p. 3. See also Hellman and Moreau 2013, p. 1; Lippert-Rasmussen 2013, p. 4.
2. They are also very important in the EU context, where anti-discrimination law has developed at a breathtaking pace in the last few decades. See, e.g., Somek 2011.
3. For the importance of this distinction, see in particular Khaitan 2015.
4. By "comparatively" disadvantaged, I mean that the member(s) of group Y are disadvantaged (advantaged) compared with either actual or hypothetical others.
5. Lippert-Rasmussen 2013, p. 169.
6. This way of proceeding also has the added advantage that most contemporary theories of discrimination (including those discussed below) also use non-moralized definitions, so it makes it much easier to compare across them.
7. Notice that, in these definitions, we may not know whether a particular instance of discrimination was direct or indirect, since we may not have any evidence regarding how a particular factor affected, consciously or unconsciously,

the deliberations leading to the policy. This is not an objection to this way of drawing the distinction, since our concern is not to devise a legal test for direct as against indirect discrimination. Rather, our aim is to identify when a policy or act that discriminates is morally wrong. And, as we will see below, I believe that whether and how a particular factor entered into a deliberation can affect the wrongfulness of the act or policy independently of other factors. Consider this example: A landlord turns away a black family because they are black, but no one knows about it. This is a case of wrongful, direct discrimination, even if no one but the landlord knows on what basis the family was turned away. The same is true if the family was turned away due to unconscious bias (in which case the bias unconsciously made a difference to the deliberations leading to the decision). I return to cases like this below.

8. Legal definitions of discrimination always include references to "protected groups" or "suspect classifications." My definition refers to groups defined by "socially salient" characteristics, since it should be part of the moral theory to determine both which socially salient characteristics matter in evaluating particular discriminatory acts or policies and why.

9. For the importance of distinguishing between covert and indirect discrimination, see Selmi 2013.

10. 403 US 217.

11. *Palmer v. Thompson,* 403 US 217, §87.

12. For a similar case, see the discussion of the racist landlord below.

13. On this point, see the helpful Moreau 2010. Cf. Gardner 1989.

14. See, e.g., Alexander 1992; Arneson 2006.

15. Cf. Larry Alexander's assessment of "reaction qualifications," namely characteristics or policies that contribute to job effectiveness (such as turning away blacks) by serving as the basis for a reaction among consumers of the end product (such as preferences against patronizing diners that cater to blacks): "The morality of the chosen treatment is primarily a function of both considering the gravity and the distribution of the social effects of acknowledging reaction qualifications and the gravity and distribution of the social effects of not acknowledging them" (Alexander 1992, p. 174).

16. I am indebted to Hellman 2008 for the need to emphasize the social meanings of acts or policies. As I will explain in more detail below, my view, however, holds that social meanings are solely a function of the attitudes actually held by discriminators (against a wider background of societal conventions and practices). For Hellman (and also Anderson and Pildes), by contrast, social meanings can inhere in acts and policies as a result solely of societal conventions, and hence independently of the attitudes of discriminators.

17. Anderson and Pildes 2000, pp. 1509–1510.

18. The example is from Loury 2009, p. 71.

19. Cf. Anderson and Pildes 2000, pp. 1512–1513.

20. As I have already mentioned, our judgment of the *(pro tanto)* wrongfulness of the city restaurant's policy would persist even if we imagined it to *decrease* the stigma associated with being black in that community.

21. Eidelson 2015, pp. 121–122, has a good discussion of cases involving special preferences grounded in special connectedness.

22. Or, at the very least to the formal structure of the work of art itself, as in formalist theories of artistic interpretation.

23. The literature is divided on this question. For example, for Anderson and Pildes, unknowingly making a rude gesture in a foreign culture counts as expressing disrespect even if the act does not express any attitude of indifference, hostility, or malice actually held by the tourist, i.e., even if the tourist didn't know the conventional meaning of the gesture (Anderson and Pildes 2000, pp. 1512–1513. Hellman agrees [Hellman 2008, pp. 35–36]). Eidelson, on the other hand, argues that the expression of an attitude in an action requires that the action "effectuate or arise out of" the attitude (Eidelson 2015, pp. 84–90). I agree with Eidelson, though I offer a different range of considerations in support of the conclusion.

24. Note that its utterance might not therefore be impermissible if it did not have any harmful psychological effects, did not propagate racist beliefs, and did not carry any negative social meaning (on account of the ignorance of the reciter). However, according to the view I am defending, it would be impermissible if it did express racist attitudes, though without any further propagation of racist beliefs.

25. We consider whether there are cases in which there are downstream societal effects but no morally objectionable attitudes expressed below.

26. The example is from Scanlon 2008, p. 73. In a discussion of this case, Scanlon writes, "No one can be asked to accept a society that marks them out as inferior in this way and denies them its principal benefits. When this occurs, individual acts of discrimination on certain grounds become impermissible because they support and maintain this practice" (73). I agree, but a crucial question is left open: Why can no one be asked to accept a society that marks them out as inferior? And: Is the discrimination wrongful because and *only insofar as* it "supports and maintains" a broader racist practice, or is its social meaning sufficient to make it wrong independently of its contribution to the broader societal practice?

27. What about a case in which the landlord has racist beliefs but resists the temptation to make a decision on this basis, makes further inquiries, and acts on the basis of the latter rather than the former? In that case, the attitude has not been transmitted to the action. As Anderson and Pildes, cited above, write, "to express an attitude through action is to act on reasons that attitude gives us."

28. If we were discussing legal remedies, we might say that the landowner owes damages to the couple, but not a contract for the flat.

29. See, most famously, Freud on jokes in Freud 1960a, but see also the more recent literature on implicit bias, such as, e.g., Greenwald and Krieger 2006; Saul 2013. For the application to discrimination law, see Jolls and Sunstein 2006.

30. For contrasting views on the connection between blameworthiness and unconscious bias, see, e.g., Levy 2005; A. Smith 2005. I do not need to take a position on this dispute, since both Attributionist and Voluntarist accounts of blameworthiness would converge in judging the paramedic as a blameless wrongdoer.

31. The most fully developed disrespect-based view is Eidelson 2015. See also Glasgow 2009; Shin 2009.

32. Hellman 2008.

33. Eidelson 2015, p. 97.

34. Eidelson 2015, p. 98.

35. Eidelson 2015, p. 98.

36. This is not a hypothetical case. The United Kingdom has recently negotiated an agreement with the EU which would allow it to do just that (though that agreement has been superseded by Brexit). I discuss the sense in which the policy is wrongfully discriminatory in Sangiovanni forthcoming-c.

37. Hellman 2008, p. 57.

38. Lippert-Rasmussen makes a similar point in Lippert-Rasmussen 2013, pp. 136–137.

39. Wiltse 2014.

40. Wiltse 2007.

41. Wiltse 2007, p. 78.

42. It is striking how long the shadow cast by this past is: black children in the United States are, today, three times more likely to die of drowning than white children. See, e.g., the "Red River" tragedy, in which six black teens died, in 2010, in shallow water in a Louisiana river. See also http://www.nytimes.com/2006/09/18/us/18pool.html?pagewanted=all and http://www.theatlantic.com/politics/archive/2015/06/troubled-waters-in-mckinney-texas/395150/.

43. Fanon 1952, p. 88.

44. See, e.g., the powerful account of the wrongness of racial inequality, and its roots in stigma, in Loury 2009, chap. 2. See also Fanon 1952, esp. chap. 5, "L'expérience vécue du Noir" (or "the lived experience of blackness," translated in the English edition, somewhat misleadingly, as "The Fact of Blackness"). See also Haslanger 2012: "A good objectifier will, when the need arises—that is, when the object lacks the desired properties—exercise his power to make the object have the properties he desires" (65).

45. Consider that, in the United Kingdom, a nationwide 2016 survey records that 42 percent of lesbian, gay, bisexual, or transgender individuals aged sixteen to twenty-five have sought medical help for anxiety or depression, 52 percent report self-harm either now or in the past, and 44 percent have considered suicide. These rates are over two times higher than the average for heterosexuals. See Metro, "Youth Chances: Integrated Report," 2016, https://www .metrocentreonline.org/pdfs/Experiences_LGBTQ_Intergrated%20 Report2015.pdf.

46. Cf. Lippert-Rasmussen 2013, p. 131.

47. Notice, however, that this denial of opportunity is not necessary to explain the wrongness of the turning away, since the turning away would still have been wrong even if (as I have argued) it would have been permissible for the landlord to turn away the couple for other reasons (which the landlord never took into account). In this case, the couple has not, in fact, been denied an opportunity they *would have otherwise had.*

48. Both Hellman and Eidelson reject harm-based views on such a narrow construal. See Hellman 2008, pp. 26–27; Eidelson 2015, p. 73.

49. Cf., e.g., Scanlon 1998, p. 112.

50. Duff makes a similar point in Duff 2001, p. 23.

51. Cf. Eidelson 2015, pp. 74–76, who argues that racism is wrong when and because it fails to respect our interest-independent standing as moral equals and hence "intrinsically" wrongs us. But in what are our entitlements to be treated with equal respect grounded? Eidelson's view, as I have argued above, is not equipped to give us an answer to this question. This brings my view closer to the harm-based view defended in Lippert-Rasmussen 2013, though without an appeal to the desert-prioritarian considerations that Lippert adduces in defense of his view. Lippert-Rasmussen's desert-prioritarianism, I believe, tends to run together the two ways in which people can be made worse off that I have been trying to separate, namely: they can be made worse off as an indirect result of downstream societal effects or as a direct result of the stigma, infantilization, etc., of particular discriminatory acts. The two harms, I have argued, need a distinct treatment to capture the distinctive wrongness of discriminatory acts that inferiorize.

52. See Morehouse College, "A Proud Tradition of Producing Outstanding Leaders," https://www.morehouse.edu/about/.

53. On misogyny, see, e.g., Greer 1971, part 4, "Hate."

54. Arendt 1971. This structure of beliefs and practices—patriarchy—has a profound effect on the world of work as well. For example, see Phillips and Taylor 1980 for the association of "unskilled" labor with women's work.

55. On the role of history and the changeability of historical patterns, see, e.g., Lerner 1986, pp. 6–7. On the (contingent) reproduction of mothering in the

modern family from a psychoanalytic perspective, see, e.g., Chodorow 1978, and especially the discussion in the afterword.

56. Beauvoir 2012, p. 15.

57. Beauvoir 2012, p. 27.

58. W. Williams 1981, p. 176.

59. See, e.g., Young 1990, p. 41, in which oppression often resides in the "unquestioned norms, habits, and symbols, in the assumptions underlying institutional rules and the collective consequences of following those rules" and in the "unconscious assumptions and reactions of well-meaning people in ordinary interactions, media and cultural stereotypes, and structural features of bureaucratic hierarchies and market mechanisms—in short, the normal processes of everyday life."

60. Okin 1989, pp. 134–135. And, according to Chodorow, who extensively catalogs the impact of modern parenting on the social and psychological development of women and men, the "sexual division of labor and women's responsibility for childcare are linked to and generate male dominance" (Chodorow 1978, p. 214).

61. 208 U.S. 412 (1908).

62. See *Lochner v. New York,* 198 US 45 (1905), which held that limits to working time were unconstitutional.

63. I leave aside here the fact that, by limiting working hours, this might have in fact put women at a relative *disadvantage* in bargaining with employers compared with men who are able and willing to work longer hours. Even if we focus on this feature of the legislation, my point still stands, since no one would argue that this relative disadvantage is the sole source of the wrongfulness of the legislation. We would still have an objection, that is, even if it turned out that men were not, on average, willing to work more hours, and this was generally known, or if it turned out that men and women did not compete, on average, for the same jobs. Interestingly, the famous Brandeis Brief (1907) attempts to answer precisely this objection at p. 82. See https://louisville.edu/law/library/special-collections/the-louis-d.-brandeis-collection/muller5.pdf.

64. 169 US 366 (1898), 397. Even the famous *Lochner* (1908) decision—which overturned maximum-hours legislation for bakers on the basis of liberty of contract—recognized the special dangers of work in mines.

65. 208 US 412, at 421–422.

66. Cf. both forms of Fricker's epistemic injustice, namely testimonial and hermeneutical, in Fricker 2007.

67. MacKinnon 1987, p. 172. See also the insightful reconstruction of MacKinnon's view in Haslanger 2012, pp. 59–67, and Langton 2000.

68. Ginsburg 2008.

69. The Court, for example, made no effort to explore the *structural* obstacles influencing women's relative bargaining position and capacity to live a life of independence. Cf. J. S. Mill in *The Subjection of Women:* "Hence, in regard to that most difficult question, what are the natural differences between the two sexes—a subject on which it is impossible in the present state of society to obtain complete and correct knowledge—while almost everybody dogmatizes upon it, almost all neglect and make light of the only means by which any partial insight can be obtained into it. . . . The [psychological and moral differences between men and women] only could be referred to be natural which could not possibly be artificial—the residuum, after deducting every characteristic of either sex which can admit of being explained from education or external circumstances" (Mill 1984, p. 277).

70. *Holden v. Hardy,* 397.

71. See, e.g., Moss-Racusin et al. 2012.

72. *Robinson v. Jacksonville Shipyards,* 760 F.Supp. 1486 (1991).

73. I agree, therefore, with MacKinnon 1979, who argues that sexual harassment is sex-based discrimination in virtue of its connection to the mobilization of norms governing gender hierarchy rather than in virtue of the fact that the harasser would not have behaved the same way with a man.

74. For this point, see Green 2000.

75. The example is mine, not Nussbaum's.

76. Nussbaum 1995, p. 273. See also Leslie Green's insightful analysis of gay porn: "If [gay men] are to be treated as *sexual* they also need to be treated as, and be able to see themselves as, the possible objects of another's desire. . . . Gay pornography contributes to gay life what is everywhere else denied—that gay sexualities exist, that gay men are sexual beings, and that men may be objects of male desire" (Green 2000, p. 48).

77. More specifically, she focuses on a specific kind of instrumentalization: "The instrumental treatment of human beings, the treatment of human beings as tools of the purposes of another, is always morally problematic *if it does not take place in a larger context of regard for humanity*" (Nussbaum 1995, p. 289; emphasis added). Notice that Nussbaum does not rule out all forms of instrumentalization, but only instrumentalization that "does not take place in a larger context of regard for humanity." But what does regard for humanity consist in? And what is its basis?

78. Nussbaum 1995, p. 273.

79. A similar example is discussed by Parfit to make the same point. See Parfit 2011, p. 213.

80. For this example, see Parfit 2011, p. 216.

81. I discuss this problem in the Kantian view at much greater length in Sangiovanni forthcoming-d; see also the discussion of consent in Chapter 2.

82. For the distinction between norms that are constitutively grounded in a role and those that are separable, see Haslanger 2012.

83. The account I defend here combines the positive elements of what Elizabeth Anderson, in a helpful review article, calls "dignity," "autonomy," and "equality" accounts, while avoiding their negatives. See Anderson 2006.

84. E.g., so-called quid pro quo sexual harassment, in which a fellow worker (usually a superior) offers some work-based advantage in exchange for sexual favors. The request mobilizes gendered structures of power to intimidate and coerce in the same way as *Robinson*. The social meaning is therefore similar: "You are subject to my sexual control as a woman; the terms that you choose for your engagement with me as a fellow worker are irrelevant; it is permissible for me to discount your value as a worker compared to the men who work here."

85. 842 F.2d 1010, 1014 (8th Circuit, 1988).

86. Consider, for example, laws against what in European contexts is called "mobbing."

87. I leave aside the possibility of a woman, say, participating in the kind of exclusion in *Robinson,* which would still count as sex-based discrimination even though it is female-female.

88. It also seems clear that cases involving the "intersection" of, say, race and sex or sexual orientation could also affect the social meaning of actions, and hence how insidious any particular attack might be.

89. *DH and Others v. Czech Republic* [2007], App. No. 57325/00 (ECHR).

90. *DH and Others v. Czech Republic,* §44. See also the recent report prepared by the European Roma Rights Centre, which details the failure of the Czech Republic to remedy the situation, "Persistent Segregation of Roma in the Czech Education System," 2008, http://www.errc.org/cms/upload/media/03/AC/m000003AC.pdf.

91. If the case *did* involve conscious and unconscious bias in the administration of the tests, then, of course, it would be a straightforward case of direct discrimination. This is why I stipulate, for the sake of argument, that there was *no* such bias.

92. Crowe 1996.

93. Crowe 2008, p. 522.

94. Young 1990, pp. 196–197.

95. Young 2011, p. 100.

96. Parfit 1984, pp. 79–82. Note that I have modified it to suit our purposes.

97. Note that I am not here denying that there are instances of structural injustice *generally* that are not instances of indirect discrimination. Someone might be a victim of an injustice for which no one, either individually or collectively, is culpable, but where the injustice is not a result of belonging to a

disadvantaged group. In this case, it would be structural injustice but without being discrimination (in my sense).

98. Recall that insofar as agents' outcome-affecting deliberations are affected by *unconscious* bias, then, I have argued, the actions count as forms of direct discrimination and infect the social meanings of the actions in question. My account of indirect discrimination helps us to distinguish the production of oppressive results via unconscious bias (and so independently of how diffuse the causal inputs to the outcome are) and the production of oppressive results that are solely the product of diffuse causes.

99. Young 2011, p. 107.

100. See Kutz 2000, pp. 186–191. But see also Gardner 2007; Lepora and Goodin 2013.

101. For a helpful account of recklessness as involving practical indifference or contempt for the interests of others, see Duff 1990, chap. 7.

102. The Sentencing Project, "Criminal Justice Facts," http://www.sentencing project.org/criminal-justice-facts/.

103. For a wide-ranging study of the stigma and associated problems of "reentry," see Loury et al. 2008, pp. 20–21; Thompson 2008.

104. See, e.g., Loury et al. 2008; Thompson 2008.

105. See, to name just one example, how associations between race and particular crimes affect juror verdicts in Jones and Kaplan 2003.

106. For one example of the effects of slavery on contemporary patterns, see Patterson 2000 on paternal abandonment. Of course, personal responsibility plays a large role. But personal responsibility, especially when averages and effects are distributed in such a racially marked way, must be evaluated in light of value of the choices and opportunities that one has. As Loury writes, "when we hold a person responsible for his or her conduct—by establishing laws, investing in their enforcement, and consigning some persons to prisons—we need also to think about whether we have done our share in ensuring that each person faces a decent set of opportunities for a good life" (Loury et al. 2008, p. 32).

107. Consider that while 60 percent of black high school dropouts have spent time in prison, only 5 percent of college-educated blacks have (Loury et al. 2008, pp. 23, 61), and consider that over two-thirds of US inmates issue from households with an annual income that amounts to less than *half* the poverty line (Loury et al. 2008, p. 60). See also Anderson 2010, pp. 1–66.

108. Thompson 2008, p. 2.

109. On the ineffectiveness of the war on drugs, see, e.g., Western 2006.

110. Loury et al. 2008, pp. 30–33.

111. We could construct a similar example for cases of unconscious bias in which the agent undertakes good-faith, but unsuccessful, efforts to rid themselves

of such biases. Note, however, that such cases would count as wrongful but blameless forms of *direct* discrimination, since unconscious bias is involved. The example I develop in the text involves *indirect* discrimination.

112. Loury et al. 2008, p. 11.

4. THE CONCEPT OF HUMAN RIGHTS

1. In this chapter, I focus on the question of what *moral* rather than *legal* human rights are. It is a further question (about which I will have more to say both below and in Chapter 5) what the relation between legal and moral human rights ought to be. See Buchanan 2013 for the importance of drawing this distinction.

2. Tasioulas 2007; Griffin 2008.

3. This is Beitz's preferred formulation. See Beitz 2009, esp. chap. 6. The distance between a morally urgent interest and a moral right seems, however, less wide than we might otherwise believe if we assume that what makes an interest "morally urgent" is not (merely) how important it is for the agent but how stringent the third-party duties required for its satisfaction are. We should assume the latter for the following reason. Someone might have, say, a very pressing and morally urgent interest (in the former sense) in a medical treatment that costs millions. But the mere fact of its urgency would not be enough to ground obligations for states to satisfy it (and generate reasons for the international community to be concerned when the state fails to satisfy it); the interest would not therefore provide a ground for a human right on Beitz's view. Interests must therefore be morally urgent in the different sense that they generate stringent third-party duties—falling on states and owed to the individuals whose interests they are—to protect or satisfy those interests. But if this is true, then "morally urgent interests" would entail the existence of a moral right (at least according to the Razian notion of a right). As Beitz himself recognizes, "not every threat to an important interest is best made the subject of a [human] right" (p. 139). From now on, in the text, I therefore drop the parenthetical reference. I thank John Tasioulas for discussion on this point.

4. Rawls 1999a; Beitz 2009; Raz 2010.

5. Tasioulas 2011, p. 39.

6. Raz 2010, p. 321. See also Griffin 2008, p. 25; Beitz 2009, p. 8.

7. The Subclass, Fidelity, and Determinacy Desiderata are commonly recognized. See, e.g., Tasioulas 2011, pp. 18–19. The Normativity Desideratum is surprisingly overlooked, with important consequences that I discuss in more detail below.

8. Cf. Dworkin 2011, p. 158.

9. Griffin 2008, p. 45. See also pp. 32–33.

10. Cf. Griffin 2008, p. 273: "We do not say that a man who free-rides when filling out his income tax return violates his fellow citizens' human rights; he is a cheat, clearly, but not a human rights violator."

11. Cf. Griffin 2008, p. 273: "Nor do we say, of a woman given an unjust prison sentence, either too little or too much, that her human rights have been violated; she has, though, not been fairly treated."

12. See, e.g., Griffin 2008, p. 263.

13. Raz makes a similar point in Raz 2010.

14. Griffin 2008, pp. 34, 53, 263; see also p. 41.

15. Griffin 2008, p. 34.

16. See, e.g., Article 12.1, which promises the "right of everyone to the enjoyment of the highest attainable standard of physical and mental health."

17. Though I won't be able to make good on this claim here, I also believe that Orthodox accounts of human rights that try to ground human rights in some account of basic human needs, or basic capabilities, also will fall afoul of both the Normativity and Determinacy Desiderata. See, e.g., Sen 2004; Miller 2012. Why can only *basic* needs ground human rights claims? Why only *basic* capabilities?

18. Griffin 2008, p. 38.

19. Tasioulas 2010, p. 662.

20. Griffin 2008, p. 92.

21. Tasioulas 2011, p. 37.

22. It is revealing that Griffin claims that prisoners' human rights are indeed infringed, but that this is justified, all things considered, on the basis that they morally deserve to be punished. See Griffin 2008, p. 64. I thank Rowan Cruft for pointing me to this passage in Griffin.

23. The brackets indicate the scope of the rights claim.

24. See Wolterstorff 2010, pp. 314–315. Tasioulas responds in Tasioulas 2011, pp. 38–41.

25. Tasioulas 2011, p. 39.

26. See Tasioulas 2011, p. 39.

27. I am indebted to discussion in Waldron forthcoming-a for the arguments I make in this section.

28. This also strikes me as applying to Beitz's discussion of women's human rights. He claims that many of the concerns defended in the Convention on the Elimination of All Forms of Discrimination against Women cannot be bona fide human rights because it would be infeasible to pursue international action to change them: "The inference is that a government's failure to comply with those elements of women's human rights doctrine that require efforts to bring about substantial cultural change does not supply a reason for action by outside agents because there is no plausibly effective strategy of action for

which it could be a reason. But if this is correct, then these elements do not satisfy one of our schematic conditions for justifying human rights: they are not appropriately matters of international concern. . . . But human rights are supposed to be matters of international concern, and if there are no feasible means of expressing this concern in political action, then perhaps to this extent women's human rights doctrine overreaches" (Beitz 2009, p. 195). Whether women have human rights turns out to vary according to how feasible international efforts at social change in fact would be.

29. See, e.g., Neier 2012, chap. 3.

30. See, e.g., Alston and Goodman 2008.

31. See, e.g., Beitz 2009, p. 109.

32. I here imagine that we have answers to the criticisms made in the text above.

33. Chalmers 2011, p. 526.

34. The violation must be systematic. To determine whether the assassination of Archduke Franz Ferdinand was a human rights violation, we need to assess whether assassinations *qua* assassinations merit universal concern, rather than the particular fact that a single such assassination led to a chain of events with global significance. I thank Adam Etinson for the need to clarify.

35. In 2007, Austrian animal rights activists fought to have a chimpanzee (named Matthew Hiasl Pan) declared a person. See also the Nonhuman Rights Project, on which see more here: http://www.nonhumanrightsproject.org /overview/.

36. Cf. Griffin 2008, p. 92, where he denies that children or the cognitively disabled have human rights.

37. Therefore, if the right to self-determination is a moral right held by a collective, then it can be, on the Broad construal, a human right. It is a further, normative and substantive question whether, in a particular context, its violation *qua* collective right merits universal moral, legal, and political concern.

38. Cf. Beitz 2009, p. 122.

39. For the distinction between "interactional" and "institutional" accounts, see Pogge 2002, chap. 2.

40. I return to the idea of a "basic" right specified in this way in Chapter 6.

41. I am indebted to Rainer Forst for how to conceive of this relation and to helpful discussion with Massimo Renzo. I note in particular the structural similarity between Forst's "right to justification" and its articulation in a system of political *cum* human rights, and my appeal to higher-order moral rights and how they are construed in different contexts of justification (on which, see more below). See Forst 2011, chap. 9.

42. For one interpretation of the context-sensitivity of gradable adjectives, see Kennedy 2007; on quantifier domain restrictions, see Stanley and Szabó 2000. I here remain neutral on how, among other things, the semantic and

pragmatic aspects of an utterance in a context combine to establish and fix the parameter, and what the best account of the parameter itself is.

43. Here I note in passing that although I am focusing in this chapter on *moral* human rights, the same thing could be said regarding *legal* human rights, i.e., legal human rights are those legal rights that ought to garner a particular kind of universal legal concern but where the type of "legal concern" envisaged varies by context (ECHR, ICCPR, etc.). I turn to legal human rights, and their relation to moral rights, in Chapter 5. So when I mention legal contexts in this chapter, I refer to moral human rights that might provide reasons for the realization of a corresponding legal right or norm or some other legal right or norm that, though not the same in content, is necessary to protect or promote the realization of an underlying moral human right.

44. Cf. Peter Benenson's 1961 *Observer* article, "The Forgotten Prisoners," which founded Amnesty International: "The force of opinion, to be effective, should be broadly based, international, non-sectarian and all-party. Campaigns in favour of freedom brought by one country, or party, against another, often achieve nothing but an intensification of persecution." http://www.amnesty usa.org/about-us/amnesty-50-years/peter-benenson-remembered/the -forgotten-prisoners-by-peter-benenson. See also Moyn 2010 and Neier 2012 on Amnesty's neutrality.

45. See also its very first campaign, launched in Benenson's "The Forgotten Prisoners," which focused on the rights of prisoners from Romania, the United States, Angola, Portugal, Czechoslovakia, Greece, and Hungary.

46. The monitoring and informational function is predominant in an organization like Human Rights Watch.

47. An example is its recent call for the United Kingdom to accept greater numbers of refugees from Syria. See also its 2007 calls to impose economic sanctions on Sudan in the Darfur conflict, http://www.globalpolicy.org /images/pdfs/sudanamnesty.pdf: "Amnesty International is urgently calling upon the international community to assert its authority and immediately adopt steps to strengthen the implementation of the UN arms embargo and stem the flow of arms to Darfur as part of a package of immediate measures to help protect civilians and uphold their human rights as is required by international law." No *military* action, on the other hand, was called for in 1997 in Zaire or in 1999 in Kosovo.

48. See Redfield 2013, pp. 104–105, on Medecins Sans Frontière's (MSF) 1994 calls for outright military intervention in Rwanda under the slogan "You can't stop genocide with doctors." The internal struggle over this decision was crucial in the development of MSF. And cf. the internal dispute between MSF and one of its founding members, Bernard Kouchner (later the head of a splinter group, the Medecins du Monde), on the right (and duty) to undertake (often coercive) interventions *in situ*. See Dechaine 2005; Redfield 2013, p. 12.

49. On the ECHR, see Letsas 2007.

50. See, e.g., Parker 1988; Simma and Alston 1988; Bianchi 2008; and, on the distinction between *erga omnes* norms and *jus cogens,* see, e.g., Bianchi 2008, pp. 501–503. I return to this in Chapter 6.

51. As a particularly interesting example of a strategic adoption of a more Political approach, consider that nongovernmental organizations (NGOs) like Amnesty and Human Rights Watch often file amicus briefs in particularly high-profile cases. See, for example, the joint amicus filed by Interights and Human Rights Watch, among others, in *Al Skeini and Others v. UK* (2011), 55721/07 ECHR, or Amnesty's amicus in *Cayara v. Peru* (1993), Series C No. 14 IACHR. In those cases, NGOs take on the perspective of the court in question and adopt a particular concept of human rights that fits that perspective (while seeking, simultaneously, to extend the reach and ambit of the court's jurisprudence). On the role of NGOs generally in filing such briefs, see Van den Eynde 2013. I thank Matthias Mahlmann, Steve Ratner, and Chris McCrudden for helpful discussion.

52. These two kinds of disagreement would be examples of what Plunkett and Sundell (2013) call "metalinguistic negotiations." I am grateful to Eliot Michaelson for discussion.

53. I am grateful to Charles Beitz for helping me to see the need for responding to his objection.

54. I thank Philip Alston for discussion on this assumption.

5. INTERNATIONAL LEGAL HUMAN RIGHTS AND EQUAL MORAL STATUS

1. With the exception of Allen Buchanan, who argues that the system of ILHRs need not have anything to do with the protection of individual moral rights at all. I discuss Buchanan's view at length below. I hence agree with Charles Beitz's useful "two-level model," as long as we see his account as a characterization of ILHRs rather than human rights *simpliciter* and as long as we allow for duty-bearers to include individuals and other nonstate actors as well (e.g., crimes against humanity). See Beitz 2009, pp. 109–110.

2. For legitimacy, see, e.g., Buchanan 2013.

3. Buchanan 2013, pp. 30–31; see also Besson 2013.

4. If I am right, then the Grounding View could be used by both Political and Orthodox views to defend their arguments against Buchanan. But note that they would still face the criticisms leveled in the previous chapter.

5. Buchanan 2013, p. 53.

6. See Human Rights Watch, "Protecting Child and Adult Gold Miners against Mercury: A Right to Health Issue," October 17, 2011, http://www.hrw.org

/news/2011/10/17/protecting-child-and-adult-gold-miners-against-mercury
-right-health-issue.

7. Buchanan 2013, p. 27; emphasis added.

8. See, e.g., Buchanan 2013, p. 68.

9. David Luban makes a similar point in Luban 2015.

10. Buchanan 2013, p. 70.

11. See Sreenivasan 2012; Buchanan 2013, pp. 58–64.

12. I discuss this response to Buchanan's objection to the Mirroring View at greater length in Sangiovanni forthcoming-a.

13. For a powerful account of the reasons Britain should not leave the ECHR, see Gearty 2016.

14. For more on this kind of argument and its problems, see the excellent Tan 2006.

15. For these criteria, see the Montevideo Convention.

16. But see Krasner 1999 for the variety of ways in which Westphalian sovereignty has historically been thwarted.

17. On the "thin" justice of extraterritorial application of human rights norms and universal jurisdiction, see Ratner 2015, chap. 8.

18. I therefore agree with David Owen's instructive analysis of the international refugee regime as a "legitimacy-repair mechanism," required by the existence of a system of states. See Owen 2016.

19. For similar lists, see Pogge 2002; Buchanan 2013.

20. The classic statement of this argument is Pogge 2002; see also Pogge 2005. It is important to note, however, that here we are focusing on the state system *in toto* rather than this or that aspect of the international *cum* global order that the state system makes possible (the arms trade, the resource and borrowing privileges, the system of pharmaceutical patents, etc.). The difficulties the argument faces when applied to the state system *in toto,* which I will discuss below, may not be as relevant when applied to narrower aspects of the international *cum* global order.

21. Cf. Leeson 2007.

22. Pogge calls this a "consequentialist baseline."

23. Though this is done mainly through international humanitarian law, there is a growing trend for human rights methods and practice to influence the development of IHL. See, e.g., Meron 2000.

24. Though see Hathaway 2002, Goodman and Jinks 2003, and B. Simmons 2009 for critique.

25. Cf. Pogge: "The topic of my inquiry can be defined through three distinctions. The first distinction concerns the different ways in which individual and collective agents can be related to unfulfilled human rights. Here, first, a human rights deficit may lie beyond an agent's capacities. In such cases, the agent bears no responsibility for the deficit (insofar as it lies in the past) and

has no responsibilities in regard to it (insofar as it lies in the future). Second, an agent may have the capacity to diminish a human rights deficit and may then bear some responsibility for it (by virtue of neglecting a positive duty to reduce it) or have a responsibility to alleviate it. Third, an agent may have a *role in bringing about* a human rights deficit and may then (by virtue of violating a negative duty not to harm) bear some responsibility for it or have a responsibility not to contribute to it in the future. I call all and only such *active* contributions [as defined by the third distinction] to the nonfulfillment of human rights, when they are foreseeable and reasonably avoidable by the agent, human rights violations. And I focus on cases of this kind" (Pogge 2014, p. 74; emphasis added). Note also that this causal contribution need only be a nonredundant but unnecessary member of a set of sufficient conditions.

26. I defend the principle of reciprocity on which the Principle of Reciprocal Protection is based, along with potential objections, in Sangiovanni forthcoming-b. Here it is enough if it has enough intuitive plausibility to trigger the judgment that our obligations to prevent violations of our equal moral status are more stringent once we begin cooperating via institutions.

27. I give a more complete answer to A. John Simmons's famous critique of fair play (1979) in Sangiovanni forthcoming-b.

28. But what about the case in which you *illegitimately* coerce someone into helping you climb the mountain? In this case, if the rock slide should fall on the coerced climber, it strikes me as uncontroversial that you must help (both out of reciprocity but also out of compensation for illegitimately putting them in harm's way). But what if the landslide falls on you? Here it seems as if the other climber has only a duty of the first kind to help. But the duty lacks the stringency associated with reciprocity not because the other climber has been forced *simpliciter*, but because the other climber has been forced *illegitimately*. They therefore have a justification for not paying any extra costs, given the wrong that has been done to them. I discuss voluntariness and fair play in greater detail in Sangiovanni forthcoming-b.

29. For an account of the myriad forms of reciprocity, see Becker 1990.

30. Sangiovanni 2007, 2015a, forthcoming-b.

31. Why not a world state? If we assume, as seems plausible, that a world state would be a global despotism, then, by entering a world state, governments would be violating a duty to citizens to protect them from tyranny. The minimal basis for regulating interaction among states *qua* states is the international order that I have referred to as the state system. (This view is similar to the one Kant provides in *Perpetual Peace*, with the important difference that it does not rely on the wrongness of unilateral imposition to generate the duty to exit. On the implausibility of the idea of subjection and the innate right to freedom that underlies Kant's commitment to the wrongness of unilateral imposition, see Sangiovanni 2012, 2015b, forthcoming-d). It is a

further question what other forms of cooperation are morally mandatory. Indeed, my argument is that, once a state system is up and running, we also have duties to set up an ILHR system.

32. See also Beitz 2009, pp. 129–136.

33. For an illuminating account, see Skinner 1999.

34. This loss of legitimacy does not entail that other states may intervene or occupy the illegitimate state. It simply means that the state has lost a right to say to other states "this is none of your business." What further actions will be morally permissible as a response to this loss is a further question, which will depend on the circumstances and the wider relations between the parties.

6. FUNDAMENTAL RIGHTS, INDIVISIBILITY, AND HIERARCHY AMONG HUMAN RIGHTS

1. Shue 1996.

2. As we have seen in Chapter 2, I adopt an interest-based view of rights that is different from Shue's, since in my view what matters are the counterpart (directed) duties. Shue goes further and says that for something to be a right, it must be socially guaranteed by an authority. This is a more demanding condition. This difference between us doesn't affect the argument I make here. All I am drawing from Shue is the concept of a basic right, not the more general concept of a right.

3. Shue 1996, p. 27; emphasis added. See also p. 75 on rights to political participation.

4. As Shue writes, when discussing political participation as a basic right, "to enjoy something only at the discretion of someone else, especially someone powerful enough to deprive you of it at will, is precisely *not* to enjoy a *right* to it" (p. 78). Cf. Pettit 1997.

5. See, e.g., Human Rights Watch, "Saudi Arabia: New Law to Criminalize Domestic Abuse," September 3, 2013, http://www.hrw.org/news/2013/09/03/saudi -arabia-new-law-criminalize-domestic-abuse, on domestic violence in Saudi Arabia and its connection to other limitations on women's liberties in that country.

6. Shue 1996, p. 29.

7. Shue notes this as well: "No one can fully enjoy any right that is supposedly protected by society if someone can credibly threaten him or her with murder, rape, beating, etc." (Shue 1996, p. 21).

8. Cf. Wolff and De-Shalit 2013.

9. On governments and famines, see Sen 1999.

10. For Sen's "missing women," see Amartya Sen, "More than 100 Million Women Are Missing," *New York Review of Books*, December 20, 1990, available at

http://www.nybooks.com/articles/1990/12/20/more-than-100-million
-women-are-missing/. Sen argues that, at least in India, women are "missing"
because of neglect in early childhood due, he conjectures, to the lower status,
diminished voice, and above all economic dependence of women, who are
seen as less "valuable" in maintaining a household than men (on whom, most
often, the family relies for subsistence).

11. This is a central lesson of Raz's theory of rights and his emphasis on "dynamic
    duties" in Raz 1986.

12. See also efforts under CEDAW at combating domestic violence. A good over-
    view is Alston and Goodman 2008, pp. 196–205.

13. Note that the language of "gross and systematic" violations is receiving
    increasing attention within the UN system, particularly in relation to inter-
    national criminal law; see, for example, the chapters and commentary on
    "serious breaches" in the "Draft Articles on State Responsibility" in Crawford
    2002, pp. 242–254. See also the useful general overview at http://opil.ouplaw
    .com/view/10.1093/law:epil/9780199231690/law-9780199231690-e1732?prd
    =EPIL.

14. An important exception is Nickel 2008, to which I am indebted.

15. Proclamation of Teheran, Final Act of the International Conference on
    Human Rights, Teheran, U.N. Doc. A/CONF. 32/41 at 3 (1968).

16. Available at http://www.un.org/documents/ga/res/32/ares32r130.pdf.

17. Available at http://www.ohchr.org/EN/ProfessionalInterest/Pages/Vienna
    .aspx.

18. See, e.g., the United Nations Population Fund at http://www.unfpa.org
    /resources/human-rights-principles: "Human rights are indivisible. Whether
    they relate to civil, cultural, economic, political or social issues, human rights
    are inherent to the dignity of every human person. Consequently, all human
    rights have equal status and cannot be positioned in a hierarchical order. De-
    nial of one right invariably impedes enjoyment of other rights. Thus, the
    right of everyone to an adequate standard of living cannot be compromised
    at the expense of other rights, such as the right to health or the right to
    education."

19. See, e.g., Shelton 2006; Bianchi 2008; De Wet and Vidmar 2012.

20. Available at http://www.un.org/documents/ga/res/32/ares32r130.pdf.

21. See also Tasioulas 2016.

22. Meron 1986.

23. Cassese 2012, p. 136.

24. *Barcelona Traction*, ICJ Reports [1970], §33.

25. *Questions Relating to the Obligation to Prosecute or Extradite (Belgium v. Sen-
    egal)*, ICJ Reports 2012.

26. International Law Commission, "Draft Articles on State Responsibility," in
    Yearbook of the International Law Commission, 1976, vol. 2, part 2 (New York:

United Nations, 1977), p. 99, quoted in Meron 1986. The same phrasing is lacking in the 2001 version of the Draft Articles.

27. See, e.g., Koji 2001.

28. Other sources for such "super-norms" include Article 103 of the UN Charter, the idea of an international public order, and general principles of international law. Because these further sources are even more controversial as sources for hierarchy among jurists than the ones already mentioned, I leave them aside.

29. See Tasioulas 2016.

30. Once again, this is not to say that international human rights law should be *only* concerned with such fundamental violations. As I argued in Chapter 4, I do not believe there is a single moral foundation for *all* human rights norms.

31. Cf. Beitz's warning against monistic grounds for human rights in Beitz 2013, p. 287.

32. I have however noted in the previous section that many, if not most, cases of famine, starvation, and other severe deprivation are, in fact, best understood not as the result of natural disaster but political choice. And, as a result of a political choice, the denial of such basic necessities must count, if anything does, as a form of inferiorizing social cruelty, and hence also as a violation of equal moral status.

33. I say more in Sangiovanni 2013 and in Sangiovanni forthcoming-b.

REFERENCES

Alexander, L. (1992). "What Makes Wrongful Discrimination Wrong? Biases, Preferences, Stereotypes, and Proxies." *University of Pennsylvania Law Review* 194: 149–219.

Alston, P., and R. Goodman (2008). *International Human Rights in Context* (Oxford: Oxford University Press).

Anderson, E. (1999). "What Is the Point of Equality?" *Ethics* 109: 287–337.

Anderson, E. (2006). "Recent Thinking about Sexual Harassment: A Review Essay." *Philosophy & Public Affairs* 34: 284–312.

Anderson, E. (2008). "Emotions in Kant's Later Moral Philosophy: Honour and the Phenomenology of Moral Value." In *Kant's Ethics of Virtue,* ed. Monika Betzler, pp. 123–147 (Berlin: de Gruyter).

Anderson, E. (2010). *The Imperative of Integration* (Princeton, NJ: Princeton University Press).

Anderson, E., and R. Pildes (2000). "Expressive Theories of Law: A General Restatement." *University of Pennsylvania Law Review* 148: 1503–1575.

Arendt, H. (1971). *The Human Condition* (Chicago: University of Chicago Press).

Arneson, R. (1999). "What, If Anything, Renders All Humans Morally Equal?" In *Singer and His Critics,* ed. Dale Jamieson, pp. 103–129 (London: Routledge).

Arneson, R. (2006). "What Is Wrongful Discrimination?" *San Diego Law Review* 43: 775–808.

Arneson, R. (2014). "Basic Equality: Neither Acceptable nor Rejectable." In *Do All Persons Have Equal Moral Worth? On "Basic Equality" and Equal Respect and Concern,* ed. Uwe Steinhoff, pp. 30–53 (Oxford: Oxford University Press).

Arpaly, N., and T. Schroeder (1999). "Praise, Blame, and the Whole Self." *Philosophical Studies* 93: 161–188.

Beauvoir, S. de (2012). *The Second Sex* [1949] (New York: Vintage).

Becker, L. (1990). *Reciprocity* (Chicago: University of Chicago Press).

Beitz, C. (2009). *The Idea of Human Rights* (Oxford: Oxford University Press).

Beitz, C. (2013). "Human Dignity in the Theory of Human Rights: Nothing but a Phrase?" *Philosophy & Public Affairs* 41: 259–290.

Besson, S. (2013). "The Egalitarian Dimension of Human Rights." *Archiv für Sozial-und Rechtsphilosophie Beiheft* 136: 19–52.

Bianchi, A. (2008). "Human Rights and the Magic of Jus Cogens." *European Journal of International Law* 19: 491–508.

Bird, C. (2013). "Dignity as a Moral Concept." *Social Philosophy and Policy* 30: 150–176.

Blackburn, S. (1998). *Ruling Passions: A Theory of Practical Reason* (Oxford: Oxford University Press).

Buchanan, A. (2010). "The Egalitarianism of Human Rights." *Ethics* 120: 679–710.

Buchanan, A. (2013). *The Heart of Human Rights* (Oxford: Oxford University Press).

Byrd, S., and J. Hruschka (2010). *Kant's Doctrine of Right: A Commentary* (Cambridge: Cambridge University Press).

Calhoun, C. (1995). "Standing for Something." *Journal of Philosophy* 92: 235–260.

Card, C. (2003). "Genocide and Social Death." *Hypatia* 18: 63–79.

Carter, I. (2011). "Respect and the Basis of Equality." *Ethics* 121: 538–571.

Casas, B. de las (1992). *In Defense of the Indians,* trans. and ed. Stafford Poole (DeKalb: Northern Illinois University Press).

Cassese, A. (2012). *Realizing Utopia: The Future of International Law* (Oxford: Oxford University Press).

Castiglione, B. (2002). *The Book of the Courtier,* trans. Charles Singleton (New York: Norton).

Chalmers, D. J. (2011). "Verbal Disputes." *Philosophical Review* 120: 515–566.

Chodorow, N. (1978). *The Reproduction of Mothering* (Berkeley: University of California Press).

Christiano, T. (2014). "Rationality, Equal Status, and Egalitarianism." In *Do All Persons Have Equal Moral Worth? On "Basic Equality" and Equal Respect and Concern,* ed. Uwe Steinhoff, pp. 53–76 (Oxford: Oxford University Press).

Cicero, M. T. (1913). *De Officiis,* trans. Walter Miller (Cambridge, MA: Harvard University Press).

Cicero, M. T. (1991). *Cicero: On Duties* (Cambridge: Cambridge University Press).

Cicero, M. T. (2001). *Cicero: On Moral Ends* (Cambridge: Cambridge University Press).

Cohen, G. A. (2013). "Notes on Regarding People as Equals." In *Finding Oneself in the Other,* ed. Michael Otsuka, pp. 193–201 (Princeton, NJ: Princeton University Press).

Cooper, J., and J. Procopé (1995). *Seneca: Moral and Political Essays* (Cambridge: Cambridge University Press).

Cooper, J. M. (2012). *Pursuits of Wisdom: Six Ways of Life in Ancient Philosophy from Socrates to Plotinus* (Princeton, NJ: Princeton University Press).

Cortes, J. D. (1879). *Essays on Catholicism, Liberalism, and Socialism, Considered in Their Fundamental Principles,* ed. William McDonald (Dublin: Gill & Son).

Crawford, J. (2002). *The International Law Commission's Articles on State Responsibility: Introduction, Text and Commentaries* (Cambridge: Cambridge University Press).

Crowe, D. (1996). *A History of the Gypsies of Eastern Europe and Russia* (London: Palgrave).

Crowe, D. (2008). "The Roma in Post-Communist Eastern Europe: Questions of Ethnic Conflict and Ethnic Peace." *Nationalities Papers* 36: 521–552.

Cruft, R. (2013). "Why Is It Disrespectful to Violate Rights?" *Proceedings of the Aristotelian Society* 113: 201–224.

Daniels, N. (1996). *Justice and Justification* (Cambridge: Cambridge University Press).

Dante, A. (2010). *La Divina Commedia: Inferno,* ed. Umberto Bosco and Giovanni Reggio (Milano: Mondadori).

Darwall, S. (1977). "Two Kinds of Respect." *Ethics* 88: 36–49.

Darwall, S. (2006). *The Second-Person Standpoint* (Cambridge, MA: Harvard University Press).

Dechaine, D. R. (2005). *Global Humanitarianism: NGOs and the Crafting of Community* (Oxford: Lexington).

De Wet, E., and J. Vidmar (2012). *Hierarchy in International Law: The Place of Human Rights* (Oxford: Oxford University Press).

Didion, J. (2007). *The Year of Magical Thinking* (New York: Vintage).

Dostoevsky, F. (1991). *The Brothers Karamazov,* trans. Richard Pevear and Larissa Volokhonsky (New York: Vintage).

Du Bois, W. E. B. (2007). *The Souls of Black Folk* (Oxford: Oxford University Press).

Duff, A. (1990). *Intention, Agency and Criminal Liability* (London: Blackwell).

Duff, A. (1996). *Criminal Attempts* (Oxford: Oxford University Press).

Duff, A. (2001). "Harms and Wrongs." *Buffalo Criminal Law Review* 5: 13–45.

Dworkin, R. (2011). *Justice for Hedgehogs* (Cambridge, MA: Harvard University Press).

Eidelson, B. (2015). *Discrimination and Disrespect* (Oxford: Oxford University Press).

Elstein, D., and T. Hurka (2009). "From Thick to Thin: Two Moral Reduction Plans." *Canadian Journal of Philosophy* 39: 515–535.

Engberg-Pedersen, T. (1990). *The Stoic Theory of Oikeiosis: Moral Development and Social Interaction in Early Stoic Philosophy* (Aarhus: Aarhus Universitetsforlag).

Enoch, D. (2006). "Agency, Shmagency: Why Normativity Won't Come from What Is Constitutive of Action." *Philosophical Review* 115: 169–198.

Fanon, F. (1952). *Black Skin, White Masks* (New York: Grove Press).

Fara, M. (2008). "Masked Abilities and Compatibilism." *Mind* 117: 843–865.

Feinberg, J. (1973). "Some Conjectures about the Concept of Respect." *Journal of Social Philosophy* 4: 1–3.

Finnis, J. (1997). "A Philosophical Case against Euthanasia." In *Euthanasia Examined: Ethical, Clinical and Legal Perspectives,* ed. John Keown, pp. 23–36 (Cambridge: Cambridge University Press).

Fiss, O. (1976). "Groups and the Equal Protection Clause." *Philosophy & Public Affairs* 5: 107–177.

Forst, R. (2011). *The Right to Justification: Elements of a Constructivist Theory of Justice* (New York: Columbia University Press).

Forst, R. (2014). "Response." In *Justice, Democracy and the Right to Justification: Rainer Forst in Dialogue,* ed. David Owen, pp. 169–217 (London: Bloomsbury).

Fourie, C., F. Schuppert, and I. Wallimann-Helmer, eds. (2015). *Social Equality: On What It Means to Be Equals* (Oxford: Oxford University Press).

Franke, K. (1997). "What's Wrong with Sexual Harassment?" *Stanford Law Review* 49: 691–772.

Frankfurt, H. (1988). *The Importance of What We Care About* (Cambridge: Cambridge University Press).

Frankfurt, H. (1999). *Necessity, Volition, and Love* (Cambridge: Cambridge University Press).

Freud, S. (1960a). "Jokes and Their Relation to the Unconscious." In *The Standard Edition of the Complete Psychological Works of Sigmund Freud,* vol. 8, ed. James Strachey (London: Hogarth Press).

Freud, S. (1960b). "Notes upon a Case of Obsessional Neurosis." In *The Standard Edition of the Complete Psychological Works of Sigmund Freud,* vol. 10, ed. James Strachey (London: Hogarth Press).

Fricker, M. (2007). *Epistemic Injustice: Power and the Ethics of Knowing* (Oxford: Oxford University Press).

Fricker, M. (2016). "What's the Point of Blame? A Paradigm-Based Explanation." *Noûs* 50: 165–183.

Gardner, J. (1989). "Liberals and Unlawful Discrimination." *Oxford Journal of Legal Studies:* 1–22.

Gardner, J. (2007). "Complicity and Causality." *Criminal Law and Philosophy* 1: 127–141.

Gardner, J., and S. Shute (2000). "The Wrongness of Rape." In *Oxford Essays in Jurisprudence, 4th Series,* ed. J. Horder, pp. 193–217 (Oxford: Oxford University Press).

Garnsey, P. (1996). *Ideas of Slavery from Aristotle to Augustine* (Cambridge: Cambridge University Press).

Gearty, C. (2016). *On Fantasy Island: Britain, Europe, and Human Rights* (Oxford: Oxford University Press).

Gibbard, A. (1990). *Wise Choices, Apt Feelings: A Theory of Normative Judgment* (Cambridge, MA: Harvard University Press).

Gibbard, A. (1999). "Morality as Consistency in Living: Korsgaard's Kantian Lectures." *Ethics* 110: 140–164.

Gibbard, A. (2003). *Thinking How to Live* (Cambridge, MA: Harvard University Press).

Ginsburg, R. B. (2008). "*Muller v. Oregon:* One Hundred Years Later." *Willamette Law Review* 45: 359–380.

Glasgow, J. (2009). "Racism as Disrespect." *Ethics* 120: 64–93.

Glover, J. (2012). *Humanity* (New Haven, CT: Yale University Press).

Goffman, E. (1956). *The Presentation of Self in Everyday Life* (Edinburgh: University of Edinburgh, Social Sciences Research Centre).

Goffman, E. (1961). "On the Characteristics of Total Institutions." In *Asylums* (New York: Penguin).

Goffman, E. (1963). *Stigma* (Englewood Cliffs, NJ: Prentice-Hall).

Goodman, R., and D. Jinks (2003). "Measuring the Effects of Human Rights Treaties." *European Journal of International Law* 14: 171–183.

Green, L. (1998). "Pornographizing, Subordinating, Silencing." In *Censorship and Silencing: Practices of Cultural Regulation,* ed. Robert Post, pp. 285–311 (Los Angeles: Getty Research Institute).

Green, L. (2000). "Pornographies." *Journal of Political Philosophy* 8: 27–52.

Greenwald, A., and L. H. Krieger (2006). "Implicit Bias: Scientific Foundations." *California Law Review* 94: 945–967.

Greer, G. (1971). *The Female Eunuch* (New York: Farrar, Strauss & Giroux).

Griffin, J. (2008). *On Human Rights* (Oxford: Oxford University Press).

Grosseteste, R. (1972). *Ethica Nicomachea: Libri I–III ("recensio pura"),* ed. R. A. Gauthier (Turnhout: Aristoteles Latinus).

Guenther, L. (2013). *Solitary Confinement: Social Death and Its Afterlives* (Minneapolis: University of Minnesota Press).

Haslanger, S. (2012). "On Being Objective and Being Objectified." In *Resisting Reality: Social Construction and Social Critique,* pp. 35–83 (Oxford: Oxford University Press).

Hathaway, O. (2002). "Do Human Rights Treaties Make a Difference?" *Yale Law Journal* 111: 1935–2042.

Hellman, D. (2008). *When Is Discrimination Wrong?* (Cambridge, MA: Harvard University Press).

Hellman, D., and S. Moreau, eds. (2013). *Philosophical Foundations of Discrimination Law* (Oxford: Oxford University Press).

Herman, B. (1989). "Murder and Mayhem: Violence and Kantian Casuistry." *The Monist* 72: 411–431.

Hill, T. (2000). *Respect, Pluralism, and Justice: Kantian Perspectives* (Oxford: Oxford University Press).

Hohfeld, W. N. (1964). *Fundamental Legal Conceptions, as Applied in Judicial Reasoning* (New Haven, CT: Yale University Press).

Hornsby, J., and R. Langton (1998). "Free Speech and Illocution." *Legal Theory* 4: 21–37.

Hume, D. (1998). *An Enquiry Concerning the Principles of Morals,* ed. Tom L. Beauchamp (Oxford: Oxford University Press).

Hurston, Z. N. (1990). *Their Eyes Were Watching God* (New York: Perennial).

Jolls, C., and C. R. Sunstein (2006). "The Law of Implicit Bias." *California Law Review* 94: 969–996.

Jones, C., and M. Kaplan (2003). "The Effects of Racially Stereotypical Crimes on Juror Decision-Making and Information-Processing Strategies." *Basic and Applied Social Psychology* 25: 1–13.

Kagan, S. (2016). "What's Wrong with Speciesism?" *Journal of Applied Philosophy* 33: 1–21.

Kant, I. (1998). *Critique of Pure Reason,* ed. Paul Guyer and Allen W. Wood (Cambridge: Cambridge University Press).

Kant, I. (1999). *Practical Philosophy,* ed. Mary Gregor (Cambridge: Cambridge University Press).

Kekes, J. (1996). "Cruelty and Liberalism." *Ethics* 106: 834–844.

Kelly, J. (1982). "Early Feminist Theory and the 'Querelle Des Femmes,' 1400–1789." *Signs* 8: 4–28.

Kennedy, C. (2007). "Vagueness and Grammar: The Semantics of Relative and Absolute Gradable Adjectives." *Linguistics and Philosophy* 30: 1–45.

Khaitan, T. (2015). *A Theory of Discrimination Law* (Oxford: Oxford University Press).

Klein, L. (2002). "Politeness and the Interpretation of the British Eighteenth Century." *The Historical Journal* 45: 869–898.

Koji, T. (2001). "Emerging Hierarchy in International Human Rights and Beyond: From the Perspective of Non-derogable Rights." *European Journal of International Law* 12: 917–941.

Kolnai, A. (1976). "Dignity." *Philosophy* 51: 251–271.

Korsgaard, C. (1996a). *Creating the Kingdom of Ends* (Cambridge: Cambridge University Press).

Korsgaard, C. (1996b). "Two Distinctions in Goodness." In *Creating the Kingdom of Ends,* pp. 249–275 (Cambridge: Cambridge University Press).

Korsgaard, C. (2003). "Realism and Constructivism in Twentieth-Century Moral Philosophy." *Journal of Philosophical Research* 28: 99–122.

Korsgaard, C. (2004). *The Sources of Normativity* (Cambridge: Cambridge University Press).

Kramer, M. (1998). "Rights without Trimmings." In *A Debate over Rights,* ed. Matthew Kramer, pp. 60–100 (Oxford: Oxford University Press).

Kramer, M. (2014). *Torture and Moral Integrity* (Oxford: Oxford University Press).

Krasner, S. D. (1999). *Sovereignty: Organized Hypocrisy* (Princeton, NJ: Princeton University Press).

Kraut, R. (2011). *Against Absolute Goodness* (Oxford: Oxford University Press).

Kristeller, P. O. (1978). "Humanism." *Minerva* 16: 586–595.

Kutz, C. (2000). *Complicity* (Cambridge: Cambridge University Press).

Langton, R. (1993). "Speech Acts and Unspeakable Acts." *Philosophy & Public Affairs* 22: 293–330.

Langton, R. (2000). "Feminism in Epistemology: Exclusion and Objectification." In *The Cambridge Companion to Feminism in Philosophy,* ed. Miranda Fricker and Jennifer Hornsby, pp. 127–145 (Cambridge: Cambridge University Press).

Lee, P., and R. P. George (2008). "The Nature and Basis of Human Dignity." *Ratio Juris* 21: 173–193.

Leeson, P. T. (2007). "Better Off Stateless: Somalia before and after Government Collapse." *Journal of Comparative Economics* 35: 689–710.

Lepora, C., and R. E. Goodin (2013). *On Complicity and Compromise* (Oxford: Oxford University Press).

Lerner, G. (1986). *The Creation of Patriarchy* (Oxford: Oxford University Press).

Letsas, G. (2007). *A Theory of Interpretation of the European Convention on Human Rights* (Oxford: Oxford University Press).

Levi, P. (1996). *Survival in Auschwitz* (New York: Simon & Schuster).

Levy, N. (2005). "The Good, the Bad and the Blameworthy." *Journal of Ethics and Social Philosophy* 1: 1–16.

Lippert-Rasmussen, K. (2013). *Born Free and Equal?* (Oxford: Oxford University Press).

Lipsius, J. (2006). *On Constancy,* trans. John Stradling (Bristol: Bristol Phoenix Press).

Lipton, P. (2004). *Inference to the Best Explanation,* 2nd ed. (London: Routledge).

Loury, G. (2009). *The Anatomy of Racial Inequality* (Cambridge, MA: Harvard University Press).

Loury, G., P. Karlan, T. Shelby, and L. Wacquant (2008). *Race, Incarceration, and American Values* (Cambridge, MA: MIT Press).

Luban, D. (2007). "Liberalism, Torture, and the Ticking Bomb." *Virginia Law Review* 91: 1425–1461.

Luban, D. (2015). "Human Rights Pragmatism and Human Dignity." In *Philosophical Foundations of Human Rights,* ed. Rowan Cruft and Massimo Renzo, pp. 263–279 (Oxford: Oxford University Press).

Lugones, M. (1990). "Hispaneando y lesbiando: On Sarah Hoagland's Lesbian Ethics." *Hypatia* 5: 138–146.

MacKinnon, C. (1979). *Sexual Harassment of Working Women* (New Haven, CT: Yale University Press).

MacKinnon, C. (1987). *Feminism Unmodified: Discourses on Life and Law* (Cambridge, MA: Harvard University Press).

Margalit, A. (1996). *The Decent Society* (Cambridge, MA: Harvard University Press).

McCrudden, C. (2008). "Human Dignity and Judicial Interpretation of Human Rights." *European Journal of International Law* 19: 655–724.

McGreevy, J. T. (2009). "Catholics, History, and Conscience." *Villanova Law Review* 54: 609–612.

McMahan, J. (2002). *The Ethics of Killing* (Oxford: Oxford University Press).

McMahan, J. (2016). "On 'Modal Personism.'" *Journal of Applied Philosophy* 33: 26–30.

Meron, T. (1986). "On a Hierarchy of International Human Rights." *American Journal of International Law* 80: 1–23.

Meron, T. (2000). "The Humanization of Humanitarian Law." *American Journal of International Law* 94: 239–278.

Mill, J. S. (1984). *Collected Works of John Stuart Mill,* vol. 21, ed. John Robson (Toronto: University of Toronto Press).

Miller, D. (2012). "Grounding Human Rights." *Critical Review of International Social and Political Philosophy* 15: 407–427.

Misner, P. (1991). "The Predecessors of *Rerum Novarum* within Catholicism." *Review of Social Economy* 49: 444–464.

Montaigne, M. (1965). *The Complete Essays of Montaigne,* ed. Donald Murdoch Frame (Stanford, CA: Stanford University Press).

Moreau, S. (2010). "Discrimination as Negligence." *Canadian Journal of Philosophy* 40: 123–149.

Morrison, T. (1987). *Beloved* (New York: Knopf).

Moss-Racusin, C., J. Dovidio, V. Brescoll, M. Graham, and J. Handelsman (2012). "Science Faculty's Subtle Gender Biases Favor Male Students." *Proceedings of the National Academy of Sciences* 109: 16474–16479.

Moyn, S. (2010). *The Last Utopia* (Cambridge, MA: Harvard University Press).

Moyn, S. (2013). "Jacques Maritain, Christian New Order, and the Birth of Human Rights." In *Intercultural Dialogue and Human Rights,* ed. Luigi Bonanante, Roberto Papini, and William Sweet, pp. 55–77 (Washington, DC: Council for Research in Values and Philosophy).

Nagel, T. (1979a). "War and Massacre." In *Mortal Questions,* pp. 53–75 (Cambridge: Cambridge University Press).

Nagel, T. (1979b). "What Is It Like to Be a Bat?" In *Mortal Questions,* pp. 165–181 (Cambridge: Cambridge University Press).

Nagel, T. (2002). *Concealment and Exposure* (Oxford: Oxford University Press).

Nathan, C. (2014). "What Is Basic Equality?" In *Do All Persons Have Equal Moral Worth? On "Basic Equality" and Equal Respect and Concern,* ed. Uwe Steinhoff, pp. 1–17 (Oxford: Oxford University Press).

Neier, A. (2012). *The International Human Rights Movement: A History* (Princeton, NJ: Princeton University Press).

Nickel, J. (2008). "Rethinking Indivisibility: Towards a Theory of Supporting Relations between Human Rights." *Human Rights Quarterly* 30: 984–1001.

Nozick, R. (1974). *Anarchy, State, and Utopia* (New York: Basic Books).

Nussbaum, M. (1995). "Objectification." *Philosophy & Public Affairs* 24: 249–291.

Nussbaum, M. (1996). *For Love of Country?* (Boston: Beacon Press).

Nussbaum, M. (2001). "Symposium on Amartya Sen's Philosophy: 5 Adaptive Preferences and Women's Options." *Economics and Philosophy* 17: 67–88.

Nussbaum, M. (2011). *Creating Capabilities* (Cambridge, MA: Harvard University Press).

Okin, S. M. (1989). *Justice, Gender, and the Family* (New York: Basic Books).

O'Malley, J. (2010). *What Happened at Vatican II* (Cambridge, MA: Harvard University Press).

O'Neill, O. (1989). *Constructions of Reason* (Cambridge: Cambridge University Press).

Owen, D. (2016). "In Loco Civitatis." In *Migration in Political Theory: The Ethics of Movement and Membership,* ed. Sarah Fine and Lea Ypi, pp. 269–291 (Oxford: Oxford University Press).

Owens, D. (2011). "The Possibility of Consent." *Ratio* 24: 402–421.

Owens, D. (2012). *Shaping the Normative Landscape* (Oxford: Oxford University Press).

Parfit, D. (1984). *Reasons and Persons* (Oxford: Oxford University Press).

Parfit, D. (2011). *On What Matters,* vols. 1 and 2 (Oxford: Oxford University Press).

Parker, K. (1988). "Jus Cogens: Compelling the Law of Human Rights." *Hastings International and Comparative Law Review* 12: 411–463.

Patterson, O. (1982). *Slavery and Social Death* (Cambridge, MA: Harvard University Press).

Patterson, O. (2000). "Taking Culture Seriously: A Framework and an Afro-American Illustration." In *Culture Matters: How Values Shape Human Progress,* ed. Lawrence Harrison and Samuel Huntington, pp. 202–218 (New York: Basic Books).

Pettit, P. (1997). *Republicanism: A Theory of Freedom and Government* (Oxford: Oxford University Press).

Phillips, A., and B. Taylor (1980). "Sex and Skill: Notes towards a Feminist Economics." *Feminist Review* 6: 79–88.

Pico Della Mirandola, G. (2012). *Oration on the Dignity of Man,* ed. Francesco Borghesi, Michael Papio, and Massimo Riva (Cambridge: Cambridge University Press).

Pinker, S. (2008). "The Stupidity of Dignity." *The New Republic,* May 28.

Plunkett, D., and T. Sundell (2013). "Disagreement and the Semantics of Normative and Evaluative Terms." *Philosopher's Imprint* 13: 1–37.

Pogge, T. (2002). *World Poverty and Human Rights* (Cambridge: Polity Press).

Pogge, T. (2005). "Real World Justice." *Journal of Ethics* 9: 29–53.

Pogge, T. (2014). "Are We Violating the Human Rights of the World's Poor? Responses to Four Critics." *Yale Human Rights and Development Journal* 17: 74–87.

Pojman, L. (1992). "Are Human Rights Based on Equal Human Worth?" *Philosophy and Phenomenological Research* 52: 605–622.

Power, S. (2002). *A Problem from Hell* (New York: Basic Books).

Prichard, H. A. (1912). "Does Moral Philosophy Rest on a Mistake?" *Mind* 21: 21–37.

Rao, N. (2007). "On the Use and Abuse of Dignity in Constitutional Law." *Columbia Journal of European Law* 14: 201–255.

Ratner, S. (2015). *The Thin Justice of International Law: A Moral Reckoning of the Law of Nations* (Oxford: Oxford University Press).

Rawls, J. (1999a). *The Law of Peoples* (Cambridge, MA: Harvard University Press).

Rawls, J. (1999b). *A Theory of Justice* (Cambridge, MA: Harvard University Press).

Raz, J. (1986). *The Morality of Freedom* (Oxford: Clarendon Press).

Raz, J. (1992). "Rights and Individual Well-Being." *Ratio Juris* 5: 127–142.

Raz, J. (2001). *Value, Respect, and Attachment* (Cambridge: Cambridge University Press).

Raz, J. (2010). "Human Rights without Foundations." In *The Philosophy of International Law*, ed. S. Besson and J. Tasioulas, pp. 321–339 (Oxford: Oxford University Press).

Redfield, P. (2013). *Life in Crisis: The Ethical Journey of Doctors without Borders* (Berkeley: University of California Press).

Roberts, D. (2011). "Shapelessness and the Thick." *Ethics* 121: 489–520.

Rosen, G. (2010). "Metaphysical Dependence: Grounding and Reduction." In *Modality: Metaphysics, Logic, and Epistemology*, ed. Bob Hale and Aviv Hoffmann, pp. 109–136 (Oxford: Oxford University Press).

Rosen, G. (2015). "Real Definition." *Analytic Philosophy* 56: 189–209.

Rosen, M. (2012). *Dignity: Its History and Meaning* (Cambridge, MA: Harvard University Press).

Rousseau, J.-J. (1997). *The Discourses and Other Early Political Writings*, ed. Victor Gourevitch (Cambridge: Cambridge University Press).

Sangiovanni, A. (2007). "Global Justice, Reciprocity, and the State." *Philosophy & Public Affairs* 35: 2–39.

Sangiovanni, A. (2008). "Justice and the Priority of Politics to Morality." *Journal of Political Philosophy* 16: 137–164.

Sangiovanni, A. (2012). "Can the Innate Right to Freedom Alone Ground a System of Public and Private Rights?" *European Journal of Philosophy* 20: 460–469.

Sangiovanni, A. (2013). "On the Relation between Moral and Distributive Equality." In *Cosmopolitanism versus Non-Cosmopolitanism*, ed. Gillian Brock, pp. 55–75 (Oxford: Oxford University Press).

Sangiovanni, A. (2014). "Scottish Constructivism and the Right to Justification." In *Justice, Democracy and the Right to Justification: Rainer Forst in Dialogue*, ed. David Owen, pp. 29–65 (London: Bloomsbury).

Sangiovanni, A. (2015a). "Solidarity as Joint Action." *Journal of Applied Philosophy* 32: 340–359.

Sangiovanni, A. (2015b). "Why There Can Be No Truly Kantian Theory of Human Rights." In *Philosophical Foundations of Human Rights,* ed. Rowan Cruft and Massimo Renzo, pp. 671–691 (Oxford: Oxford University Press).

Sangiovanni, A. (2016). "How Practices Matter." *Journal of Political Philosophy* 24: 3–23.

Sangiovanni, A. (forthcoming-a). "Are Moral Rights Necessary for the Justification of International Legal Human Rights?" *Ethics & International Affairs.*

Sangiovanni, A. (forthcoming-b). *The Bounds of Solidarity: International Distributive Justice, Reciprocity, and the European Union* (Cambridge, MA: Harvard University Press).

Sangiovanni, A. (forthcoming-c). "Non-Discrimination, In-Work Benefits, and the EU." *European Journal of Political Theory.*

Sangiovanni, A. (forthcoming-d). "Rights and Interests in Ripstein's Kant." In *Freedom and Force: Essays on Kant's Legal Philosophy,* ed. Sari Kisilevsky and Martin Stone (London: Hart).

Sartre, J.-P. (1983). *Huis Clos et les Mouches* (Paris: Gallimard).

Saul, J. (2006a). "On Treating Things as People: Objectification, Pornography, and the History of the Vibrator." *Hypatia* 21: 45–61.

Saul, J. (2006b). "Pornography, Speech Acts and Context." *Proceedings of the Aristotelian Society* 106: 229–248.

Saul, J. (2013). "Implicit Bias, Stereotype Threat, and Women in Philosophy." In *Women in Philosophy: What Needs to Change,* ed. Katrina Hutchison and Fiona Jenkins, pp. 39–60 (Oxford: Oxford University Press).

Scanlon, T. (1998). *What We Owe to Each Other* (Cambridge, MA: Harvard University Press).

Scanlon, T. (2008). *Moral Dimensions* (Cambridge, MA: Harvard University Press).

Scanlon, T. (2014). *Being Realistic about Reasons* (Oxford: Oxford University Press).

Scheffler, S. (2003). "What Is Egalitarianism?" *Philosophy & Public Affairs* 31: 5–39.

Scheffler, S. (2015). "The Practice of Equality." In *Social Equality: On What It Means to Be Equals,* ed. Carina Fourie, Fabian Schuppert, and Ivo Wallimann-Helmer, pp. 21–45 (Oxford: Oxford University Press).

Schofield, M. (1999). *The Stoic Idea of the City* (Chicago: University of Chicago Press).

Selmi, M. (2013). "Indirect Discrimination and the Anti-Discrimination Mandate." In *Philosophical Foundations of Discrimination Law,* ed. Deborah Hellman and Sophia Moreau, pp. 250–269 (Oxford: Oxford University Press).

Sen, A. (1999). *Development as Freedom* (Oxford: Oxford University Press).

Sen, A. (2004). "Elements of a Theory of Human Rights." *Philosophy & Public Affairs* 32: 315–356.

Sensen, O. (2011). "Human Dignity in Historical Perspective: The Contemporary and Traditional Paradigms." *European Journal of Political Theory* 10: 71–91.

Shelton, D. (2006). "Normative Hierarchy in International Law." *American Journal of International Law* 100: 291–323.

Shin, P. (2009). "The Substantive Principle of Equal Treatment." *Legal Theory* 15: 149–172.

Shklar, J. N. (1984). *Ordinary Vices* (Cambridge, MA: Harvard University Press).

Shklar, J. N. (1989). "The Liberalism of Fear." In *Liberalism and the Moral Life*, ed. Nancy Rosenblum, pp. 21–39 (Cambridge, MA: Harvard University Press).

Shue, H. (1996). *Basic Rights: Subsistence, Affluence, and U.S. Foreign Policy*, 2nd ed. (Princeton, NJ: Princeton University Press).

Simma, B., and P. Alston (1988). "The Sources of Human Rights Law: Custom, *Jus Cogens*, and General Principles." *Australian Year Book of International Law* 12: 82–108.

Simmons, A. J. (1979) *Moral Principles and Political Obligations* (Princeton: Princeton University Press).

Simmons, B. (2009). *Mobilizing for Human Rights: International Law in Domestic Politics* (Cambridge: Cambridge University Press).

Skinner, Q. (1999). "Hobbes and the Purely Artificial Person of the State." *Journal of Political Philosophy* 7: 1–29.

Smith, A. (1982). *The Theory of Moral Sentiments*, ed. A. L. Macfie and D. D. Raphael (Indianapolis: Liberty Classics).

Smith, A. (2005). "Responsibility for Attitudes: Activity and Passivity in Mental Life." *Ethics* 115: 236–271.

Somek, A. (2011). *Engineering Equality: An Essay on European Anti-Discrimination Law* (Oxford: Oxford University Press).

Sreenivasan, G. (2010). "Duties and Their Direction." *Ethics* 120: 465–494.

Sreenivasan, G. (2012). "A Human Right to Health? Some Inconclusive Scepticism." *Aristotelian Society Supplementary Volume* 86: 239–265.

Stanley, J., and Z. Gendler Szabó (2000). "On Quantifier Domain Restriction." *Mind & Language* 15: 219–261.

Steinhoff, U., ed. (2014). *Do All Persons Have Equal Moral Worth? On "Basic Equality" and Equal Respect and Concern* (Oxford: Oxford University Press).

Stern, R. (2011). "The Value of Humanity: Reflections on Korsgaard's Transcendental Argument." In *Transcendental Philosophy and Naturalism*, ed. Joel Smith and Peter Sullivan, pp. 74–95 (Oxford: Oxford University Press).

Strawson, G. (2004). "Against Narrativity." *Ratio* 17: 428–452.

Strawson, P. (2008). "Freedom and Resentment." In *Freedom and Resentment and Other Essays*, pp. 1–29 (London: Routledge).

Stump, E. (2008). *Aquinas* (London: Routledge).

Sussman, D. (2005). "What's Wrong with Torture?" *Philosophy & Public Affairs* 33: 1–33.

Tan, K.-C. (2006). "The Duty to Protect." In *Humanitarian Intervention*, ed. Terry Nardin and Melissa Williams (New York: NYU Press).

Tasioulas, J. (2007). "The Moral Reality of Human Rights." In *Freedom from Poverty as a Human Right,* ed. T. Pogge (Oxford: Oxford University Press).

Tasioulas, J. (2010). "Taking Rights Out of Human Rights." *Ethics* 120: 647–678.

Tasioulas, J. (2011). "On the Nature of Human Rights." In *The Philosophy of Human Rights: Contemporary Controversies,* ed. Gerhard Ernst and Jan-Christoph (Berlin: Walter de Gruyter).

Tasioulas, J. (2016). "Custom, *Jus Cogens,* and Human Rights." In *Custom's Future: International Law in a Changing World,* ed. Bradley Curtis, pp. 95–117 (Cambridge: Cambridge University Press).

Thompson, A. (2008). *Releasing Prisoners, Redeeming Communities* (New York: NYU Press).

Van den Eynde, L. (2013). "An Empirical Look at the Amicus Curiae Practice of Human Rights NGOs before the European Court of Human Rights." *Netherlands Quarterly of Human Rights* 31: 271–313.

Velleman, D. (1999a). "Love as a Moral Emotion." *Ethics* 109: 338–374.

Velleman, D. (1999b). "A Right of Self-Termination?" *Ethics* 109: 606–628.

Velleman, D. (2006). *Self to Self* (Cambridge: Cambridge University Press).

Veyne, P. (1993). "Humanitas: Romans and Non-Romans." In *The Romans,* pp. 342–369 (Chicago: Chicago University Press).

Vinci, L. da (1804). *Trattato Della Pittura* (Milan: Società tipografica de'classici italiani).

Vlastos, G. (1984). "Justice and Equality" [1962]. In *Theories of Rights,* ed. Jeremy Waldron, pp. 141–176 (Oxford: Oxford University Press).

Vogt, K. (2008). *Law, Reason, and the Cosmic City: Political Philosophy in the Early Stoa* (Oxford: Oxford University Press).

Waal, F. de (2009). *Primates and Philosophers: How Morality Evolved* (Princeton, NJ: Princeton University Press).

Waldron, J. (2002). *God, Locke, and Equality: Christian Foundations of John Locke's Political Thought* (Cambridge: Cambridge University Press).

Waldron, J. (2012). *Dignity, Rank, and Rights* (Oxford: Oxford University Press).

Waldron, J. (forthcoming-a). "Human Rights: A Critique of the Raz-Rawls Approach." In *Human Rights: Moral or Political?,* ed. Adam Etinson (Oxford: Oxford University Press).

Waldron, J. (forthcoming-b). *One Another's Equals: The Basis of Human Equality* (Cambridge, MA: Harvard University Press).

Wallace, R. J. (1994). *Responsibility and the Moral Sentiments* (Cambridge, MA: Harvard University Press).

Wallace, R. J. (2007). "Reasons, Relations, and Commands: Reflections on Darwall." *Ethics* 118: 24–36.

Watson, G. (2007). "Morality as Equal Accountability: Comments on Stephen Darwall's *The Second-Person Standpoint.*" *Ethics* 118: 37–51.

Wenar, L. (2013). "The Nature of Claim-Rights." *Ethics* 123: 202–229.

Westen, P. (1982). "The Empty Idea of Equality." *Harvard Law Review* 95: 537–596.

Western, B. (2006). *Punishment and Inequality in America* (New York: Russell Sage Foundation).

Westlund, A. (2003). "Selflessness and Responsibility for Self: Is Deference Compatible with Autonomy?" *Philosophical Review* 112: 483–523.

Williams, B. (2005). "The Idea of Equality." In *In the Beginning Was the Deed: Realism and Moralism in Political Argument,* ed. G. Hawthorn, pp. 97–115 (Princeton, NJ: Princeton University Press).

Williams, W. (1981). "The Equality Crisis: Some Reflections on Culture, Courts, and Feminism." *Women's Rights Law Reporter* 7: 175–200.

Wiltse, J. (2007). *Contested Waters: A Social History of Swimming Pools in America* (Chapel Hill: University of North Carolina Press).

Wiltse, J. (2014). "The Black–White Swimming Disparity in America: A Deadly Legacy of Swimming Pool Discrimination." *Journal of Sport & Social Issues* 38: 366–389.

Wolff, J. (1998). "Fairness, Respect, and the Egalitarian Ethos." *Philosophy & Public Affairs* 27: 97–122.

Wolff, J. (2015). "Social Equality and Social Inequality." In *Social Equality: On What It Means to Be Equals,* ed. Carina Fourie, Fabian Schuppert, and Ivo Wallimann-Helmer, pp. 209–227 (Oxford: Oxford University Press).

Wolff, J., and A. De-Shalit (2013). *Disadvantage* (Oxford: Oxford University Press).

Wolterstorff, N. (2010). *Justice: Rights and Wrongs* (Princeton, NJ: Princeton University Press).

Wood, A. (1998). "Kant on Duties regarding Nonrational Nature: Allen W. Wood." *Aristotelian Society Supplementary Volume* 72: 189–210.

Wood, A. (1999). *Kant's Ethical Thought* (Cambridge: Cambridge University Press).

Woolf, V. (1974). *The Death of the Moth and Other Essays* (London: Harcourt).

Young, I. M. (1990). *Justice and the Politics of Difference* (Princeton, NJ: Princeton University Press).

Young, I. M. (2011). *Responsibility for Justice* (Oxford: Oxford University Press).

INDEX